Rick Stein's
SEAFOOD ODYSSEY

Rick Stein's
SEAFOOD ODYSSEY

Rick Stein

For Jill, Edward, Jack and Charles

Food photography by James Murphy
Illustrations by Charlotte Knox

This book was published to accompany the television series entitled
Rick Stein's Seafood Odyssey which was first broadcast in 1999.
The series was produced by Denham Productions for BBC Features, Bristol.
Producer and Director: David Pritchard
Executive Producer for the BBC: Jeremy Gibson

First published by BBC Worldwide Limited, 80 Wood Lane, London, W12 0TT
© Rick Stein 1999 Reprinted 1999 (three times)
Paperback edition first published 2000, reprinted 2000, 2001 (three times)
First published with this cover 2002, reprinted 2002, 2004
The moral right of the author has been asserted

Food photography © James Murphy 1999
Illustrations © Charlotte Knox 1999
Photographs on pages 28, 44, 120, 140 and 196 by Debbie Major © BBC Worldwide 1999;
on pages 3, 68, 92 and 164 by David Pritchard © David Pritchard 1999; and on pages 1 and
6 by Andrew Campbell © BBC Worldwide 1999

ISBN 0 563 38440 9 (hardback)
ISBN 0 563 55186 0 (paperback)

Commissioning Editor: Viv Bowler
Project Editors: Anna Ottewill and Charlotte Lochhead
Copy Editor: Jane Middleton
Art Directors: Ellen Wheeler and Lisa Pettibone
Designer: Isobel Gillan
Home Economist: Debbie Major
Stylist: Antonia Gaunt

Set in Gill Sans and Rotis Semi Sans
Printed and bound in Great Britain by Butler & Tanner Limited, Frome and London
Colour separations by Radstock Reproductions Limited, Midsomer Norton
Jacket printed by Lawrence Allen Limited, Weston-super-Mare
Cover printed by Belmont Press Ltd, Northampton

Acknowledgements
How could I ever have finished this book without the help of Debbie Major? She not only tested and
typed all of the recipes, but also did all the hard work of preparing the food for the TV series that
accompanies this book. I hope to work with her on cookery books for ever. Thanks to Paul Ripley and
the chefs at the Seafood Restaurant for getting hold of all the ingredients for the recipes. To all the BBC
staff: Viv Bowler, Charlotte Lochhead, Anna Ottewill, Isobel Gillan, Jane Middleton, Ellen Wheeler and
Lisa Pettibone; thanks for their sensitive handling of an overworked chef and, once again, so sorry about
the deadlines. Thanks to the TV crew. What a great trip we had filming the series – the book would not
be the same without it – so big thanks to Julian Clinkard, David Holmes and Emma Mansfield. And finally
thanks to the director, David Pritchard; working with David is how everyone would like to work all the
time. It doesn't feel like work – you're just having the best time of your life.

Photograph page 2: *Barbecued Spiced Sardines* (see p. 35)

Contents

Introduction

The Dinosaur Hall at the Natural History Museum in South Kensington, London, is an odd place in which to think about a new cookery book. Last October, I was at a lecture there given by Sir David Attenborough to celebrate fifty years of the BBC's Natural History Unit. There were film clips of bears sliding along the polar ice, lions and crocodiles fighting at a water hole in Africa, and killer whales snatching sea lions from a beach in Argentina. The hall was filled with the tanned and the fit, all famous in the world of nature and geography and all just back from exotic adventures in Borneo or Patagonia. In that splendid hall, as I watched their films and listened to their stories of foreign places, a germ of an idea for a new book was born.

Isn't this, I thought, an endearing British enthusiasm? We love to explore the world and, like magpies, bring back objects or knowledge, ideas and memories to share and enrich our own lives. As I thought more about this, I realized that this is exactly what I do, too. I spend all my spare time travelling on a seafood odyssey in search of new and exciting dishes. But my quest is not just for the new. In Britain, because we don't have a great tradition of time-honoured fish recipes, I have had to look elsewhere in the world to build up a satisfactory repertoire of dishes that would keep my Seafood Restaurant customers happy. At any point in time the menu in Padstow will contain a number of dishes I have lovingly collected and brought back from my travels. As I write today the current choice ranges from *Barbecued Spiced Sardines with Pilau Rice* and *Oysters in Tempura Batter with Sesame Seeds and Lime,* to *Razor Clams a la Plancha, Linguine ai Frutti di Mare,* or *Chargrilled Tuna with Salsa Verde.*

I suppose I don't have to travel to gather these culinary gems; I could just browse through cookery books for new ideas. Of course I do that too, but I find I need to go and explore, to taste, to have a look for myself. Recently, in the kitchen, one of my chefs asked me to try the Goan *Shark Vindaloo* he'd made. The shark was glistening white in the midst of a dark red-brown, thick, deep sauce in which hovered some slivers of bright green chilli. The flavour was hot with the scent of cloves and tart with palm vinegar, or palm toddy as they call it in India. I felt a stab of excitement, a bit like hearing the first few notes of a classic rock 'n' roll tune like 'Shake, Rattle and Roll' and feeling that blast of nostalgia.

'That's it,' I said. 'That's exactly it.' And I was back in Goa … wailing Indian music on a humid, balmy night, the smell of incense, burning waste paper, and dogs barking somewhere in the dark … I am passing the dusty roadside general store, which smells hot and damp inside and is stacked with jars of curry paste, bottles of palm vinegar and kerosene, with hessian sacks spilling red and yellow spices and rice, great baskets of chillies and lots of mice.

Travelling changes you. The way I cook now, the recipes I write, the way I look at food, can never be the same as a result of my travels and my quest to find new seafood dishes. I suppose a certain purity, innocence and simplicity in the way I used to cook have been lost because of what I have learnt on the way, but I can't go back. I keep thinking that it would be nice to retire into some sort of Cornish fish cuisine, but it's just not enough any more. I need to keep travelling to find those perfect, simple dishes from all over the world.

Homer's *Odyssey* is about a long, much-diverted voyage home from Troy to Ithaca. Odysseus's homecoming and the setting to rights of his household and land is where the odyssey ends. However, Tennyson, in his poem 'Ulysses', wrote:

I am a part of all that I have met;
Yet all experience is an arch wherethro'
Gleams that untravell'd world whose margin fades
For ever and for ever when I move.

The poem suggests that a homecoming, and living happily ever after, is not really the end of the story. Tennyson was not the first to have wondered whether if, once you have tasted the excitement of travel, you can ever truly go home again.

Yet it is always home I dream of when I'm away, and it gives me that comfortable feeling of being where I love to be. When I think of home I cannot imagine ever going for a walk along the cliffs of Cornwall or through the winding lanes without foraging for wild parsley, mushrooms, sloes, fennel, blackberries or whatever happens to be in season. Neither can I imagine a trip anywhere in the world without wanting to know all about the fresh local food and cooking. Who wants to be just a tourist? I arrive somewhere and head straight for the market or the fish docks. I love getting lost in the markets and I love trying out the local specialities. When I was last in Thailand, in Hua Hin, I spent half a day just trying dried and pickled fish. Last time I was in Mexico I went to a market in Zitácuaro, west of Mexico City, and spent a morning in the market talking about chillies — *poblano, serrano, habanero, chilaca*, and many more. And, as much as I like reading cookery books, nothing comes near to the thrill of finding a new fish dish in some faraway place. The *Morton Bay Bug Risotto* that

I found in Brisbane was so much better for eating it there, or the *Pasta con le Sarde* which, although it appears in every Italian recipe book, I'd never truly appreciated until I sat down and ate it in Sicily.

I have chosen to travel to seven parts of the world for my *Seafood Odyssey*. I could have chosen many more, but difficult decisions had to be made. What is it about these particular areas that makes them so special to me? I think the chapter titles probably sum up what I think: India – colour, vibrancy and spice; Thailand and the Far East – the seafood of market stalls and streets; Italy – passion and flavour, to name a few. These places have a unique value to me. They all go together to make up my style of cooking. There are also a couple of everlasting influences I wanted to include in this book. To the classic cookery of France my debt, after twenty-four years of cooking, is still greatest, and dishes like *Marmite Dieppoise* and *La Mouclade* will last for ever in my repertoire. The fish cookery of Britain is also worthy of note, and I have included memories of *Potted Shrimps* and warming home-cooked *Fish Pie* in this chapter as well as some of my own dishes, dreamed up in my restless imagination yet owing much to the country where I live. It is not at all insignificant that while filming the television series that accompanies this book, we chose to visit the unassuming town of Leigh-on-Sea in Essex and its cockle and seafood sheds. While there, we found passionate enthusiasm for the British way with seafood, and I discovered that this was just as appealing as the passion and exuberance of the cooking I found in Italy or the excitement and ingenuity of the cooking I experienced in Australia.

RICK STEIN

Notes about the recipes

- All eggs are medium unless otherwise stated and, if you can, buy genuine free range eggs which have beautiful bright yellow yolks and a much better flavour.
- All herbs are fresh.
- All spoon measurements are level and 1 teaspoon = 5 ml, 1 tablespoon = 15 ml.
- All conversions are approximate. Follow one set of measurements; do not mix metric and imperial.
- Oven temperatures and cooking times are flexible and may vary according to equipment used.
- If you do not have a kitchen thermometer to test the heat of your oil for deep-frying, drop a small piece of bread into the hot oil. If it browns and rises to the surface in about 1–2 minutes, the oil is hot enough to deep-fry in.

Notes about the fish classification

How would you cook a jewfish, a barramundi, a pompano, a striped bass, a pomfret or a hammerhead shark? Can you barbecue flounder? Is barracuda good in a fish stew? Can you cook British cold-water lobster in the same way as those from Tasmania or Kaikoura on the east coast of New Zealand's South Island? Can you make Maryland crab cakes with a mud crab?

Many people are perplexed about what to do with fish they aren't familiar with, particularly if those fish come from another country. I don't have this problem because I find that fish all over the world cook in the same sorts of ways. I have grouped fish into broad culinary categories to show you what I mean (see pages 10–25. These groups are, I suppose, a little strange, but they suit me for cookery purposes even if a marine biologist might be surprised by them. The shellfish fall into distinct categories without any interference from me, and the fish groupings in this book are based on the eating qualities of the fish.

I have to admit to making one mistake in my categorization. There is an interloper in the flaky fish category: the Australian sand whiting should really be in the round fish group. How my mistake came about is rather a nice story. The beautiful watercolour paintings of fish and shellfish in this book were done by the artist Charlotte Knox, who has produced a series of perfectly detailed identification paintings at the same time as imbuing each species with individuality and character. While she was doing the artwork, I persuaded a fish expert and friend of mine, Annie Foord, to bring an Australian sand whiting from Sydney so that Charlotte could paint it accurately. Up to that point I had only ever tasted cooked Australian sand whiting and, because it had such delicate white flesh, I had thought it was an antipodean relative of the North Atlantic cod family. As such, I firmly believed I was eating whiting as I knew it to be in Europe. It wasn't until I saw the fish whole that I realized I should strictly have classified it as a round fish. But I opted to keep it in the flaky fish category because, despite its shape, its flesh is less firm and lends itself to being treated more as one would a flaky fish. There are in fact quite a few Australian fish with the same names as European and North American fish, but they are not the same thing at all – coral trout, blue-eyed cod and Murray cod to name a few

Finally, a note about oily fish – or rather a paean of praise for them. The oil in these fish gives them lots of flavour, but it makes the fish smell when they are cooking. People don't like this smell, which is understandable, but I see oily fish as providing the greatest highs with its lows. A dozen of the first sprats of the season sprinkled with coarsely chopped rosemary, garlic, parsley, capers, olives and some flaked sea salt, with a glass of Fleurie and some crusty sour-dough bread, and eaten by nibbling along their backs and biting each fillet away from the backbones, is sheer delight. Those of you who are put off by the oil just don't know what you are missing.

Flaky fish

All these fish have very white, soft flesh which parts in thick, appetizing flakes when cooked. The muscle tissue is designed for rather leisurely activity at the bottom of the sea, with occasional bursts of energy for catching prey.

BELOW (from the top) Hake, Sand Whiting and Ling.
RIGHT (from the left) Whiting, Haddock and Cod.

Meaty fish

Normally large, these have similar qualities to meat. Tuna, for instance, is best when cooked rare like steak, but shark has a taste almost like veal. Swordfish has a meaty texture and monkfish is firm, again like steak.

BELOW (from the top) Kingfish and Tuna.
RIGHT (clockwise from the top) Thornback Ray, Swordfish, Monkfish and Porbeagle Shark.

Oily fish

Sleek and designed to travel long migratory distances, the muscle tissue on these fish is dark and oily for strength and endurance. The oil gives them lots of flavour, which can become unpleasant in stale fish. These are the best fish to salt or smoke.

BELOW (from the top) Brown Trout, Sea Trout and Salmon scattered with Sardines and
   smaller Whitebait.
RIGHT (from the top) Bonito, Herring, Mackerel and Eel.

Flat fish

These live at the sea bottom. They range in eating quality from soft and delicate, like dabs and flounder, to the best eating fish on earth – halibut, turbot and Dover sole. Easy to prepare into completely boneless fillets.

BELOW (clockwise from the top left) Dabs (x3), Dover Sole and Halibut.
RIGHT (clockwise from the top) Turbot, Lemon Sole, Brill, Plaice.

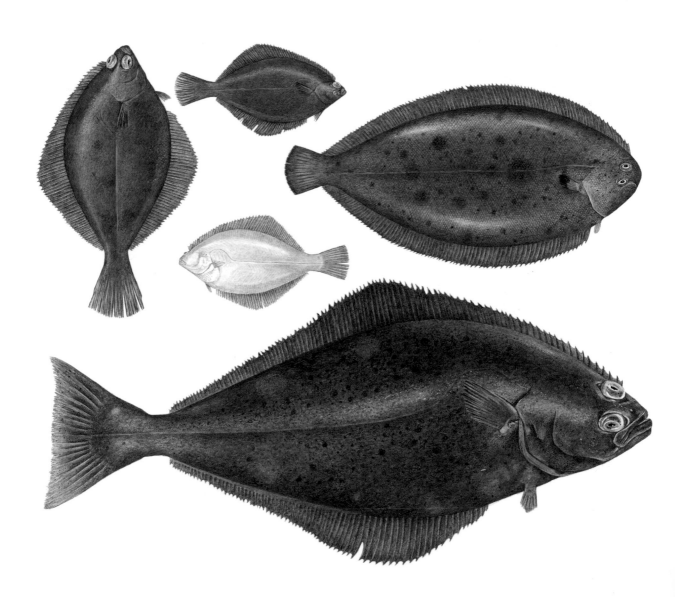

Round fish

Just right to barbecue or steam, braise, bake or roast. Round fish have a much firmer texture than flaky fish but still have an appealing moist delicacy about them, combined with a fair amount of oil, which gives them plenty of flavour.

BELOW (from the top, left to right) Gilt-head Bream, Red Mullet, John Dory and Barramundi.
RIGHT (from the top, left to right) Mahi Mahi, Grey Mullet, Red Snapper, Sea Bass and Pomfret.

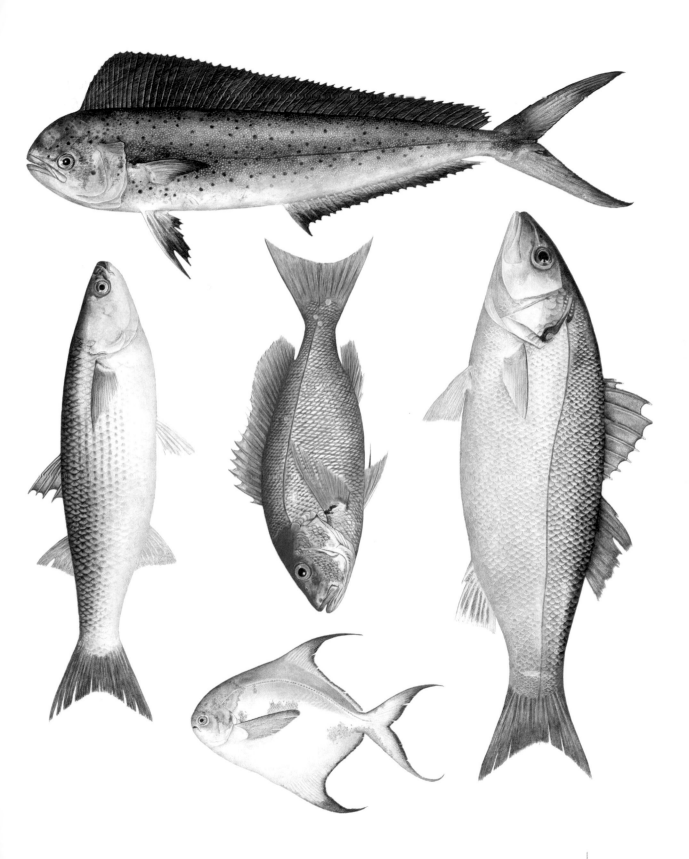

Shellfish

These fit into a perfectly precise category, both biologically and for cooking purposes.
Definitely the most expensive seafood the world over, but full of sweet, round flavour.
Difficult to say which I like best: possibly the cold-water northern European lobster.

BELOW (from the left) Lobster and Spiny Lobster.

RIGHT (from the left, top row) Mud Crab and Spider Crab; (middle row) Asian Swimming Crab
and (above) North Atlantic Prawn and Brown Shrimp with (below) uncooked and cooked
Tiger Prawns, and Blue Crab; (bottom row) Moreton Bay Bug, Brown Crab and Langoustine.

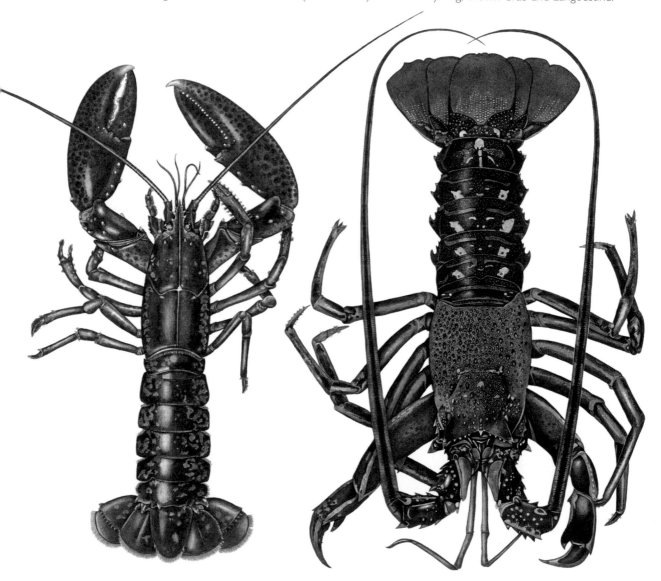

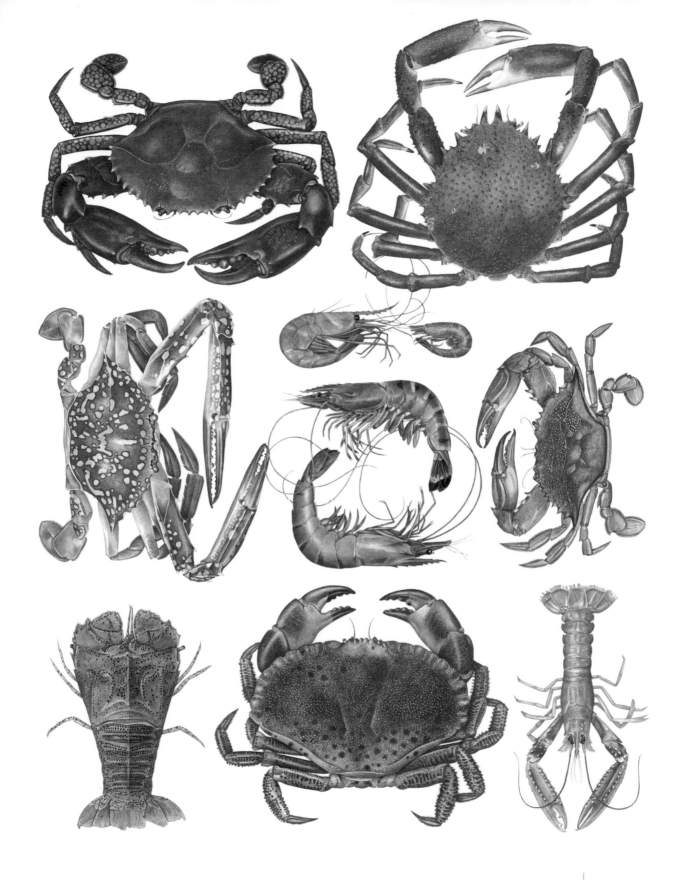

Squid, Cuttlefish and Octopus

Called cephalopods, from the Greek, meaning 'feet coming out of head'. Very good to eat, though European octopus needs some form of tenderizing. The smell and taste of these cooking is the most tantalizing of all seafood aromas from the kitchen.

BELOW (from the left) Squid and Cuttlefish.
RIGHT Octopus.

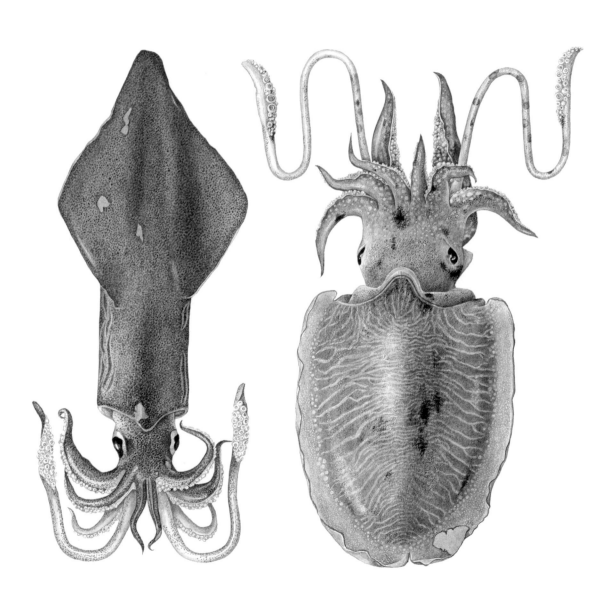

Molluscs

All these live in two shells, called bivalves. The less you cook these the better, and all can be eaten raw. All are the warp and weft of seafood connoisseurs. They are what I would call the taste of the sea.

BELOW (top and bottom row) Razor Clams; (middle rows, from the left, show clams open and closed) Carpet Clam, Little Neck Clam and Smooth Venus Clam

RIGHT (from the left, top row) Cockles and Scallop; (middle row) Oysters and Mussels; (bottom row) Scallops uncleaned and cleaned.

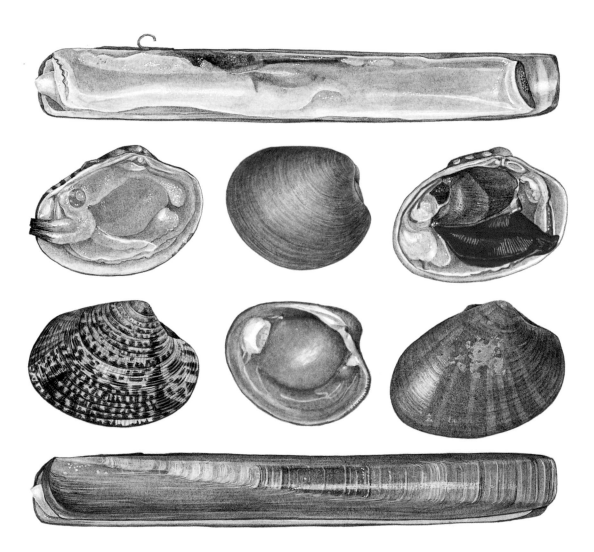

Fish preparation

Cleaning round fish

Trim off the fins with kitchen scissors. Then, working over several sheets of newspaper or under cold running water, scale the fish by scraping it from tail to head with a blunt, thick-bladed knife, a fish scaler or even a scallop shell, which works very well. To remove the guts, slit open the belly from the anal fin to the head. Pull out most of the guts with your hand and cut away any remaining pieces with a small knife. Wash out the cavity with cold water.

For large fish you may wish to remove the gills. Pull open the gill flaps and cut them away from the two places where they join the fish – at the back of the head and under the mouth.

Filleting round fish

You will need a fish filleting knife. This has a thin, flexible blade designed to glide over the backbones of fish. For fish up to about 500 g (1 lb), lay the fish on a board with its back towards you. Cut down through the fillet just behind the head, then turn the knife blade towards the tail and cut the whole fillet away from the backbone in one clean sweep, using the flat of the knife against the backbone as a guide. Turn the fish over and repeat this on the other side.

For larger fish, make the same cut behind the head but remove the head before cutting down the length of the back from head to tail until you reach the backbone. Lift up the part of the fillet you have already cut to make it easier to see where you are going, then cut away the fillet from the bones on the other side of the backbone. Turn the fish over and do the same thing on the other side. Some big fish, like salmon, can be filleted using the method for smaller fish above, but use a big serrated bread or ham knife. Other fish, like hake, have plates rather than rib bones, and the filleting has to be done much more delicately.

Cleaning flat fish

To remove the guts, locate the gut cavity by pressing on the white side of the fish just below the head until you find a place that is much softer. Make a small incision across this area (if you wish to remove any roe, make a slightly longer incision) and pull them out. Trim off the fins with kitchen scissors.

Dover sole and brill are the only flat fish that need scaling. Follow the method for round fish.

Filleting flat fish

You will get 4 fillets from one flat fish, 2 from either side of the backbone. Lay the fish on a chopping board and cut around the back of the head. Now cut through the skin down the centre of the fish from head to tail, very slightly to one side of the raised backbone. Starting at the head end, slide a knife under each fillet in turn and carefully cut it away from the bones, keeping the knife as close to the bones as you can and folding the released fillet back as you go. Turn the fish over and repeat.

Skinning fillets of fish

Place the fillet skin-side down on a chopping board. Put your fingertips on the tail end and work a filleting knife between the skin and the flesh. Work your way up the fillet, keeping the blade of the knife as flat and as close to the skin as you can.

Preparing monkfish tails

First remove the skin from the tail: grasp the thick end of the tail in one hand and the skin in the other and briskly tear off the skin, which should come away quite easily. Fillet the monkfish by cutting either side of the thick backbone. Pull off as much membrane as possible from each fillet with your fingers, then carefully cut away the rest, taking care not to cut away too much of the flesh.

Cleaning cockles, clams and mussels

Wash well in plenty of cold water and discard any that won't shut when lightly tapped. Scrape any barnacles off mussels and pull out the fibrous beards, with which the mussel clings to rocks, ropes or wooden stakes.

Incidentally, don't bother to steep these bivalve molluscs in flour, oatmeal or anything else, mixed with water. They won't self-cleanse like this – trust me! They need air, which they won't get in a bucket of cloudy water.

Preparing raw prawns

Twist the head away from the body and discard or use for stock. Break open the soft shell along the belly and carefully peel it away from the flesh. For some recipes you may wish to leave the last tail segment of the shell in place, as it looks more fun.

With some large prawns you may need to remove the intestinal tract, which looks like a dark vein running down the back of the prawn flesh. Run the tip of a small knife down the back of the prawn to expose the gut and then pull it away.

Preparing scallops

Wash the scallops in plenty of cold water to remove any sand and weed from the shells. Hold each one in turn, flat shell uppermost, and slide the blade of a filleting knife between the shells. Keeping the blade flat against the top shell, feel for the ligament that joins the shell to the muscle meat of the scallop and cut through it. Lift off the flat top shell and pull out all the material in the scallop shell except the white scallop meat and the bright orange coral. If you want to cook the scallop in the shell, rinse away any sand from inside the shell and drain away all excess water. Otherwise, cut the scallop meat away from the bottom shell and lift out.

Opening oysters

Hold the oyster in one hand well wrapped in a tea towel. Push the point of a knife into the oyster's hinge. Work the knife and oyster backwards and forwards, applying a little pressure. The hinge will break open quite easily. Slide the knife under the top shell and sever the ligament that joins the oyster to the shell. Working over a bowl so that you collect all the juices, remove the oysters from their shells and pick out any little bits of shell that might have escaped.

Killing a live crab

Turn the crab on its back with its eyes facing you. Drive a thick skewer or a long, thin-bladed knife between the eyes into the centre of the crab. Then lift up the tail flap and drive the skewer though the underside of the crab. When the crab is dead it will go limp.

Removing the meat from a cooked crab

Break off and discard the tail flap, then twist off the two larger claws and the legs. Break the legs at the joints and discard all but the first, largest joints. Crack the leg shells with the back of a knife or a hammer and pick out the white meat with a crab pick. Break open the claws and remove this meat too, discarding the very thin flat bone from the centre of the claws. Insert the blade of a large knife between the body and the back shell and twist to release it. Pull off the feathery-looking gills or 'dead man's fingers' from the body and discard. Cut the body into four and pick out all the white meat from the little channels. Remove the stomach sac from the back shell by pressing on the little piece of shell located just behind the eyes. Discard both the bone and the stomach. Scrape out the brown meat from the back shell and keep it separate from the white meat.

Removing the meat from a cooked lobster

Twist off the claws and legs and discard the legs. Break the claws into pieces at the joints and crack the shells with the back of a knife or a hammer. Remove the meat in the largest possible pieces. Cut the lobster in half lengthways, remove the intestinal tract and discard. Remove the meat from the tail section. Cut it into largish chunks. Remove the soft, greenish tomalley (liver) and any red roe from the head section and set them aside with the rest of the meat. Pull out the dead man's fingers (gills) and the stomach sac and discard; you can either leave in or remove the rest of the head matter.

If you want to remove the tail meat in one piece, detach the head from the tail and then cut the head in half and deal with as before. Turn the tail section over and cut along either side of the flat under-shell with scissors. Lift back the flap of shell and lift out the meat. Remove the intestinal tract with the tip of a small sharp knife and discard before slicing the tail meat.

Preparing squid

Gently pull the head away from the body, taking the milky-white intestines with it. Cut off the tentacles from the head and squeeze out the beak-like mouth from the centre. Cut it off and discard along with the head. Pull out the plastic-like quill from the body and discard. Then pull off the fins from either side of the pouch. Pull off and discard the purple, semi-transparent skin from both the body and the fins, then wash out the pouch with water.

Cleaning cuttlefish

Cut off the tentacles just in front of the eyes and remove the beak-like mouth from the centre of the tentacles. Pull the skin off the tentacles if they are large. Cut the head section from the body and discard the head. Cut open the body section from top to bottom along the darker-coloured back and remove the chalky-white cuttlebone and the entrails. Discard these. However, if you want to use the ink for a recipe, locate the pearly-white ink pouch in among the entrails and remove it first, being careful not to pierce it as you do so. Scrape the inside of the fish clean and then remove the skin from the outside of the body.

colour, vibrancy and spice • *I first arrived in Goa in southern India after a long charter flight, about ten years ago. The sun felt as though it was slamming us into the tarmac as we walked through a mirage of heat to join a long line, heading for a shed with no air-conditioning. The officials inside all had khaki army uniforms, highly polished shoes with no socks, clipboards and big sticks. One ordered my son Charles to stand up when he was discovered sitting, a little fatigued, on our luggage.*

We emerged from the airport after about two-and-a-half hours of rigorous bureaucracy, into a world of intense colour and brightness. We hadn't slept much on the flight and, after another two hours on a slow noisy bus and a rusty old riverboat, we finally arrived at our hotel. Slumped in a chair by the pool I ordered kingfish curry, rice, salad and Kingfisher beer and when the food arrived it totally transformed us from jaded zombies into bright, cheerful optimists. The fish was

India

meaty and full of flavour, the curry sauce deep red and fragrant with cloves, coriander and ginger with hints of curry leaves, chillies, okra and whole spice. The salad was so simple – just tomatoes and onions sliced wafer thin, sprinkled with lime juice – and the rice was light, dry, fluffy and scattered with deep-fried onion flakes. The beer – ice cold and not too strong – was revitalizing and refreshing, and the naan bread was blistered from the tandoor oven, shiny and brushed with butter.

I discovered then that I could put up with just about anything India had to throw at me, airport officials included, if the food was as good as this. In Goa, especially, I couldn't help but be excited by the rows of giant mackerel-like kingfish coming off the outrigger fishing boats on Baga Beach, or the enormous prawns and piles of gleaming clams and mussels at the fish stalls at Calangute or Mapusa market. I had to revel in the abundance of seafood I found there, I marvelled at its freshness and I was enchanted by its flavours.

Kingfish Curry

Kingfish are the cod of the Indian Ocean, in the sense that they are large fish in plentiful supply which cut up into beautiful meaty steaks. However, they've got much more flavour than cod, being related, albeit distantly, to mackerel and tuna. Watching the landing of kingfish on a beach in Goa is one of those occasions when you have to pinch yourself, it's so much like a picture out of National Geographic magazine. The fishing boats are made out of roughly hewn planks held together with twine and pitch, with an outrigger made from the branch of a tree and joined to the boat using another two tree branches. The fishermen's wives, with their lungis tucked up, arrange rows and rows of majestic kingfish along the sand and packs of wandering dogs sniff at them. In the distance, two bronzed men in thongs, and some Rajasthani girls in reds and purples getting ready for the day's trade on the beach.

Kingfish are perfect for a curry. I particularly like the okra in this dish, which is cooked just long enough not to be too slimy, and the whole spices, which are lightly fried to bring out their nutty aromas and which look great in the finished sauce.

serves 4

4 × 175–225 g (6–8 oz) skinned pieces of
   thick kingfish fillet or shark fillet
3 tablespoons groundnut oil
½ teaspoon black mustard seeds
½ teaspoon cumin seeds
½ teaspoon fennel seeds
¼ teaspoon fenugreek seeds
1 onion, thinly sliced
1 quantity of *Goan Masala Paste* (see p. 241)
1 teaspoon turmeric powder

6 curry leaves
2 small red finger chillies, seeded and sliced
   across diagonally
12 small okra, topped and tailed
3 tomatoes, skinned and quartered
400 ml (14 fl oz) coconut milk
4 tablespoons *Tamarind Water* (see p. 238)
150 ml (5 fl oz) water
Salt

method

Lightly salt the pieces of fish. Heat the oil in a pan that is just large enough to take the fish in one layer. Add the whole spices and fry them for about 30 seconds. Add the sliced onion and fry until golden. Add the masala paste and turmeric and fry for 3–4 minutes to cook out the rawness of the garlic and ginger in the spice paste. Add the curry leaves, chillies, okra, tomatoes, coconut milk, tamarind water, water and salt to taste, and simmer for 5 minutes. Add the pieces of fish and simmer for another 5 minutes. Serve with some *Steamed Basmati Rice* (see p. 226).

alternative fish

This also works well with other big fish like tuna, bonito or some of the really big game fish such as marlin or sail fish. But you could make it with pieces of the humble cod too, if you wish.

Sardine and Potato Curry Puffs

Oily fish such as sardines and herrings are only great grilled whole if they are extremely fresh – 'stiff fresh', as they say in the fishmongering trade. Some of the previously frozen sardines sold at supermarket counters and optimistically labelled 'suitable for barbecuing' are, in my opinion, only suitable for adding to the barbecue as fuel. But the same sardines, or even mackerel, trout and herrings, that aren't tip-top for grilling are ideal for a hot, robustly flavoured dish like this. The point is that the oil in the fish will develop more flavour as the fish ages.

makes 12

100 g (4 oz) potato, peeled and cut into 1 cm (½ inch) cubes

1 tablespoon groundnut or sunflower oil, plus extra for deep-frying

2 garlic cloves, crushed

1 cm (½ inch) fresh root ginger, finely grated

½ onion, thinly sliced

1 tablespoon good-quality garam masala paste or *Goan Masala Paste* (see p. 241)

225 g (8 oz) sardines, cleaned, filleted (see p. 26) and cut across into strips 2.5 cm (1 inch) wide

1 red finger chilli, seeded and finely chopped

1 tablespoon lemon juice

¼ teaspoon salt

2–3 spring onions, sliced

2 tablespoons chopped coriander

450 g (1 lb) fresh puff pastry

Lemon wedges and coriander sprigs, to garnish

method

Boil the potato in salted water until just tender, then drain. Heat the oil in a large frying pan and fry the garlic, ginger and onion for 1 minute. Add the masala paste and fry for 1 minute, then add the pieces of sardine and fry for another minute. Finally put in the potato, chilli, lemon juice and salt and cook for 1 minute. Take the pan off the heat, stir in the spring onions and coriander and leave to cool.

Roll out the pastry on a lightly floured surface and cut out twelve 10 cm (4 inch) circles. Spoon a heaped teaspoon of the filling mixture on to each circle. Brush half of the pastry edge with a little water, then fold it over the filling and press together well to seal the edge. Mark along the edge with a fork to make an even tighter seal.

Heat some oil for deep frying to 190°C/375°F. Deep-fry the puffs 3 or 4 at a time for 7–8 minutes, turning them over every now and then, until they are golden brown. Drain on kitchen paper. Keep warm in a low oven while you cook the rest. Pile them on to a plate and serve warm, garnished with some lemon wedges and coriander.

alternative fish

These would work well with mackerel, pilchards, sprats, herrings and any other oily fish with lots of flavour.

Prawn Caldine

This is one of the best dishes I cooked when I was filming in India. Unusually for a Goan seafood dish, it is particularly light and fragrant, with distinctive little wisps of green chilli in the sauce. We found a spot under some banyan trees in which to film. This overlooked a wide estuary where the locals were picking clams – some commercially, others just out on a Sunday excursion. We named the spot 'Clam Pickers' Bluff' and spent much of the day trying to dislodge particularly noisy crows from the trees by hurling stones at them. It was pretty unsuccessful, and they finally made off with the last of the finished caldine. The director has now called for a catapult to be part of the crew's kit when we next have to film in India.

serves 4

550 g (1¼ lb) headless raw prawns

2 tablespoons coconut vinegar or
   white wine vinegar

1 teaspoon turmeric powder

1 teaspoon black peppercorns

1 tablespoon coriander seeds

1 teaspoon cumin seeds

2 tablespoons white poppy seeds
   or ground almonds

4 tablespoons groundnut oil

1 onion, thinly sliced

3 garlic cloves, cut into slivers

2.5 cm (1 inch) fresh root ginger,
   finely chopped

400 ml (14 fl oz) coconut milk

4 tablespoons *Tamarind Water* (see p. 238)

150 ml (5 fl oz) water

5 mild green finger chillies, halved, seeded and
   cut into long, thin shreds

2 tablespoons chopped coriander

Salt

method

Peel the prawns, leaving the last tail segment in place (see p. 26). Mix the prawns with the vinegar and ½ teaspoon of salt and leave for 5 minutes or so. This enhances the flavour. Meanwhile, put the turmeric powder, peppercorns, coriander seeds, cumin seeds and white poppy seeds, if using, into a spice grinder and grind to a fine powder.

Heat the oil in a medium-sized pan. Add the onion, garlic and ginger and fry gently for 5 minutes. Stir in the ground spices and fry for 2 minutes. Add the ground almonds if you aren't using poppy seeds, plus the coconut milk, tamarind water, water, three-quarters of the sliced chillies and ½ teaspoon of salt. Bring to a simmer and cook for 5 minutes. Add the prawns and simmer for only 3–4 minutes so they don't overcook. Stir in the rest of the sliced chillies and the coriander and serve with some *Steamed Basmati Rice* (see p. 226).

alternative fish

You can use any type of raw prawns for this dish; it would work well with goujons of fish like brill or John Dory, too.

Coconut Chilli Prawns with Cumin Puris

The combination of chilli, coconut and coriander is what I would call the holy trinity of Indian fish cookery. These are the flavours that everybody goes wild about. Even though this dish appears to be pretty exotic, I designed it to use ingredients that I could get in the high street. The real pleasure here is the cumin puris, which are freshly made using wholemeal flour flavoured with cumin seeds.

serves 4

3 tablespoons sunflower oil

2.5 cm (1 inch) fresh root ginger, finely grated

3 garlic cloves, crushed

2 tablespoons ready-made rogan josh or
   medium curry paste

450 g (1 lb) peeled large raw prawns

50 g (2 oz) creamed coconut, roughly chopped

150 ml (5 fl oz) hot water

2 tablespoons chopped coriander

2 birdseye chillies, seeded and very
   finely chopped

2 spring onions, thinly sliced

FOR THE CUMIN PURIS:

100 g (4 oz) wholemeal flour

100 g (4 oz) plain flour

$\frac{1}{2}$ teaspoon salt

2 tablespoons sunflower oil, plus extra
   for brushing

1 teaspoon cumin seeds

150 ml (5 fl oz) water

method   First make the puris: sift the flours and salt into a large bowl, add the oil and rub it into the flour with your fingertips until well mixed in. Stir in the cumin seeds. Gradually mix in the water to make a soft, slightly sticky dough, then turn out on to a well-floured work surface and knead for 5 minutes. Rub the ball of dough with a little more oil, put it in a clean bowl, cover and leave for 30 minutes.

Pre-heat the grill to high. Knead the dough again for about 3 minutes, until smooth. Divide into 12 balls, dust each one quite heavily with flour and then roll out into a 12.5 cm (5 inch) disc. Brush them on both sides with oil and grill the puris for 1 minute on each side.

Heat the 3 tablespoons of oil in a large pan, add the ginger and garlic and fry for 30 seconds. Add the curry paste and fry for 2 minutes, until it looks as if it is splitting away from the oil. Add the prawns to the pan and stir-fry over a high heat for 3 minutes, until firm and pink. Add the creamed coconut and hot water and stir every now and then until the coconut has melted. Simmer for 1 minute. Mix the coriander with the chillies and spring onions. Stir into the prawns and serve immediately with the cumin puris.

alternative fish

As a last resort, you could stir some cooked peeled large prawns into the sauce just to heat through, if that's all you can get.

Barbecued Spiced Sardines with Pilau Rice

Much as I love simply grilled sardines and pilchards straight off the barbecue, I also enjoy them cooked in the same way but stuffed with a little intensely aromatic Goan masala paste (pictured on p. 2). And the pilau rice cooked by my friend Rui in Goa is to die for! However, there's such a difference between fresh and frozen sardines that I must say here that this dish should only be made with fresh ones. A fresh sardine, still firm and, as the Cornish say, 'sweet as a nut', is a delight. Barbecued frozen sardines are such a disappointment, you're left thinking how horrible oily fish are, when in fact it isn't true.

serves 4

12 sardines, cleaned (see p. 26)

1 quantity of *Goan Masala Paste* (see p. 241)

1 quantity of *Kachumber Salad* (see p. 227),
   to serve

FOR THE PILAU RICE:

Sunflower oil for frying

6 large shallots, thinly sliced

3 cloves

3 green cardamom pods

5 cm (2 inch) piece of cinnamon stick

1 bay leaf

350 g (12 oz) basmati rice

½ teaspoon salt

600 ml (1 pint) water

method

Pre-heat your barbecue. Cut the heads off the sardines and then fillet them, leaving them attached at the tail end. Spread the cut face of one fillet with a teaspoon of the masala paste. Push the fish back into shape and tie in place, at what was the head end, with some string.

For the rice, heat a good deep layer of sunflower oil in a large frying pan. Add the shallots and fry, stirring now and then, until crisp and golden. Lift out with a slotted spoon on to plenty of kitchen paper and leave to drain.

Heat 2 tablespoons of oil in a large pan, add the whole spices and bay leaf and cook for a few seconds until they start to smell aromatic. Stir in the rice, salt and water, bring to the boil, then cover and cook over a low heat for 10 minutes.

Remove the rice from the heat and leave for another 5 minutes. Meanwhile, place the sardines on the barbecue and cook them for 1–2 minutes on each side, until crisp and lightly golden. Toss the fried shallots with a little salt and then stir them into the cooked rice. Serve with the sardines and *Kachumber Salad* (see p. 227).

alternative fish

This dish is also great with small mackerel, hooked out of the sea on a warm summer's evening, just off Gulland Island, to the west of Stepper Point and Padstow.

Shark Vindaloo

The traditional meat for a vindaloo is pork, and although my Goan friend, Rui, said that making a vindaloo out of shark is quite common I didn't really think it would be more than just a second-division dish. But it is quite unbelievably good and Rui's vindaloo paste, which starts with some roasted onion to darken and sweeten it, adds real depth to the dish.

serves 4

900 g (2 lb) small skinned shark steaks
3–4 tablespoons groundnut or sunflower oil
1 onion, chopped
2 tomatoes, roughly chopped
4 tablespoons *Vindaloo Curry Paste* (see p. 241)
300 ml (10 fl oz) water
8 small green chillies
Coconut vinegar or white wine vinegar, to taste
Salt

method

Season the shark steaks with salt. Heat the oil in a large, deep frying pan, add the onion and fry until richly browned. Add the tomatoes and cook until they form a deep golden paste. Now stir in the vindaloo paste and fry gently for 5 minutes, stirring, until it has slightly caramelized. Pour in the water and leave the sauce to simmer for 10 minutes, giving it a stir every now and then. Meanwhile, slit the green chillies open along their length and scrape out the seeds but leave them whole.

Add the shark steaks and chillies to the sauce and simmer for 10 minutes, carefully turning the steaks over half-way through. Add vinegar and salt to taste and serve with some pilau rice (see the recipe for *Barbecued Spiced Sardines* on p. 35).

alternative fish

Try this with monkfish, swordfish, kingfish or any of the other meaty fish mentioned on pages 12–13.

Prawn-stuffed Papads

Like so many of my Goan recipes, this comes from Rui Madre de Deus, at the Ronil Beach Resort Hotel in Baga. It makes the most delightful appetizer and is ideal as a nicely spicy canapé for a drinks party. You have to be a bit careful with the papads, or poppadoms, though. When we were making them in India we found that it's easy enough to buy freshly made poppadoms there that are quite flexible, but in the UK you need to buy a good brand. Try to get them from an Indian grocer's because they will be slightly bendy (and far cheaper than the supermarket boxed ones). Liberally brush them with water, then leave them for a couple of minutes until they are moist enough to fold. This recipe can make as many as 48 pieces, depending on the number of poppadoms you use.

makes 42

2 tablespoons groundnut or sunflower oil, plus extra for shallow-frying

225 g (8 oz) onions, finely chopped

225 g (8 oz) tomatoes, skinned and chopped

275 g (10 oz) peeled raw prawns, finely chopped

3–4 green finger chillies, seeded and finely chopped

2 garlic cloves, crushed

2.5 cm (1 inch) fresh root ginger, finely grated

1 teaspoon turmeric powder

1 teaspoon chilli powder

Juice of $\frac{1}{2}$ lime

$\frac{1}{2}$ teaspoon salt

14–16 × 15 cm (6 inch) uncooked plain poppadoms

1 small egg, beaten

method

Heat the oil in a frying pan, add the onions and fry over a high heat, stirring now and then, until they are richly golden. Add the tomatoes and continue to fry until everything has reduced down to a golden-coloured paste. Add the chopped prawns, green chillies, garlic, ginger, turmeric, chilli powder, lime juice and salt. Fry for about 1 minute, until the prawns are cooked, then take off the heat.

Pour about 5 mm ($\frac{1}{4}$ inch) of oil into another frying pan and heat it to 200°C/400°F. Taking 2–3 poppadoms at a time, brush them generously with water on both sides and leave to soften for 2 minutes. Place 2 good tablespoons of the prawn filling down the centre of each one and brush the edge with a little beaten egg. Roll them up and press the open ends together to seal.

Once you have filled all the papads, shallow-fry them 3 or 4 at a time for 1–1$\frac{1}{2}$ minutes, turning them frequently, until crisp and golden. Place on kitchen paper to remove any greasiness, then slice off the ends and cut each one into 3 pieces. Spear each piece with a cocktail stick and serve hot.

alternative fish

This would be an ideal occasion for using lobster, preferably Canadian or North American because of the price, and a little will go a long way. You need that sweet, concentrated flavour, so you could make these equally well with some cooked white crab meat or good-quality cooked and peeled North Atlantic prawns. However, with all these alternatives, the fish is already cooked, so just stir it in and then take it off the heat straight away.

Goan Lobster with Cucumber and Lime Salad

This is a cracker — and the remarkable thing about this dish is that although the spices, chilli, garlic and ginger make it quite hot and aromatic, they don't seem to hide the flavour of the lobster. I would suggest using North American cooked lobsters as they are readily available and considerably cheaper than British lobsters.

serves 4

2 × 750–900 g (1½–2 lb) cooked lobsters

2 tablespoons groundnut oil

1 onion, chopped

3 garlic cloves, crushed

2.5 cm (1 inch) fresh root ginger, finely grated

2 mild green chillies, seeded and chopped

3 tablespoons *Goan Masala Paste* (see p. 241) or
    a good-quality bought curry paste

FOR THE CUCUMBER AND LIME SALAD:

1 cucumber

2 limes

Salt

method

Pre-heat the oven to 150°C/300°F/Gas Mark 2. Remove the meat from the cooked lobsters (see p. 27). Place the shells on a baking tray and warm them through in the oven.

To make the salad, peel the cucumber and cut it into thick slices. Overlap the cucumber slices on a plate and sprinkle with the juice of one of the limes and some salt. Slice the other lime into wedges to serve with the lobster.

Heat the oil in a large, deep frying pan. Add the onion, garlic, ginger and chillies and fry for about 5 minutes, until soft. Add the masala paste and fry for 2–3 minutes. Fold in the lobster meat and cook gently until it has heated through.

Spoon the mixture back into the lobster shells and serve with the cucumber and lime salad, the lime wedges and maybe some warm naan bread.

alternative fish

Any spiny lobster is ideal for this dish i.e. the native lobsters of Australia, New Zealand, South Africa, the west coast of America and for that matter India.

Rui's Turmeric Fish with Masala Dhal

My friend Rui, from Goa, cooked this dish for Jill and me and our sons when he came to Cornwall last summer. We went wild about it but Rui, who is very modest, couldn't understand what all the fuss was about – he said that he'd just cooked it up from the spices he'd found in the kitchen cupboards. But no one in England would have done it quite like this. So we asked him to cook it once more when we filmed in Goa, in the back garden of a beautiful old blue and white Portuguese house. I was worried that he might lose it a bit in front of the camera but he was a natural and the dish was as good then as it was back in Padstow. Rui stirs some quickly fried mustard seeds, ginger, onions, tomatoes and green chilli into the dhal right at the end of cooking. Now that's real fun.

serves 4

1 teaspoon salt

Juice of 1 lime

1 teaspoon turmeric powder

4 × 175–225 g (6–8 oz) skinned pomfret
   or sea bass fillets

3 tablespoons vegetable oil

FOR THE MASALA DHAL:

250 g (9 oz) red lentils

600 ml (1 pint) water

225 g (8 oz) onions

225 g (8 oz) tomatoes

175 g (6 oz) ghee or *Clarified Butter* (see p. 239)

2 garlic cloves, finely chopped

1 tablespoon turmeric powder

1 teaspoon chilli powder

150 ml (5 fl oz) coconut milk

15 g ($\frac{1}{2}$ oz) black mustard seeds

2.5 cm (1 inch) fresh root ginger,
   finely chopped

2 green finger chillies, seeded and finely chopped

A pinch of asafoetida (optional)

3 tablespoons roughly chopped coriander

Salt

method

For the dhal, cover the lentils with the water and leave them to soak. Coarsely chop half the onions and finely chop the rest. Cut half the tomatoes into small chunks and finely dice the rest. Heat half the ghee or clarified butter in a heavy-based pan. Fry the garlic, coarsely chopped onions and tomato chunks for 5 minutes, until the mixture has cooked to a golden-brown paste. Pour in the lentils and their soaking water and bring to the boil. Add the turmeric, chilli powder and coconut milk and simmer until the lentils have broken down and the mixture has thickened (about 30 minutes). Season to taste with some salt and remove from the heat.

To finish the dhal, heat the rest of the ghee or butter in a large, deep frying pan. Add the mustard seeds, cover the pan with a lid and fry until the seeds begin to pop. Add the ginger, the rest of the onions and tomatoes, the green chillies and the asafoetida, if using. Cook for 5 minutes and then pour everything into the lentil mixture and stir well. Keep warm while you fry the fish.

Mix the salt, lime juice and turmeric together and rub well into the fish fillets. Heat the oil in a large, non-stick frying pan, add the fillets and fry for 2–3 minutes on each side. Stir the coriander into the dhal and serve with the fish. This would be great served with either the *Kachumber Salad* or *Tomato, Onion and Lime Salad* on p. 227.

alternative fish

You can get pomfret pretty easily now in the UK but any chunky fish, such as John Dory, would work equally well; in fact Rui used thick lemon sole fillets when he cooked it in Padstow, which were very good. You could also use large fillets of plaice or thin fillets of small cod and haddock.

the seafood of market stalls and streets • Hua Hin is about 120 miles from Bangkok on the Gulf of Thailand. The king has a summer palace there. The first time I went, there was a lot of open country between it and the capital; now there's not much at all. The first time I went I stepped over a snake at a ramshackle petrol-pump forecourt; this time I had noodle soup in a shining brand-new service station. But despite progress, most of Hua Hin is still pretty good. My hotel still has a garden full of enormous topiary elephants, strung with little fairy lights, and the night market is still there. During the day the market is just another busy, noisy street full of traffic, but come nightfall it is transformed into a festival of food stalls, noisy, colourful and a siren song to the appetite. The first time I went to the market, with my friend Johnny, we sat at a blue table with a thin green plastic tablecloth and ordered tom yung gung, hot and sour seafood soup. It was the hottest thing I'd ever tasted. I wanted to go back and film the whole street in order to capture the frenetic excitement of cooking and

Thailand
and the Far East

eating on the streets. Just one example, I remember a smiling Thai lady mixing raw, shelled mussels with a tapioca and ground-rice batter and pouring it on to a hot flat griddle. As the mixture started to cook she broke it up a little, then cracked an egg on to it. Alongside, she fried some chopped garlic, then she added bean sprouts, chilli vinegar, fresh coriander, shredded spring onion, fish sauce, sugar and salt. She flipped the omelette over on to the vegetables, and scooped it all up to serve it with a chilli dipping sauce. The whole performance took about 45 seconds but, although it was fast, it was food cooked with real care for a discerning public. This chapter is filled with those sorts of dishes, not just from Thailand but from all over South-east Asia, recipes like Hot and Sour Fish Soup, Green Papaya Salad, stir-fried Singapore Seafood Noodles ... the world's best street food.

Hot and Sour Fish Soup

One of the endearing things about life in Thailand is that all the houses are open to the street, so you can walk past somebody's front room and see a whole family watching the telly and eating. It's as if one wall has been entirely removed. I was wandering through the streets of a town a few years back and found a family sitting on a terrace in front of their house eating breakfast. I suppose I was quite rude because I watched them a little bit too long, but they asked me if I'd like to try some of their meal – and this was it! There were also some pickled vegetables and rice and they gave me rainwater to drink. I couldn't even begin to describe how the vegetables were cooked but I've since found this recipe for the soup and it's very good.

serves 4

4 red birdseye chillies, roughly chopped

2.5 cm (1 inch) fresh galangal or root ginger, roughly chopped

1 teaspoon *blachan* (dried shrimp paste)

3 garlic cloves, roughly chopped

6 shallots, roughly chopped

½ teaspoon palm sugar or light muscovado sugar

3–4 tablespoons *Tamarind Water* (see p. 238) or lemon juice

1 litre (1¾ pints) *Chicken Stock* (see p. 232)

3 tablespoons Thai fish sauce (*nam pla*)

75 g (3 oz) snake beans or French beans, topped, tailed and cut into small pieces

100 g (4 oz) monkfish fillet, cut into small pieces

100 g (4 oz) prepared squid (see p. 27), cut into small pieces

2 heads of bok choi, sliced across into 2.5 cm (1 inch) pieces, or 50 g (2 oz) baby leaf spinach

TO GARNISH:

A handful of coriander leaves

1 red finger chilli, seeded and thinly sliced

method

Put the birdseye chillies, galangal or ginger, *blachan*, garlic, shallots and sugar into a mortar or a food processor and work to a coarse paste, adding a little of the tamarind water if necessary.

Bring the chicken stock and the rest of the tamarind water to the boil in a pan. Add the spice paste and simmer for 10 minutes. Strain through a muslin-lined or very fine sieve and add the Thai fish sauce and the beans. Simmer for 1 minute. Add the monkfish and squid and simmer for 1 minute. Add the bok choi or spinach and simmer for a further minute. Ladle the soup into warmed bowls and serve sprinkled with the coriander leaves and red chilli.

alternative fish

You can use any fillets of small fish such as lemon sole, plaice, flounder, prawns, scallops and even cooked mussels dropped in at the end and brought back to the boil.

Crab and Sweetcorn Soup

My reason for including this in the book is that apart from the fact that it is the first oriental dish I ever ate at a Chinese restaurant, in Peterborough, England, in 1964 as it happens, it is also a world classic and is so often ruined by sickly-sweet cans of creamed corn, tasteless crab and gloopy cornflour. I thought it would be interesting to restore the dish to its simplicity and reliance on good fresh ingredients. Paradoxically, when you first taste it you'll probably find it a bit under-flavoured, unencumbered as it is with msg and too much soy. But then the subtlety will grow on you.

serves 4

1.2 litres (2 pints) *Chicken Stock* (see p. 232)

2 ears of sweetcorn

225 g (8 oz) fresh white crab meat

5 teaspoons cornflour

1 teaspoon very finely chopped fresh
   root ginger

2 spring onions, cut into 2.5 cm (1 inch) pieces
   and finely shredded lengthways

1 tablespoon light soy sauce

1 tablespoon Chinese rice wine or dry sherry

1 teaspoon salt

1 egg white, lightly beaten

Freshly ground black pepper

method

Bring the chicken stock to the boil in a pan. Meanwhile, stand the sweetcorn up on a board and slice away the kernels with a large sharp knife. Add the sweetcorn to the stock and simmer for 5 minutes.

Check over the crab meat for any little pieces of shell, keeping the meat in the largest pieces possible.

Mix the cornflour to a smooth paste with a little cold water, stir it into the soup and simmer for 2 minutes. Stir in the crab meat, ginger, spring onions, soy sauce, rice wine or sherry, salt and some pepper to taste. Simmer for 1 minute.

Now give the soup a good stir, remove the spoon and slowly trickle in the beaten egg white so that it forms long thin strands in the soup. Simmer for about 30 seconds and then serve.

Hard-fried Fish in Red Curry with Steamed Jasmine Rice

When we filmed this we just happened to have some very large John Dory in the restaurant, which we bought cheaply from a Padstow fisherman who was keen to exchange them for a few £5 notes so that he could get down to the pub. They made wonderful steaks but this dish is also really good for cheaper fish such as farmed salmon as there's so much flavour in the sauce. You could use expensive fish like sea bass, turbot or wild salmon if you happen to know a fisherman with a lunchtime thirst!

serves 4

2 tablespoons groundnut or sunflower oil, plus
    extra for deep-frying
3 tablespoons *Thai Red Curry Paste* (see p. 240)
200 ml (7 fl oz) coconut milk
1 tablespoon Thai fish sauce (*nam pla*)
1 teaspoon palm sugar or light muscovado sugar
4 × 225 g (8 oz) John Dory steaks
Juice of ½ lime
Salt and freshly ground black pepper
1 quantity of *Steamed Thai Jasmine Rice*
    (see p. 226), to serve

method

Heat the 2 tablespoons of oil in a large, deep frying pan. Add the red curry paste and fry for about 2 minutes, until the spices separate from the oil. Add the coconut milk, fish sauce and sugar and simmer very gently for 10 minutes, until thickened.

Meanwhile, heat some oil for deep-frying to 190°C/375°F. Deep-fry the fish steaks two at a time, for 2 minutes until crisp, golden and cooked through. Lift on to a tray lined with kitchen paper and keep warm in a low oven while you cook the rest. Once the excess oil has drained off the fish, place the steaks on to 4 warmed serving plates. Stir the lime juice into the sauce with some seasoning to taste, spoon it over the fish and serve with the *Steamed Thai Jasmine Rice*.

alternative fish

Steaks of haddock, hake or salmon or even steaks of monkfish, skinned and cut across the bone, would be a great idea. You could also try shark and swordfish steaks.

Chargrilled Prawns with a Simple Thai Dipping Sauce

The prawns in Thailand are unbelievable – so big that they're just like mini lobsters – and I was very keen to come up with a dish that didn't spoil the impact of the whole prawn. That's the thing I feel so strongly about with a lot of seafood. What, after all, is a mussel or oyster out of its shell, or a pile of lobster meat, compared with the same meat back in its shell? So I decided to barbecue the prawns over a traditional Thai charcoal barbecue, which costs literally pence over there. Talk about practicality – it was just a clay pot moulded into a large tin can for strength but it worked beautifully.

serves 4

12–16 unpeeled large raw prawns
A little sunflower oil for brushing

FOR THE THAI DIPPING SAUCE:
2 tablespoons Thai fish sauce (*nam pla*)
Juice of 1 lime
2 tablespoons water
3 red birdseye chillies, thinly sliced

method

Pre-heat your grill or barbecue and allow it to get very hot. Brush the prawns with sunflower oil and cook them for 2 minutes on each side, until they are cooked through and nicely charred on the outside. The dipping sauce is simply made by mixing all the ingredients together.

alternative fish

Use small lobsters or crayfish instead.

Paper-wrapped Prawns in Honey and Ginger

This is a delightful, easy little appetite stimulator, the sort of thing you might serve up with a few ice-cold bottles of Tiger beer. Keeping the ingredients to a minimum does nothing to diminish the excitement of the taste when you open up these little deep-fried parcels.

serves 4

32 peeled large raw prawns

5 cm (2 inches) fresh root ginger, unpeeled

2 tablespoons clear honey

2 tablespoons Chinese rice wine or dry sherry

2 tablespoons dark soy sauce

6 spring onions, thinly sliced

1 teaspoon ground Sichuan peppercorns

Sunflower oil for deep-frying

method

Place the prawns in a bowl. Finely grate the piece of root ginger on to a plate. Collect it all up and squeeze out the juice into the bowl, then stir in the honey, rice wine or sherry and soy sauce. Cover and leave to marinate in the fridge for 1 hour.

Cut out sixteen 18 cm (7 inch) squares of non-stick baking paper. Put a square of paper on a work surface with a corner pointing towards you. Place 2 prawns in the centre and sprinkle over a few of the chopped spring onions and some of the ground Sichuan pepper. Fold the corner nearest you into the centre of the square so that it just covers the prawns. Next fold over the left-hand corner, then the right-hand one. Fold the parcel in half and then tuck in the flap to make a little parcel. Repeat with the rest of the paper squares and prawns.

Heat some oil for deep frying to 190°C/375°F. Fry the parcels a few at a time for about 2 minutes. Remove with a slotted spoon, place on a paper-lined tray and leave to drain while you cook the rest. Serve immediately, letting your guests unwrap their own packages.

Nasi Goreng with Mackerel

The secret of a good nasi goreng is rice that has been cooked well so that the grains are separate, and which has been left to cool but not refrigerated. Leftover rice that has been stored in the fridge overnight does not taste as good. Like so many rice or noodle street dishes from South-east Asia, nasi goreng is a bit of a 'put whatever you like into it' sort of dish. However, it should always include a good curry paste, some thinly sliced omelette and plenty of crisp fried onion flakes. I always put prawns in my nasi goreng and I love some broken-up well-flavoured fish like mackerel in it too.

serves 4

225 g (8 oz) long grain rice

2 × 175–225 g (6–8 oz) mackerel, cleaned
   (see p. 26)

2 large eggs

Sunflower oil for frying

6 large shallots, thinly sliced

175 g (6 oz) peeled cooked North
   Atlantic prawns

1 tablespoon light soy sauce

5 cm (2 inch) piece of cucumber, quartered
   lengthways and sliced

4 spring onions, chopped

Salt and freshly ground black pepper

FOR THE NASI GORENG PASTE:

3 tablespoons groundnut oil

4 large garlic cloves, roughly chopped

2 large shallots, roughly chopped

15 g (½ oz) roasted salted peanuts

6 red finger chillies, roughly chopped

1 tablespoon tomato purée

½ teaspoon *blachan* (dried shrimp paste)

1 tablespoon *ketjap manis* (sweet soy sauce)

method

First make the nasi goreng paste: put the paste ingredients into a food processor and blend until smooth.

Cook the rice in boiling salted water for 15 minutes, until just tender. Drain, rinse well and then spread it out on a tray and leave until cold.

Pre-heat the grill to high. Season the mackerel on both sides with salt and pepper. Lay them on a lightly oiled baking tray or the rack of a grill pan and grill for 4 minutes on each side. Leave them to cool and then flake the flesh into large pieces, discarding the bones.

Next, beat the eggs with salt and pepper then heat a little oil in a frying pan and make three omelettes. The object is to get them as thin as possible. Cook each one till the egg has lightly set on top, then flip over and cook a few seconds on the other side. Roll the omelettes up, leave to cool then thinly slice.

Pour 1 cm (½ inch) of sunflower oil into a frying pan. Add the shallots and fry over a medium heat until crisp and golden brown. Lift them out with a slotted spoon and leave to drain on kitchen paper.

Spoon 2 tablespoons of the oil from frying the shallots into a large wok and get it smoking hot. Add 2 tablespoons of the nasi goreng paste and stir-fry for 2 minutes. Add the cooked rice and stir-fry over a high heat for another 2 minutes, until it has heated through. Add the prawns, the strips of omelette, the fried shallots and the flaked mackerel and stir-fry for another minute. Add the soy sauce, cucumber and most of the spring onions, toss together well and then spoon on to a large warmed plate. Sprinkle with the remaining spring onions and serve straight away.

alternative fish

Try grilled and flaked sea trout, fresh sardines, red mullet, snapper or bream.

Green Papaya Salad

I must confess I've slightly sneaked this one into the book because I like it so much and the connection between it and seafood is just a small quantity of dried shrimps. However, it really is one of the world's great dishes – green papaya, lightly crushed with some chilli, peanuts, tomatoes, green beans, garlic, lime juice and fish sauce. You may find it difficult to get hold of the underripe papaya needed here but you should be able to find it in Asian or Thai grocers. If you really can't get it, the same dish can be made with very underripe mango. In Thailand, they serve the green mango salad with horseshoe crabs. You only eat the roes and in fact you only eat the roes of one species – eat those of any other and you die. You can also die from the roes of the edible one too if you are allergic to them, a fact conveyed to me just before I tried them. I've written this recipe for only one serving because that's how they do it in Thailand, simply because it is impossible to bruise and mix all the ingredients for more than one salad at a time.

serves 1

1 small green (underripe) papaya

1 teaspoon palm sugar or light
    muscovado sugar

A pinch of chopped garlic

A pinch of chopped red birdseye chilli

5 × 10 cm (4 inch) pieces of snake bean or
    5 French beans

A few roasted unsalted peanuts

A pinch of chopped dried shrimps

1 tablespoon Thai fish sauce (*nam pla*)

1 tablespoon *Tamarind Water* (see p. 238)

4 cherry plum tomatoes, halved

Juice of 1 lime

method

Peel the papaya and finely shred it on a mandoline into long, thin shreds. Work your way around the fruit until you get to the core and seeds which you discard.

Moisten the palm sugar (which is always very hard) with a little cold water.

Put the garlic, red chilli and green beans into a mortar or mixing bowl and lightly bruise with the pestle or the end of a rolling pin. Add the sugar, peanuts, dried shrimps, fish sauce, tamarind water, tomatoes and lime juice and bruise everything once more, turning the mixture over with a fork as you do so. Add a good handful of the shredded papaya (about 50 g/2 oz) and turn over and bruise one last time. Serve straight away.

alternative fish

There is no alternative to the dried shrimps. However, underripe mango is an excellent substitute for green papaya.

Steamed Crab with Lemongrass Dressing

Here's another example of trying to give something a bit of a spin, but not too much. Just a little lemongrass, lime juice, fish sauce and chilli, poured over some freshly steamed crab, is all you need. It is just as well this recipe is simple too, because we filmed it on a restaurant jetty in Thailand in temperatures you'd swear were well over 100°C. We were sweating so fast we must have drunk a gallon each of lime soda. Now that's a great drink – fresh lime juice, soda water and a good pinch of salt to help ward off sunstroke. And when it comes out on television it'll look as though we were having the time of our lives, when we actually thought we were about to expire.

serves 4

8–12 Asian swimming crabs or 2 × 900 g (2 lb) brown crabs, live or cooked

FOR THE LEMONGRASS DRESSING:
1 lemongrass stalk, outer leaves removed and the core finely chopped

Finely grated zest and juice of 1 lime
2 tablespoons Thai fish sauce (*nam pla*)
150 ml (5 fl oz) water
1 green finger chilli, seeded and finely chopped
½ teaspoon caster sugar
1 tablespoon roughly chopped coriander

method

Mix all the ingredients for the lemongrass dressing together. If using live crabs, kill them as described on p. 27. For both uncooked and cooked crabs, break off the tail flap and discard. Break off the claw arms, cut them in half at the joint and crack the shells of each piece with a hammer. Now, with a large-bladed knife, chop the body section of the crab in half and gently tug on the legs to pull the body away from the back shell. Use a knife as an added lever if you need to but it should come out quite easily, with the legs still attached. Turn each piece over and pick off the dead man's fingers (soft gills). Discard the back shells or save them for making stock.

Take a large pan and put some sort of trivet in the bottom on which you can rest a plate – a couple of pastry cutters or another upturned plate will do. Pour in some water so that it doesn't quite cover the trivet and bring to the boil.

Pile the pieces of crab on to a heatproof plate and lower it into the pan. Cover and steam for 8 minutes, by which time the crab should be cooked. If you are using cooked crabs, give it just 3–4 minutes to heat through.

To serve, arrange the pieces of crab on a large warmed serving plate. Spoon over the lemongrass dressing and serve straight away.

alternative fish

Lobster, steamed and served with this dressing, is a bit of a work of art. If you throw all the dressing ingredients in a large pot of mussels and steam them open, you'll be amazed too.

Deep-fried Dabs with Tamarind, Garlic and Chilli Sauce

A lot of the flat fish around the coast of Britain, and indeed America and Australia, are rather lacking in flavour. Usually, small dabs, plaice and flounder don't have much to say for themselves but when served up with a sauce like this one they certainly do. Until I first went to Thailand, the idea of deep-frying whole fish with no coating seemed a travesty of good cooking principles but, using very good, clean oil and frying the fish until the skin is very crisp, it was a bit of a revelation. The trick is to get the oil hot enough so that the outside of the fish is crisp but the centre remains moist.

serves 4
Groundnut or sunflower oil for deep-frying
4 × 275–350 g (10–12 oz) dabs, cleaned
   (see p. 26)

FOR THE SAUCE:
50 ml (2 fl oz) *Tamarind Water* (see p. 238)
3 tablespoons Thai fish sauce (*nam pla*)
½ small onion, roughly chopped
2 red finger chillies, seeded and finely chopped
2 garlic cloves, finely chopped
1 cm (½ inch) fresh galangal or root ginger,
   finely chopped
1 teaspoon palm sugar or light soft brown sugar
2 tablespoons water
2 tablespoons chopped coriander

method
First prepare the sauce: put the tamarind water, fish sauce and onion into a mortar or food processor and pound or whizz to a coarse paste. Pour into a bowl and stir in the chillies, garlic, galangal or ginger, sugar, water and chopped coriander.

Heat some oil for deep-frying to 180°C/350°F. Deep-fry the dabs one at a time for about 5 minutes, until very crisp on the outside and cooked through. Remove and drain on kitchen paper. Place on 4 warmed plates and spoon over some of the sauce. Serve the rest separately in a small bowl.

alternative fish

Small plaice, flounder or lemon sole.

Stir-fried Prawns and Squid with Mushrooms and Thai Holy Basil

One day I'd like to write a book about street food. I'm irresistibly drawn to the food of market stalls, the smell of hot burritos or tacos in a dusty northern town of Mexico, the streets in Panjim, Goa, lined with stalls piled high with samosa-like pastries, the noodle carts in Gurney Drive in Penang, Malaysia. America has fantastic street food, too – thoroughly bad for you but endlessly satisfying – but the best of all is in Thailand. This dish was knocked up by a 23-year-old girl on a market stall in Hua Hin and I believe it cost about 50 pence. You could have gone on eating there for ever, her repertoire was so great. There was no menu but she cooked whatever you asked for on just two gas burners, which she controlled with a deftness learned only from working under the sort of pressure that would make even a chef at the Seafood Restaurant decide to pack it all in. An enthusiasm for food and cooking doesn't need language to communicate itself. Once she realized how interested I was in what she was cooking, she took me through all the ingredients she used and got hold of someone who could speak a bit of English from a stall across the road. The thing that impressed me most was the quality of the stock, which was made with pork, whole bulbs of garlic and coriander root. My wine-making friend in Australia, Len Evans, refers to cooks, wine makers, food writers and everyone else in the trade as not the 'food mafia' but the 'food rafia'. We're all connected by a mutual thread of excitement and wherever you go in the world, if you're talking about food and drink you feel at home.

serves 4

3 tablespoons sunflower oil

3 garlic cloves, crushed

175–225 g (6–8 oz) peeled raw prawns

350 g (12 oz) prepared squid (see p. 27), sliced across into rings

175 g (6 oz) button mushrooms, cut into small chunks

3 red birdseye chillies, finely chopped

1 tablespoon light soy sauce

1 tablespoon *ketjap manis* (sweet soy sauce)

1 tablespoon oyster sauce

1 tablespoon Thai fish sauce (*nam pla*)

A large handful of Thai holy basil or ordinary basil leaves

1–2 tablespoons *Chicken Stock* (see p. 232)

Thickly sliced cucumber and spring onions, to garnish

method

Heat a wok or a large deep frying pan until hot. Add the oil and garlic and fry for a few seconds. Add the prawns and stir-fry until they have turned pink. Then add the squid and stir-fry for 1–2 minutes.

Add the mushrooms and red chillies and stir-fry for another few seconds. Add the light soy sauce, sweet soy sauce, oyster sauce and fish sauce and turn everything over once or twice.

Add the basil and the stock and toss for a few seconds. Serve on *Steamed Thai Jasmine Rice* (see p. 226), garnished with the cucumber and spring onions.

alternative fish

You could use any fish that won't fall apart in the stir-frying – monkfish, scallops, John Dory, or even lobster if you're feeling a bit flush.

Singapore Chilli Crab

Last time I was in Singapore, staying at Raffles Hotel, I hopped into a taxi with my friend Johnny. 'You want girls?' said the taxi driver. 'Certainly not!' we said. 'We want Singapore chilli crab.' We had only gone about 200 yards and he stopped quickly, turned up Purvis Street and there we were, at the best place for chilli crab. My life seems to be measured out in memorable meals and this was one of them. We had piles of chilli crab, Tiger beers and rice. The loo was through the kitchen and I swear a rat nipped past me as I made my way to it, with my brain encumbered by Tigers. A great night and a fantastic dish. Make it with cooked crab if you must.

serves 4

2 × 900 g (2 lb) live or cooked crabs

4 tablespoons groundnut or sunflower oil

4 fat garlic cloves, finely chopped

2.5 cm (1 inch) fresh root ginger,
   finely chopped

4 tablespoons tomato ketchup

3 red finger chillies, finely chopped

2 tablespoons dark soy sauce

150 ml (5 fl oz) water

A few turns of the black pepper mill

2 spring onions, cut into 5 cm (2 inch) pieces
   and finely shredded lengthways

method

If using live crabs, kill them as described on p. 27. For both uncooked and cooked crabs, break off the tail flap and discard. Break off the claws, cut them in half at the joint and crack the shells of each piece with a hammer. Take a large-bladed knife and chop the body section of the crab in half. Gently tug on the legs to pull the body away from the back shell. Use a knife as an added lever if you need to but it should come away quite easily, with the legs still attached. Turn each piece over and pick off the dead man's fingers (soft gills). Pour any liquid out of the back shells into a bowl and reserve. You can't use the brown meat for this dish as it makes the vibrant chilli sauce look and taste muddy. You just have to throw it, and the back shells, away or save it for stock.

Heat the oil in a large wok. Add the crab pieces and stir-fry for 3 minutes, adding the garlic and the ginger after 1 minute. Add the juices from the back shell, tomato ketchup, red chillies, soy sauce, water and black pepper. Cover and simmer over a medium heat for 5 minutes if the crab is fresh or 2–3 minutes if using cooked crab. Spoon the crab on to 1 large plate or 4 soup plates, sprinkle over the shredded spring onions and serve straight away.

alternative fish

Good alternatives would be large raw prawns or lobster.

Steamed Stuffed Squid with Sweet Chilli Sauce

What really pleases me about this starter is that when I first ate it I thought I could have been sitting in a restaurant in Hong Kong, or somewhere like Fung Shing in Soho, London, eating a classic Sichuan dish, and yet I made it up myself.

serves 4

4 small prepared squid (see p. 27), with
    pouches no longer than 15 cm (6 inches)
25 g (1 oz) peeled raw prawns
100 g (4 oz) minced pork
1 cm ($\frac{1}{2}$ inch) fresh root ginger, finely grated
2 garlic cloves, crushed
1 tablespoon light soy sauce
1 tablespoon chopped coriander
$\frac{1}{4}$ teaspoon caster sugar
1$\frac{1}{2}$ teaspoons sesame oil

$\frac{1}{2}$ teaspoon salt
Freshly ground Sichuan pepper
2 spring onions, chopped, plus 1 spring onion,
    finely shredded, to garnish

FOR THE SAUCE:
2 tablespoons dark soy sauce
2 tablespoons sweet chilli sauce
2 teaspoons rice vinegar or white wine vinegar
1 teaspoon sesame oil

method

Rinse out the squid pouches. Roughly chop the tentacles and fins and put them in a food processor with the prawns and minced pork. Blend to a coarse mixture. Scrape the mixture into a bowl, add the rest of the ingredients (except for the shredded spring onion and the sauce ingredients) and mix together well. Spoon the mixture into the squid pouches and secure the open ends with cocktail sticks.

Put a trivet or an upturned plate in a large pan. Pour in about 2.5 cm (1 inch) of water and bring to a gentle simmer. Put the squid on a heatproof plate and rest it on the trivet so that it is above the water. Cover the pan with a tight-fitting lid and steam the squid for 20–25 minutes, until cooked through.

Meanwhile, put the ingredients for the sauce into a small pan. Just before the squid are ready, warm the sauce through. Lift the squid on to a board and cut each one across into about 6 thin slices. Arrange them on 4 warmed plates, spoon over some of the sauce and garnish with the spring onion shreds.

alternative fish

Unfortunately there is no other natural container like a squid pouch with which to make this dish. However, the filling is so good you could use it as a stuffing for either won ton wrappers, which you can deep-fry, or dim sum wrappers for steaming, served with the same sauce.

Singapore Seafood Noodles

The essence of this dish is the dried shiitake mushrooms and smoked bacon with noodles and some seafood, such as prawns, scallops and squid. Chinese scallops with bacon, if you like.

serves 4

25 g (1 oz) dried shiitake mushrooms

15 g (½ oz) dried shrimps (optional)

120 ml (4 fl oz) hot water

175 g (6 oz) vermicelli noodles (also known as stir-fry noodles)

2 tablespoons sunflower oil

2 fat garlic cloves, finely chopped

2.5 cm (1 inch) fresh root ginger, finely grated

100 g (4 oz) rindless smoked back bacon, cut into thin strips

1 tablespoon good-quality garam masala paste

100 g (4 oz) prepared squid (see p. 27), thinly sliced

100 g (4 oz) queen scallops, also known as 'queenies'

175 g (6 oz) peeled cooked tiger prawns

3 tablespoons dark soy sauce

1 tablespoon Chinese rice wine or dry sherry

4 spring onions, thinly sliced

method

Soak the dried mushrooms and the dried shrimps, if using, in the hot water for 30 minutes, until soft. Drain, reserving the soaking liquid, and thinly slice the mushrooms.

Drop the noodles into a pan of boiling water, cover and take off the heat. Leave to soak for 1 minute, then drain, toss with a little of the oil to separate the strands.

Heat the rest of the oil in a large wok. Add the garlic and ginger and stir-fry for a few seconds. Add the bacon, curry paste and squid and stir-fry for 2 minutes. Add the mushrooms, dried shrimps and scallops and stir-fry for another minute. Add the prawns, reserved soaking water, soy sauce and rice wine or sherry, followed by the noodles, and toss together gently over a high heat, using 2 forks, for about 1 minute, until everything is hot and well mixed. Toss in the spring onions and serve.

alternative fish

Cooked peeled North Atlantic prawns, cooked shelled mussels, white crab meat, lobster and firm fish such as monkfish or Dover sole fillet.

Pad Thai Noodles with Prawns

This dish, which every Thai restaurant has on its menu, almost doesn't have a proper recipe, it varies so much from place to place. Sometimes it comes out luminous orange, sometimes it's very wet, sometimes too dry, others are disgustingly sweet and on some occasions it's far too hot. I must have eaten about ten versions while trying to track down the perfect recipe, including five in Thailand, but I finally found the best one in south London, of all places, at the Pepper Tree restaurant on Clapham Common. I think that it should be sweet but not too sweet, tart but not too tart and dry but not too dry. And above all, the noodles should still have a little bit of bite to them, just like pasta, and some beansprouts and spring onions should be thrown on top at the last minute. Then you're in danger of falling into an eating frenzy.

serves 2

175 g (6 oz) flat rice noodles

50 ml (2 fl oz) groundnut oil

2 garlic cloves, finely chopped

½ teaspoon dried chilli flakes

10 peeled large raw prawns

2 eggs, beaten

2–3 tablespoons Thai fish sauce (*nam pla*)

2–3 tablespoons *Tamarind Water* (see p. 238)

1 tablespoon palm sugar or light
   muscovado sugar

1 tablespoon dried shrimps, coarsely chopped

½ tablespoon *Thai Pickled Radish*
   (optional, see p. 248)

4 heaped tablespoons roasted peanuts,
   coarsely chopped

4 spring onions, cut into 5 cm (2 inch) pieces
   and finely shredded lengthways

50 g (2 oz) fresh beansprouts

2 tablespoons roughly chopped coriander

method

Soak the noodles in cold water for 1 hour, then drain and set to one side. Heat the oil in a wok over a high heat. Add the garlic, chilli flakes and prawns and stir-fry for 2–3 minutes, until the prawns are just cooked. Pour in the beaten eggs and stir-fry for a few seconds, until they just start to look scrambled. Lower the heat, add the noodles, fish sauce, tamarind water and sugar and toss together for a minute or two until the noodles are tender. Add the dried shrimps, pickled radish, half the peanuts, half the spring onions, half the beansprouts and all the coriander and toss for another minute. Serve sprinkled with the rest of the peanuts, spring onions and beansprouts.

alternative fish

Like other South-east Asian rice and noodle dishes – nasi goreng, Singapore noodles etc. – you can add more or less what you like to this, such as thinly sliced squid, sliced scallops or even mussels.

Steamed Grey Mullet with Black Beans and Shiitake Mushrooms

Steaming fish with ginger and serving it with soy sauce and spring onions is the classic, simple Chinese treatment that never fails to delight. If you used just these ingredients in the following recipe you would be pretty happy. But I'm addicted to fermented salted black beans – they have an unbeatable, salty savouriness which goes so well with steamed fish like this. Adding a few shiitake mushrooms and some golden fried garlic makes for great eating.

serves 4

A handful of dried shiitake mushrooms
   (about 15 g/½ oz)
5 cm (2 inches) fresh root ginger
1 star anise
1 × 900 g–1.5 kg (2–3 lb) or 2 × 450–550 g
   (1–1¼ lb) grey mullet, cleaned (see p. 26)
50 ml (2 fl oz) dark soy sauce

1 tablespoon Chinese rice wine or dry sherry
1 tablespoon salted black beans,
   coarsely chopped
2 tablespoons sunflower oil
1 teaspoon roasted sesame oil
4 spring onions, thinly sliced on the diagonal
3 garlic cloves, thinly sliced

method

Put the dried mushrooms into a bowl, cover with warm water and leave to soak for 30 minutes.

Meanwhile, construct yourself a steamer. For large or small fish you can place 2 or 3 large metal pastry cutters in a fish kettle and then rest the rack on top. Alternatively, for small fish, you could place a trivet or an upturned plate in a pan large enough to hold the fish and then rest another plate on top, or cross 4–6 chopsticks or bamboo skewers in the base of a wok and rest a plate on top.

Drain the mushrooms, reserving the liquid. Discard the woody end of the mushroom stalks and thinly slice the caps. Pour the soaking water from the mushrooms into the steamer and add just enough water so that the level does not come above the rack or plate. Bring to the boil.

Peel the piece of ginger, cut it in half and then cut it across into thin slices. Add the peelings and half the slices to the steaming water, together with the star anise.

Slash both sides of the fish right down to the bone: 4 times for a large fish and twice for small ones. Push a little of the remaining sliced ginger into the slashes, put the fish in the steamer and scatter over any remaining ginger and the sliced mushrooms. Cover with some foil or a well-fitting lid and steam a large fish for 20–25 minutes or smaller fish for 15 minutes.

Meanwhile, put the soy sauce, rice wine or sherry and black beans into a small saucepan and the sunflower and sesame oil into a small frying pan.

When the fish is cooked, lift it out of the steamer on to a warmed serving dish, making sure you take the mushrooms with it. Ladle 85 ml (3 fl oz) of the steaming liquid into the pan containing the soy sauce mixture and bring to a gentle simmer. Spoon it over the fish and then sprinkle over the sliced spring onions. Heat the sunflower and sesame oil in the frying pan, add the garlic and fry gently for a few seconds, until lightly golden. Pour this straight over the fish. Serve with some *Steamed Rice* (see p. 226).

alternative fish

Whole bass, bream or snapper. Also, this dish is about the only one that I think makes carp at all acceptable for eating.

a cook's heaven • *Last year, I was offered the job of a lifetime, to go to Australia to judge the best restaurant in the country for the Australian Gourmet Traveller. I ate my way around the country, not just in smart restaurants but in good cafés, wine bars and even a tea room in Perth. I remember barbecued pork in Chinatown, Sydney, and oysters with bloody Mary by the river in Brisbane, a relaxed restaurant out at Petaluma, a winery in the Adelaide hills. On the trip I became addicted to a white wine called Mad Fish Bay, and I also learnt a great deal about Australian cooking. But perhaps even more interesting were the food markets I visited, like the fish market in Sydney or the Footscray market in Melbourne. It was these which formed my opinion that Australia is a cook's heaven.*

The Footscray market, especially, really astonished me. It was so multicultural as to be almost bewildering. There were Vietnamese fishmongers and Chinese butchers; Thai vegetable stalls selling morning glory, snake beans, pea aubergines, lesser ginger and a fungi called rat

Australia

ears; Lebanese takeaway food stalls; Armenian and Turkish and a couple of Arabs wandering through in flowing robes; there was even an Australian butcher selling huge legs of lamb at ridiculously knocked-down prices so that he could get off to a football match. His stall was next to a Vietnamese butcher's who had various extraordinary organs like udders (which I was assured were very nice salted, braised and thinly sliced, with spring onion, chilli and rice paddy spinach called kang kung, in the popular Vietnamese soup called pho, so I tried it). The choice and availability of such a diversity of food is what makes Australia a cook's heaven. Most of it is grown locally so that even strange vegetables from Laos or Cambodia are as fresh as the basil and dill which you buy in giant, heavenly aromatic bunches.

Lindy Milan's Tuna with Anchovy Sauce

Two Australian cookery books I like, Plates and Flavours, are written by a friend of mine, Lindy Milan, who well understands how people really use recipes. First, the actual books are ruggedly constructed; secondly, virtually every recipe has an extremely appetizing picture to go with it because, let's face it, except for seriously accomplished cooks, everyone cooks by looking at the pictures these days; thirdly, the recipes are simple, laid out very clearly, and there aren't too many of them; and finally and most importantly, they're very good recipes using ingredients that you would want to cook with. I can't be more analytical about the difference between a good cookery writer and a boring one – all I can say is you've either got it or you ain't, and Lindy's got it in ladlefuls.

serves 6

6 × 225 g (8 oz) thick tuna loin steaks

3 garlic cloves, peeled

A small bunch of parsley sprigs

A small bunch of coriander sprigs

A handful of basil leaves

2–3 tablespoons olive oil

50 g (2 oz) small black olives, such as Ligurian ones

FOR THE SAUCE:

375 ml (13 fl oz) *Fish Stock* (see p. 232) or beef stock

200 ml (7 fl oz) red wine

6 anchovy fillets in oil, rinsed and finely chopped

2 tablespoons double cream

method

Pre-heat the oven to 200°C/400°F/Gas Mark 6. For the sauce, bring the fish stock and wine to the boil in a pan and leave to simmer until reduced to 200 ml (7 fl oz).

Meanwhile, trim any dark flesh from the tuna. With the food processor running, drop the garlic and herbs into the machine through the tube and roughly chop them up. (Alternatively, chop them by hand.) Dip the edges of the tuna steaks in this mixture.

Remove the stock and wine reduction from the heat and cool slightly. Whisk in the anchovies so that they dissolve into the sauce. Return to a gentle heat and add the cream. Taste for seasoning and adjust if necessary. It is unlikely it will need any salt but it may need a little more cream. Keep warm.

Heat the olive oil in an ovenproof frying pan and cook the tuna steaks on one side only for 1 minutes, until brown and crisp. Turn them over, put the pan in the oven and cook for 5 minutes, no more.

Transfer the tuna steaks to 6 warmed plates and pour over the sauce. Scatter over the olives and serve with *Garlic and Olive Oil Mash* (see p. 172) and *Blanched French Beans with Tomatoes and Thyme* (see p. 222).

alternative fish

Swordfish, shark or any meaty fish will work, because this is a 'fish as meat' kind of dish.

Lemongrass Plaice with Coriander Salsa and Coconut Rice

Coconut rice is a must. I've taken fillets of rather underwhelmingly-flavoured plaice, coated them with a delicate green lemongrass, chilli and coriander paste, then grilled them to serve with the rice and a slightly sweet salsa. This dish suggests some of the lighter cooking from areas like Kuala Lumpur and Singapore, which are reflected in Australian cuisine. We in the West tend to think of those places as having traditional time-honoured dishes yet, in fact, they are just as likely to experiment with quick cooking techniques and light flavours as we are.

serves 4

12 × 50 g (2 oz) skinned plaice fillets

FOR THE LEMONGRASS AND CHILLI PASTE:

5 lemongrass stalks, outer leaves removed and
   the core roughly chopped

6 red birdseye chillies, roughly chopped

6 garlic cloves, roughly chopped

3 kaffir lime leaves or strips of lime zest

A small bunch of coriander

120 ml (4 fl oz) sunflower oil

1½ tablespoons Thai fish sauce (*nam pla*)

1½ teaspoons freshly ground black pepper

FOR THE COCONUT RICE:

1 tablespoon *Clarified Butter* (see p. 239)

175 g (6 oz) Thai jasmine rice

300 ml (10 fl oz) coconut milk

50 ml (2 fl oz) water

½ teaspoon salt

1 small bay leaf

FOR THE TOMATO AND CORIANDER SALSA:

2 tomatoes, cut into small dice

2 spring onions, sliced

1 tablespoon red wine vinegar

A pinch of caster sugar

A pinch of cayenne pepper

A pinch of salt

2 tablespoons chopped coriander

method

First make the lemongrass and chilli paste: put the paste ingredients into a food processor and blend until smooth.

For the coconut rice, heat the clarified butter in a pan, add the rice and stir around until all the grains are coated in the butter. Add all but 2 tablespoons of the coconut milk, plus the water, salt and bay leaf. Bring to the boil, cover and reduce the heat to low. Cook for 15 minutes, until all the liquid has been absorbed and the rice is tender.

Meanwhile, mix together all the ingredients for the salsa and set to one side.

Mix the lemongrass and chilli paste with the reserved coconut milk. Lay the plaice fillets on a lightly oiled baking tray and brush each one with some of the mixture, then grill the fish for 3 minutes. Serve with the coconut rice and salsa.

alternative fish

This recipe lets you liven up fillets of plaice, haddock, cod or coley or you can use any flat fish fillets such as lemon sole or flounder, or fillets from small codling, haddock or Australian flat-head.

Moreton Bay Bug and Fennel Risotto with Lemon Oil

This comes from my Australian Restaurant of the Year that I chose last year – E'cco in Brisbane. The chef, Philip Johnson, cooked in London for a while but I put his influences down to being more European than a lot of Australian chefs. When I met Philip again this year, we talked about anchovies, olive oil and balsamic vinegar. It reminded me of a time when I heard of a famous painter talking about what he'd discussed when he'd met another painter … the price of paint, of course. Philip's cooking was simple but imaginative and, above all, fun.

This dish was the one that did it for me. Moreton Bay bugs and the almost-identical Balmain bugs are a type of shellfish known as flat-head lobsters, which appear in Italy as cigales. Generally, their flavour is bordering on the indifferent but if you only cook them lightly and make them into a beautiful risotto flavoured with lemon and fennel, you can turn a judge's heart. I don't expect many people to be able to get hold of flat-head lobsters. However, raw prawns or even lobster make an excellent substitute, and we have used the latter to photograph the dish opposite.

serves 4

10 uncooked Moreton Bay bug tails or
   2 × 450 g (1 lb) uncooked lobster
1.2–1.25 litres (2–2¼ pints) *Chicken Stock*
   (see p. 232)
1 teaspoon fennel seeds
2 tablespoons olive oil
½ fennel bulb, thinly sliced
¼ teaspoon dried chilli flakes
2 shallots, very finely chopped
1 garlic clove, crushed
350 g (12 oz) Carnaroli or arborio rice

50 g (2 oz) Parmesan cheese, finely grated
15 g (½ oz) butter
1 tablespoon lemon juice
2 tablespoons chopped fennel herb (or the
   frondy tops from the fennel bulbs)
Salt and freshly ground black pepper

TO GARNISH:
Sprigs of fennel herb
Parmesan shavings
Lemon extra virgin olive oil

method

If you are using Moreton Bay bugs, break open the shell along the underside of each one and lift out the meat. Cut the bug meats across into slices 2 cm (¾ inch) thick. If you are using lobster, kill them by dipping them into plenty of rapidly boiling salted water. Bring back to the boil and simmer for 5 minutes. Lift out of the pan then crack the shells. Remove the meat as described in p. 27 and cut into chunks. By boiling them for this time, the lobster will be killed and the meat easy to remove from the shell, though still part raw.

Bring the chicken stock to the boil in a pan and leave over a low heat. Heat a dry, heavy-based frying pan over a high heat, add the fennel seeds and toss them around for

continued overleaf

a few seconds until they start to darken slightly and smell nicely aromatic. Tip into a mortar or spice grinder and grind to a fine powder.

Heat the olive oil in a pan, add the fennel, ground fennel seeds, chilli flakes, shallots and garlic and cook until the shallots are soft and translucent – about 7 minutes. Season with a little salt and pepper. Add the rice and stir until it is well coated in the oil. Increase the heat, add a ladleful of the hot chicken stock and bring to the boil. Reduce the heat to very low and leave it to simmer, adding another ladleful of stock as each one is absorbed and stirring frequently, until the rice is almost cooked – approximately 20–25 minutes. Add the sliced bug tails or whole prawns and simmer for 2–3 minutes or until they are just cooked through.

Fold in the Parmesan, butter, lemon juice and some seasoning to taste. Stir in the fennel herb and make sure the mixture is not too wet – increase the heat and cook to allow the excess liquid to evaporate if it is.

Spoon the risotto into bowls, top with the sprigs of fennel herb and Parmesan shavings and garnish with a little black pepper and a drizzle of lemon oil.

alternative fish

Bugs are the same family as lobster, spiny lobster and freshwater crayfish and all would be suitable for this dish. Large, peeled raw prawns would also work very well, but leave them whole. You'll need to use about 12. The risotto is nearly as good made with lightly cooked lobster meat, folded in at the very end just to heat through.

Grilled Cod with Laksa Noodles and Sambal Blachan

The idea behind this dish is very straightforward. Take a lovely thick fillet of grilled cod and set it on top of a spice and coconut laksa with egg noodles, so the soft delicate cod flakes taste sweet against the fiery fragrance of coconut and chilli.

serves 4

120 ml (4 fl oz) sunflower oil, plus extra
  for brushing
1 quantity of *Laksa Spice Paste* (see p. 240)
450 ml (15 fl oz) *Chicken Stock* or *Fish Stock*
  (see p. 232)
4 × 175–225 g (6–8 oz) pieces of unskinned
  cod fillet
50 g (2 oz) dried medium egg noodles
400 ml (14 fl oz) coconut milk
100 g (4 oz) fresh beansprouts
4 spring onions, thinly sliced on the diagonal

A handful of chopped mixed mint, basil
  and coriander
1 lime, cut into 4 wedges
Salt and freshly ground black pepper

FOR THE SAMBAL BLACHAN:
2 kaffir lime leaves (optional)
8 red finger chillies, sliced
1 teaspoon salt
1 teaspoon *blachan* (dried shrimp paste)
Zest and juice of 1 lime

method

For the *sambal blachan*, if using lime leaves, remove the spines and shred the leaves very finely. Put them in a food processor with the chillies, salt, shrimp paste, lime zest and juice and blend to a coarse paste. Spoon into a small serving bowl.

Heat the oil in a large pan, add the laksa paste and fry for 10 minutes, stirring constantly, until it smells very fragrant. Add the stock and simmer for 10 minutes.

Pre-heat the grill to high. Brush both sides of the cod with a little sunflower oil and season with some salt and pepper. Place on a lightly oiled baking tray, skin-side up, and grill for 8 minutes.

Meanwhile, drop the noodles into a pan of boiling salted water, cover and remove from the heat. Leave to soak for 4 minutes, then drain.

Add the coconut milk to the soup and simmer for 3 minutes. Add the noodles, beansprouts, spring onions and 1 teaspoon of salt.

To serve, spoon the laksa into 4 large warmed soup plates and place a piece of cod in the centre of each. Scatter the chopped mint, basil and coriander around the edge and then spoon a little of the *sambal blachan* over the cod. Serve the rest separately, with the lime wedges.

alternative fish

Try this with a thick fillet of snapper, a halibut steak or a thick fillet of haddock.

Squid, Mint and Coriander Salad with Roasted Rice

This starter was inspired by a visit to a Vietnamese market in Cabramatta, a suburb of Sydney, Australia. There were no translations for any of the dishes and all I could do was point to pictures of the things I wanted. The food was a riot of unfamiliar flavours and smells but one thing I particularly remember is the fantastic textural effect of adding roasted rice to salads and other dishes. I don't think we in the West have really begun to appreciate the subtleties of texture that the Chinese and Thai understand. The Chinese, for example, have 20 gradations of tenderness, from literally melting in the mouth to so rubbery you could hardly cut it with a knife – like sea cucumbers, a delicacy whose qualities I have yet to appreciate.

serves 4

225 g (8 oz) prepared small squid (see p. 27)

2 tablespoons groundnut oil

A good pinch of cayenne pepper

2 teaspoons long grain rice

1 Romaine lettuce heart, cut across into
   wide strips

4 spring onions, trimmed, halved and
   finely shredded

A handful of mint leaves

A handful of coriander sprigs

Salt and freshly ground black pepper

FOR THE DRESSING:

1 red finger chilli, thinly sliced into rings

50 ml (2 fl oz) white wine vinegar

Juice of 1 lime

2 tablespoons Thai fish sauce (*nam pla*)

2 tablespoons water

$\frac{1}{2}$ teaspoon caster sugar

1 lemongrass stalk, outer leaves removed and
   the core very finely chopped

method

Cut along one side of each squid pouch and open it out flat. Score the inner side into a diamond pattern with the tip of a small, sharp knife, then cut the squid into 5 cm (2 inch) squares. Separate the tentacles, if large. Season with a little salt and pepper.

For the dressing, cover the chilli slices with vinegar and leave to steep for half an hour.

Heat the oil in a wok. Add the squid and stir-fry for 2 minutes. Transfer to a plate, sprinkle with the cayenne and leave to cool, but don't refrigerate.

Meanwhile, heat a small, heavy-based frying pan over a high heat. Add the rice and toss for a few minutes until it is richly browned and smells nutty. Tip into a mortar or mug and pound it with a pestle or a rolling pin end to break it up. Don't grind it into fine powder.

To serve, toss together the lettuce, spring onions, mint and coriander and spread on a large oval platter. Scatter over the squid and any oil left in the pan. Lift the chilli slices out of the vinegar but keep the vinegar for the next time. Mix with the rest of the dressing ingredients, spoon over the squid and sprinkle with the roasted rice. Serve straight away.

alternative fish

Cuttlefish or peeled raw prawns would work very well.

Pan-fried Whiting with Capers and Nut-brown Butter

This dish comes from a restaurant that I visit every time I go to Australia, in Pittwater, north of Sydney. It's called the Claireville Kiosk and it's one of those lovely old single-storey clapperboard houses with a fly-screen door that always opens with a squeak. The food is always dead simple but if ever there was a perfect combination, it's sand whiting, nut-brown butter and tiny capers with some good, freshly chopped parsley and a little lemon juice. Maybe I'm getting boring in my old age but a dish like this just gets me so excited. We filmed it up in Noosa in Queensland, Australia. It was one of those occasions when the sun's setting fast, the light's going, the tide's coming in and the director wants a beer. You've got to get it right in the first take without burning yourself or cutting yourself and then try to say something meaningful to sum up while the sun's slipping away nicely. But it's such a good dish the whole lot just falls into place – no worries!

serves 4

3 tablespoons sunflower oil

4 × 275–350 g (10–12 oz) sand whiting or
  ordinary whiting, cleaned (see p. 26)

25 g (1 oz) plain flour, seasoned with a little
  salt and pepper

100 g (4 oz) butter

2 tablespoons small capers, drained

Juice of 1 lemon

2 tablespoons chopped parsley

Salt and freshly ground black pepper

method

Heat the oil in a large frying pan. Dip the fish into the seasoned flour and pat off any excess. Put the fish in the pan and fry over a medium–high heat for 4 minutes on each side. Carefully slide a fish slice under the head and tail of each fish in turn and place on 4 warmed plates. Keep warm.

Pour away the oil and wipe out the pan. Add the butter and return the pan to a medium heat. Leave the butter to melt and then cook until it has turned light brown and smells slightly nutty.

Add the capers, lemon juice, parsley and some seasoning and let it bubble for a few seconds, then pour some over each fish. Serve with the *Fine Leaf and Herb Salad with Lemon Oil Dressing* (see p. 228).

alternative fish

In England you can use small whiting but, sadly, they don't have the flavour of their Australian counterpart. I think a trout would be as good a fish as any for this but if you can get hold of Arctic char, you'll reach equivalent perfection to the Aussie sand whiting.

Deep-fried Skate with Thai Mayo

We started by calling this mayonnaise Asian tartare sauce at the restaurant, but it soon became known as Thai mayo by the chefs, and the name stuck.

serves 4

4 × 250 g (9 oz) skate wings

Sunflower oil for deep-frying

1 quantity of *Tempura Batter* (see p. 85), made without the sesame seeds

Salt

Lime wedges and coriander sprigs, to garnish

FOR THE THAI MAYO:

1 lemongrass stalk, outer leaves removed and the core finely chopped

4 tablespoons chopped coriander

2.5 cm (1 inch) fresh root ginger, finely grated

3 garlic cloves, crushed

Finely grated zest of 1 lime

1 green chilli, seeded and finely chopped

1 quantity of *Mayonnaise* made with sunflower oil and the juice of 1 lime instead of vinegar (see p. 235)

method

For the Thai mayo, simply stir all the ingredients into the mayonnaise and put in the fridge until needed.

Trim away the frill from the edges of the skate wings with kitchen scissors and then sprinkle lightly on both sides with a little salt.

Heat some oil for deep-frying to 190°C/375°F. Dip the skate wings into the batter and fry 1 or 2 at a time for 4–5 minutes, until crisp and golden brown. Place on a tray lined with plenty of kitchen paper and keep warm in a low oven while you cook the remaining skate. Serve immediately, garnished with lime wedges and a small bunch of coriander sprigs, accompanied by the Thai mayo and maybe some *Roughly Cut Chips* (see p. 224).

alternative fish

Any skinned large fillets of flaky white fish such as cod, haddock and hake would work equally well. So would plaice, sole or any other kind of fish that you would find in a fish and chip shop.

Seared Red Mullet with Sweet Red Pepper Dressing

A friend of mine, Sarah Burns, rang me up from Australia the other day and said 'I'm in Brett's Fishmongers in Seaforth. I've got some barra fillet, you're the fish cook, what do I do with it?'.

Barramundi she meant. She organizes the Restaurant of the Year for Australian Gourmet Traveller, which I judged last year. She is very knowledgeable about restaurant food and fond of light elegant fish dishes, so it was going to be a tricky assignment. The answer in such cases is not to try too hard. This first course is what I came up with. I couldn't get any barramundi in Cornwall, so I used red mullet and kept it simple. I've since tried it with barramundi and it's great. There's another recipe for barra on page 90 and I think Sarah would like that too.

serves 4

4 little red peppers or mild red chillies

Olive oil for brushing

4 × 100 g (4 oz) unskinned fillets of red mullet

Salt and freshly ground black pepper

Sea salt flakes, coarsely ground black pepper
   and a handful of small flat-leaf parsley
   sprigs to garnish

FOR THE RED PEPPER DRESSING:

750 g (1 ½ lb) red peppers, seeded and chopped

85 ml (3 fl oz) sherry vinegar

Extra virgin olive oil for drizzling

method

For the dressing, liquidize the red peppers until smooth. Tip the purée into a fine-meshed sieve placed over a bowl and gently shake out as much juice as possible. You should be left with about 450 ml (15 fl oz) of juice. Put this into a pan and boil until it has reduced to 25 ml (1 fl oz). It needs to be deep red and exceedingly concentrated.

Meanwhile, boil the sherry vinegar until reduced to 1 tablespoon and pre-heat the grill to high. Grill the little peppers, turning them, until they are black all over. Leave to cool, then peel off the skin. Leave the stalk on but remove the seeds by making a small incision and scraping them out with a teaspoon. Brush with a little olive oil and season with salt.

Stir the reduced sherry vinegar, ¼ teaspoon of salt and some black pepper into the reduced pepper juice and keep warm. Heat a ridged cast iron griddle or a dry, heavy-based frying pan until smoking hot. Brush the fish fillets on both sides with lots of olive oil and season with a little salt. Put them in the pan, skin-side down, and cook for 1 ½ minutes, then turn over and cook for a further 1 ½ minutes.

Place the fillets on 4 warmed plates. Spoon the red pepper juice round the fish on the plate, then put your thumb over the top of a bottle of extra virgin olive oil and drizzle a lick or two of that over the top. Finish with some flakes of sea salt and coarsely ground black pepper, and garnish with the parsley sprigs.

alternative fish

This work well with any smart, trendy fish – John Dory or sea bass and of course barramundi.

Warm Salad of Seared Monkfish and Tiger Prawns
with a Fennel Butter Vinaigrette

I originally wrote this first course for a very glossy advertising brochure for Wedgwood china but the idea came from a trip to Umbria in Italy, where there is no seafood whatsoever. However, they do serve plates of rabbit roasted with white wine, garlic, olive oil and fennel seeds. Roasted until all the accompaniments have reduced to a highly concentrated coating for the rabbit, which is sensational. I thought at the time that those fennel seeds would work beautifully with seafood, especially monkfish, some prawns, some small salad leaves from my garden, a little sherry vinegar, olive oil and a shred or two of the dried Mexican chilli, so good with seafood, called pasilla. *So this recipe was commissioned by an Anglo-Irish company and based on an idea from Italy but it belongs in the Australian chapter since it is a good example of what is called fusion cooking. This is the often unsuccessful throwing together of ingredients from two or more cuisines. Of course, this one works perfectly.*

serves 4

2 × 100 g (4 oz) thin monkfish fillets taken
   from a small monkfish tail

3 tablespoons olive oil

1 tablespoon lemon juice

1/2 teaspoon crushed black peppercorns

1/2 teaspoon crushed fennel seeds

1/2 teaspoon finely shredded pasilla chilli or
   dried chilli flakes

12 unpeeled raw tiger prawns

3 tablespoons sherry vinegar

100 g (4 oz) *Clarified Butter* (see p. 239)

1 large plum tomato, skinned, seeded and
   diced (see p. 238)

2 tablespoons coarsely chopped fennel herb

150 g (5 oz) mixed baby salad leaves

Salt and freshly ground black pepper

method

Trim away any membrane from the outside of the monkfish fillets. Mix together 2 tablespoons of the olive oil, 1 teaspoon of salt, the lemon juice, peppercorns, fennel seeds and chilli in a shallow dish. Add the monkfish fillets, turn once or twice in the mixture and set aside to marinate for 1 hour, turning them now and then.

Twist the heads off the tiger prawns if necessary and then peel them, leaving the last tail segment in place.

Heat the rest of the oil in a heavy-based frying pan. Take the monkfish fillets out of the marinade and cook over a high heat for 2 minutes on each side, until lightly browned. Place on a plate and keep warm. Add the prawns to the pan and toss over a high heat for 2 minutes, until cooked through and lightly browned. Take the prawns out and keep warm with the monkfish.

Remove the pan from the heat and add the sherry vinegar and the rest of the marinade and let it bubble as the heat dissipates. Add the clarified butter, diced tomato and chopped fennel herb. Season to taste with salt and pepper.

To serve, cut the monkfish diagonally into slices 1 cm (½ inch) thick. Arrange the salad leaves, sliced monkfish and prawns in the centre of 4 large plates and spoon the dressing around the edge.

alternative fish

Try Dover sole instead of monkfish and scallops instead of prawns.

Oysters in Tempura Batter with Sesame Seeds and Lime

One of the key imperatives for me in this book is to try and keep my own recipes, of which this first course is one, as simple as possible because that's such a feature of the classic seafood dishes I've found all over the world. In recipe writing, the inclination to gild the lily is almost irresistible but here I think I've resisted it.

serves 4

20 oysters
Sunflower oil for deep-frying

FOR THE TEMPURA BATTER:
50 g (2 oz) plain flour
50 g (2 oz) cornflour
A small pinch of salt
4 teaspoons toasted sesame seeds
175 ml (6 fl oz) ice-cold soda water
Lime wedges, to serve

FOR THE DIPPING SAUCE:
4 tablespoons dark soy sauce
4 tablespoons water
Juice of 1 lime

method

Open all the oysters (see p. 27) and pour off all the liquor. Carefully cut the meats out of the bottom, deeper shells. Keep these deeper shells for serving.

Mix together the ingredients for the dipping sauce and pour into 4 small dipping saucers or bowls.

Heat some oil for deep-frying to 190°C/375°F. Make the batter by sifting the flour, cornflour and salt into a bowl. Stir in the sesame seeds, then stir in the ice-cold soda water (it must be very, very cold and from a new bottle for this batter to be successful) until only just mixed in but still a bit lumpy. If it seems a bit thick add a drop more water. You want the batter to be very thin and almost transparent. Dip in the oysters, one at a time, drop them into the hot oil and fry for 1 minute, until crisp and golden. Lift out and drain very briefly on kitchen paper. Then put the oysters back in their shells and arrange on 4 plates. Serve with the lime wedges and dipping sauce.

Roasted Fillet of Hake with Crisp Parsley and Garlic Crumbs and Warm Olive Oil Mayonnaise

I'm a great fan of slightly thinned mayonnaise as a sauce for a thick fillet of fish. And the garlic, parsley and olive oil breadcrumb coating for the fish, crisped in the oven, goes very well with the sauce. This dish is crying out for a chilled bottle of Sancerre rosé.

serves 4

4 × 200–225 g (7–8 oz) thick pieces of skinned hake fillet

3 slices of day-old white bread (about 175 g/6 oz)

15 g (¹/₂ oz) flat-leaf parsley leaves

3 garlic cloves, finely chopped

4 tablespoons olive oil

2 tablespoons hot water

¹/₂ quantity of *Mayonnaise* made with olive oil (see p. 235)

Salt, freshly ground black pepper and freshly ground white pepper

method

Pre-heat the oven to 240°C/475°F/Gas Mark 9. Season the hake fillets well with salt and black pepper and place them on a well-oiled shallow baking tray.

For the parsley and garlic crust, remove the crusts from the bread, break it into pieces and put it in a food processor. Add the parsley, garlic, 1 teaspoon of salt and some black pepper and whizz to fine crumbs. With the machine still running, gradually add the oil through the hole in the lid until just mixed in. Carefully press the crumb mixture on to the top of each piece of fish. Bake for 10–12 minutes, until the crust is golden brown and the fish is cooked through.

Put the hake on to 4 warmed plates. Gradually mix the hot water into the mayonnaise to make a smooth sauce and season with a little salt and freshly ground white pepper to taste. Spoon the sauce around the fish and serve with some *Boiled Potatoes* or *Steamed Potatoes* (see p. 223).

alternative fish

This also works really well with cod and haddock.

Grilled Tuna with Roasted Fennel
and Tomatoes and Apple Balsamic Vinegar

I think the best restaurant in Noosa, Australia, at the time of writing is Season. It's just the sort of restaurant I like – simple but high-quality ingredients perfectly cooked without pretension. This dish was on the menu last time I was there but this is not their recipe, just my idea of how they might have done it. If you cannot get apple balsamic vinegar, use ordinary balsamic vinegar instead.

serves 4

2 fennel bulbs
450 g (1 lb) large plum tomatoes
Olive oil
4 × 175–225 g (6–8 oz) thick tuna loin steaks
Sea salt flakes and coarsely crushed
 black pepper

FOR THE SAUCE:
1 tablespoon apple balsamic vinegar
$\frac{1}{2}$ teaspoon fennel seeds, lightly crushed
$\frac{1}{2}$ teaspoon coarsely crushed black pepper
85 ml (3 fl oz) extra virgin olive oil
$\frac{1}{2}$ teaspoon sea salt flakes

method

Pre-heat the oven to 240°C/475°F/Gas Mark 9. Cut each fennel bulb lengthways through the root into 5 thin slices so they stay together in one piece. Drop them into a pan of boiling water, bring back to the boil and cook for 1 minute. Drain on kitchen paper.

Remove the cores from the tomatoes, cut them in half and place cut-side up in a lightly oiled shallow roasting tin. Sprinkle over some salt and pepper. Lay the fennel slices on an oiled baking tray, sprinkle with a little oil and some salt and pepper. Roast the tomatoes and the fennel for 20 minutes, then remove the tray of fennel slices. Reduce the oven temperature to 150°C/300°F/Gas Mark 2 and leave the tomatoes to roast for a further 1$\frac{1}{2}$ hours.

For the sauce, put the apple balsamic vinegar, fennel seeds, black pepper and olive oil into a small pan and set aside.

Shortly before the tomatoes have finished roasting, pre-heat the grill to high. Brush the tuna steaks on both sides with olive oil, season well with salt and pepper and place on the rack of the grill pan or on a baking tray. Grill for just 3 minutes on each side. Put the fennel back in the oven to heat through. Set the pan of dressing over a very low heat just to warm through.

To serve, put the roasted vegetables on 4 warmed plates. Put the tuna on top and sprinkle with a little sea salt and crushed black pepper. Stir the sea salt flakes into the dressing and spoon it around the outside of each plate.

alternative fish

Try this with swordfish or porbeagle shark.

Jack's Mud Crab Omelette

Jack was a customer at Two Small Rooms, a delightful restaurant in Brisbane. He visited the restaurant every Saturday night and ordered this omelette every time, followed by a steak. There's not much more to the story really except to say he was one of those much-loved customers who don't complain and keep coming back, then one day they don't. The longer you run a restaurant the more of those there are. It's a great way of writing a dish up on a menu so that Jack's memory lives on.

Mud crabs come from the mangrove swamps of the northern part of Australia. They look a bit like European brown crabs with equally powerful and dangerous claws. The meat, however, is more like the blue crabs of Australia and Asia – more fibrous and easier to extract. A mud crab salad and a glass or two of Mad Fish Bay white – just perfect.

serves 4

FOR THE NAM PRIK SAUCE:

Juice of 1 lime

1 large garlic clove, peeled

1 tablespoon *nam prik*

½ teaspoon *sambal oelek*

25 ml (1 fl oz) *ketjap manis*

100 g (4 oz) palm sugar or light
   muscovado sugar

2 tablespoons chopped coriander

1 teaspoon chopped mint

FOR THE VEGETABLE STIR-FRY:

1 tablespoon sunflower oil

40 g (1½ oz) beansprouts

40 g (1½ oz) mangetout peas, thinly shredded

½ red pepper, cut into fine strips

⅓ medium carrot, cut into fine strips

½ small red onion, thinly sliced

4 fresh shiitake mushrooms, thinly sliced

4 oyster mushrooms, torn into fine strips

15 g (½ oz) pickled ginger, finely shredded

FOR THE OMELETTES:

4 tablespoons sunflower oil

12 large eggs, beaten

225 g (8 oz) fresh white crab meat

Salt and freshly ground black pepper

method

For the sauce put the lime juice and garlic into a liquidizer and whizz until smooth. Add all the other ingredients and blend well. Add enough water to make a smooth, sauce-like consistency, then pass through a fine sieve.

For the vegetable stir-fry, heat the oil in a frying pan or wok, add all the vegetables and stir-fry for 1–2 minutes until just cooked but still crunchy. Add the pickled ginger and toss for a few seconds to heat through.

Drizzle some of the *nam prik* sauce over each serving plate in a zigzag pattern and then put the stir-fried vegetables in the centre of each one.

For the omelettes, heat a 20–23 cm (8–9 inch) omelette pan over a medium heat, add 1 tablespoon of the oil and, when it is hot, a quarter of the beaten eggs. Move the mixture over the base of the pan with the back of a fork until it begins to set, then stop stirring and cook until it is just a little moist on top – about 2 minutes in all. Put a quarter of the crab meat down the centre of the omelette and season to taste with salt and pepper. Fold the omelette over twice and place on the stir-fried vegetables. Serve straight away and cook the remaining omelettes in the same way.

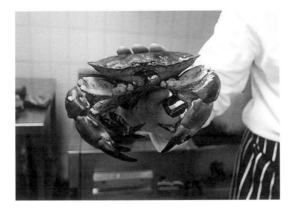

Grilled Whole Barramundi with Black Olive and Basil Butter

One of the questions I'm constantly asked is what should you accompany plain grilled fish with. As grilling is probably the easiest way of cooking fish at home, I am very keen to provide lots of lovely butters and piquant little sauces that can be whipped up in minutes. This is one of them – the sort of dish I would knock up in the evening for us at home, when I'm not thinking serious seafood recipes.

serves 4

4 × 175–225 g (6–8 oz) barramundi, cleaned (see p. 26)
A little olive oil
Salt and freshly ground black pepper

FOR THE BLACK OLIVE BUTTER:

100 g (4 oz) unsalted butter, softened
25 g (1 oz) pitted black olives, roughly chopped
3 garlic cloves, finely chopped
1 tablespoon lemon juice
A handful of basil leaves, roughly chopped
2 anchovy fillets in oil, drained

method

For the butter, simply put everything into a food processor with ½ teaspoon of salt and some pepper and blend until the olives are finely chopped but not completely smooth. Spoon the mixture on to a sheet of clingfilm and shape into a roll 2.5 cm (1 inch) thick. Wrap up tightly in the clingfilm and chill in the freezer or fridge until firm.

Pre-heat the grill to high. Trim down the tails of each fish and then brush them with olive oil and season well with salt and pepper. Lay them on a baking tray or the rack of the grill pan and cook for 4 minutes on each side. Meanwhile, unwrap the black olive butter and cut off 12 slices.

Remove the fish from under the grill, put 3 slices of the butter on each one and slide them back under the grill very briefly until it just begins to melt.

Put the fish on warmed serving plates and spoon any cooking juices around them. Serve with the *Soft Green Lettuce Salad with Olive Oil Dressing* (see p. 228).

alternative fish

Any small chunky fish such as snapper, bream or any type of mullet would work well here.

Fillets of Lemon Sole with Ciabatta Breadcrumbs and Salsa Verde Mayonnaise

Of all fish, lemon sole is best suited to deep-frying in breadcrumbs. The only other way of eating it is cooked on the bone, as in the recipe for Grilled Lemon Sole with Lemongrass Butter on p. 178. I love salsa verde and thought a little of it folded into some mayonnaise would go very well with lemon sole fillets coated in breadcrumbs made with Italian ciabatta, preferably one with black olives. It's now a dish that features on the Seafood Restaurant menu five times a week. When you start to eat this, served with a bowl of crisp chips, a salad sparingly dressed with perfect extra virgin olive oil and a glass of crisp Italian wine like Vernaccia di San Gimignano, well, you feel jolly full of beans.

serves 4

Sunflower oil for deep-frying

1 loaf of black olive ciabatta

50 g (2 oz) plain flour

2 large eggs, beaten

12 × 65 g (2½ oz) skinned lemon sole fillets

Salt and freshly ground black pepper

Lemon wedges, to serve

FOR THE SALSA VERDE MAYONNAISE:

3 heaped tablespoons parsley leaves

1 heaped tablespoon mint leaves

3 tablespoons capers, drained

6 anchovy fillets in oil, drained

1 garlic clove

6 tablespoons *Mayonnaise* made with olive oil (see p. 235)

1 teaspoon Dijon mustard

1 tablespoon lemon juice

½ teaspoon salt

method

For the salsa verde mayonnaise, coarsely chop the parsley, mint, capers, anchovy fillets and garlic all together and mix with the mayonnaise, mustard, lemon juice and salt.

Heat some oil for deep-frying to 190°C/375°F. Turn the ciabatta into fine breadcrumbs. Season the fish fillets with a little salt and pepper, then coat each one with flour, then beaten egg, then breadcrumbs.

Deep-fry, 2 pieces at a time, for about 2 minutes, until crisp and golden. Drain on kitchen paper and keep warm while you fry the rest. Serve straight away with the salsa verde mayonnaise, some lemon wedges and the *Fine Leaf and Herb Salad with Lemon Oil Dressing* (see p. 228).

alternative fish

This would also work well with other flat fish fillets such as plaice, or try using cod, haddock or Australian flat-head.

passion and flavour • *Naples is a place of such enthusiasm for food.
The feeling there about cookery can only be described as passion. They care so
much about the flavour of the raw ingredients they use, about the quality of
tomatoes, basil, mozzarella cheese, pasta and good olive oil.*

*The Neapolitans have a fish market to end all fish markets, at Pozzuoli, on the
Bay of Naples. It's a delight; colourful stalls designed to attract the public with
spectacle, theatre and serious persuasion from the vendors. Most traders keep
some of their fish alive and everything is of a quality that makes you jump for joy.
The market is right on the end of the quay with a backdrop of Naples and
Vesuvius, and there is a vegetable market there too. Here the tables are piled high
with deep red plum tomatoes from San Marzano, grown on volcanic soil which
gives them an almost bitter-sweet flavour. The Italians talk about the soil where
tomatoes are grown as reverently as wine growers talk
about the earth and gravel beneath their vines; the
terroir. There's basil next to the tomatoes with leaves
as big as cabbage leaves, and there are aubergines,
some unforgettable white peaches and enormous lemons
from Prócida, so mild that they slice them and serve them as a salad with mint,
a little chilli, garlic and olive oil. There is a farmer with his pickup filled with big
bottles of his own olive oil and tubs of olives, capers preserved in sea salt and some
small pickled chillies, very mild, almost like a green pepper.*

*Cooking in Italy is about timeless tradition. Nothing here changes too fast or
too much. There is change, but just a little, in order to keep food interesting …
alive. What really makes the difference, for the Italians, is having wonderfully fresh
ingredients bursting with flavour. We all want what they've got, we all beat a
path to their door.*

Italy

Pasta Puttanesca

Puttanesca sauce was the main reason for a trip to Naples I made recently, accompanied by the TV crew. It actually means 'prostitute's pasta' and the name intrigued me. I don't know if I'd sell many portions of it in the restaurant if I called it Tart's Spaghetti. We never did get to the bottom of why it's so named, but one theory – the director's, I believe – was that it had to be a sauce you could knock up quickly during a busy working day. What is indisputable, however, is that it's a great sauce for pasta. Don't mess around with canned tomatoes for this dish – use sweet cherry tomatoes (or mini plum ones if you can get them) and squeeze each one before you cut it in half to get rid of the excess juice. Leave most of the seeds and skin in the sauce.

serves 4

450 g (1 lb) small cherry, plum or vine-ripened tomatoes

4 tablespoons olive oil

3 garlic cloves, chopped

1 sprig of rosemary, leaves finely chopped

4 sage leaves, thinly shredded

A good pinch of dried chilli flakes, or 1 red finger chilli, seeded and finely chopped

50 g (2 oz) salted capers, excess salt rubbed off

100 g (4 oz) small black olives, pitted

2 × 50 g (2 oz) cans of anchovy fillets in oil, drained and chopped

1 tablespoon chopped oregano

450 g (1 lb) dried bucatini or spaghetti

3 tablespoons chopped flat-leaf parsley

Salt and freshly ground black pepper

method

Bring 3.4 litres (6 pints) of water and 2 tablespoons of salt to the boil for the pasta.

For the sauce, squeeze the tomatoes into the sink to get rid of most of the juice, then cut each one in half. Heat the oil in a pan with the garlic, rosemary and sage and cook gently for about 1 minute without browning. Add the chilli, tomatoes, capers, olives, anchovies, oregano and some black pepper and leave to simmer gently for 10 minutes.

Meanwhile, add the pasta to the pan of boiling water and cook for about 7 minutes or until *al dente*. Drain, then tip it into a large warmed serving bowl. Pour over the sauce, add the chopped parsley and toss together well. Serve straight away, with plenty of red wine.

Bagna Cauda

This is perhaps the perfect vehicle for a dip for raw vegetables such as fennel, celery and carrots. It is much better eaten at midday because if you have it for dinner the quantity of garlic will keep you up all night. As a lunch dish, with lots of nice gutsy red wine and good bread, it's great fun – as long as you've got nothing to do all afternoon apart from the good intention of a long walk.

serves 4

1 fennel bulb

1 red pepper

2 carrots

2 celery sticks

2 heads of chicory

50 g (2 oz) can of anchovy fillets

6 garlic cloves, crushed

150 ml (5 fl oz) olive oil

50 g (2 oz) unsalted butter

method

Trim the fennel and slice. Remove the stalk and seeds from the pepper and cut into long sticks. Cut the carrots and celery into long sticks, too. Break the chicory into leaves. Arrange all the vegetables on a large serving plate.

Drain the oil from the anchovies into a small, heavy-based pan or a fondue pot. Very finely chop the anchovies and add them to the pan with the garlic, olive oil and butter. Stir over a very gentle heat without boiling for 5 minutes, until the garlic and anchovies have dissolved.

Bring the pot to the table with the vegetables and plenty of good bread. Tell everyone to dip in.

Baked Whole Sea Bass with Roasted Red Peppers, Tomatoes, Anchovies and Potatoes

In the past I've been a bit reluctant to write recipes for baking whole fish. The reason for my resistance is that, all too often, the accompanying vegetables end up bland and serve only to emphasize any lack of flavour in the fish. So what I've done here is part-cook the vegetables so that their flavour is really concentrated by the time the bass is cooked. I've also chosen to use vibrant flavours – good plum tomatoes, sweet red peppers, salty anchovies and saffron-infused potatoes.

serves 4

A good pinch of saffron

900 g (2 lb) potatoes, peeled and cut into slices
   1 cm (½ inch) thick

4 plum tomatoes, skinned and cut lengthways
   into quarters

50 g (2 oz) anchovy fillets in oil, drained

150 ml (5 fl oz) *Chicken Stock* (see p. 232)
   or water

4 red peppers, each one seeded and cut into
   8 chunks

8 garlic cloves, each sliced into three

8 small sprigs of oregano

85 ml (3 fl oz) olive oil

1 × 1.5–1.75 kg (3–4 lb) sea bass, cleaned
   (see p. 26)

Salt and freshly ground black pepper

method

Pre-heat the oven to 200°C/400°F/Gas Mark 6. Place the saffron in a tea cup, pour over 2 tablespoons of hot water and leave to soak. Put the potatoes in a pan of boiling salted water and par-boil for 7 minutes. Drain well and arrange them in a narrow strip over the base of a large roasting dish large enough to hold the sea bass, either lengthways or diagonally. The potatoes should form a bed for the fish, leaving plenty of room on either side for the red peppers.

    Scatter the tomatoes and anchovy fillets over the potatoes, then pour over the saffron water and stock. Scatter the pieces of red pepper down either side of the

continued overleaf

potatoes and sprinkle over the garlic, oregano sprigs and olive oil. Season everything well with salt and pepper and bake in the oven for 30 minutes.

Slash the fish 5–6 times down each side and then slash it in the opposite direction on just one side to give an attractive criss-cross pattern. Rub it generously with some olive oil, season well with salt and pepper and then rest it on top of the potatoes. Return the dish to the oven and bake for a further 35 minutes, until the fish is cooked through.

Serve with roasted vegetables and the *Soft Green Lettuce Salad with Olive Oil Dressing* (see p. 228).

alternative fish

A large snapper, a striped bass or a medium-sized kingfish.

A Casserole of John Dory with Tomatoes, Olive Oil and Parsley

Of all the cuisines in the world, the Italian has the most civilized balance to its meals. You start with a very light and simple antipasto — *maybe some slices of prosciutto ham and fresh figs, or sliced Sorrento tomatoes with buffalo mozzarella, olive oil and basil. Then comes the bulk dish — some pasta or a* risotto nero *with cuttlefish, for example. Then a very simple and relatively small choice piece of meat or fish, followed by, say, grilled peaches with mascarpone cheese. This John Dory casserole is designed to fit into this sort of meal. You will end up with about 100–150 g (4–5 oz) each of beautifully cooked fish on the bone, with a tomato, olive oil and garlic sauce. As part of a typical four-course meal it would be quite memorable, as it was for me when I ate it on the island of Procida near Naples.*

serves 4

2 garlic cloves, sliced

150 ml (5 fl oz) extra virgin olive oil

3 plum tomatoes, roughly chopped

1 teaspoon salt

1 tablespoon chopped flat-leaf parsley

1 × 1 kg (2¼ lb) John Dory, cleaned (see p. 26)

method

Put the garlic and olive oil into a pan that is large enough to hold the fish and leave over the heat until the garlic begins to sizzle. Add the tomatoes and break them up with the back of a wooden spoon. Add the salt and parsley and simmer very gently for 20 minutes.

Add the John Dory to the pan, cover and simmer for 6–7 minutes, basting it every now and then with the cooking liquid. Then carefully turn the fish over and cook for a further 6–7 minutes, basting regularly, until the fish is just cooked.

To serve, remove the fillets from the fish, place them on a warmed serving dish and spoon the sauce around.

alternative fish

This would also work well with red mullet, sea bass or bream.

Chickpea, Parsley and Salt Cod Stew

One of the rather satisfactory facts about food in Italy is that inland you don't get much seafood. I enjoy eating food that comes from where I expect it to come from. Salt cod, however, is found everywhere in Italy because it's preserved fish.

This is right up my street – not too many ingredients and with lovely strong, rustic flavours. I prefer to salt my own cod for it rather than use the very dry bought variety. I always remember a remark in the film Amadeus, *when the emperor of Austria tells Mozart that* The Marriage of Figaro *has too many notes in it, and I think this is true of a lot of recipes. Mozart replies acidly that the opera had just as many notes as it needed and no more, and this is true of this dish.*

serves 4

750g (1½ lb) thick piece of unskinned cod fillet

350 g (12 oz) dried chickpeas

1 × 175 g (6 oz) potato, peeled

85 ml (3 fl oz) olive oil

8 garlic cloves, finely chopped

1 teaspoon dried chilli flakes

4 plum tomatoes, roughly chopped

3–4 tablespoons chopped flat-leaf parsley

Salt and freshly ground black pepper

method

Salt the cod overnight (see p. 238). Cover the chickpeas in plenty of water and leave them to soak overnight, too.

The next day drain the chickpeas and pour over enough fresh water to cover them by about 5 cm (2 inches). Bring to the boil, add the peeled potato and simmer until tender, adding hot water now and then if necessary to make sure they stay just covered. Drain and set aside, saving the cooking liquid.

Drop the salt cod into a pan of boiling water and simmer for 6–8 minutes or until just cooked. Drain and, when cool enough to handle, flake the flesh into large pieces, discarding the skin and any bones.

Heat the olive oil in a large pan, add the garlic and chilli flakes and cook for a minute or two without browning. Add the tomatoes, chickpeas and potato, which should be broken up into small pieces with the back of a wooden spoon. Add a little of the cooking liquid from the chickpeas and 300 ml (10 fl oz) of water and simmer for 20–30 minutes, until the stew has reduced and thickened a little. Gently fold in the salt cod and parsley and season liberally with freshly ground black pepper. Taste the stew for salt but you probably won't need any.

alternative fish

All fish from the cod family, such as haddock, hake, pollack or coley, are pleasant to eat when salted. I think the cheaper the fish the more appropriate it is for salting. Pollack, for example, is much better salted than as a fresh fish.

Roast Stuffed Monkfish with Saffron, Lemon, Tomato and Capers

Because monkfish has no bones except the backbone, has firm flesh and is almost shaped like a leg of lamb, it lends itself especially to being cooked like a joint of meat. Indeed, the French have long had a recipe for it, spiked with slivers of garlic and roasted like a gigot d'agneau. So go to your fishmonger's and ask them to sort out a nice 1.5 kg (3 lb) tail; get them to skin it for you, cut out the backbone, trying to leave the two fillets attached where possible, and remove all the pink membrane from the fillets. Then all you need to do is stuff it with some anchovies, preserved lemon, roasted red peppers and sun-dried tomatoes, roll it in an aromatic crust of crushed black peppercorns, thyme and sea salt, roast it, slice it and serve it up with an olive oil, lemon and caper sauce. Sunday lunch will never be the same again.

serves 6

1.5 kg (3 lb) monkfish tail, prepared as
  described above

1 tablespoon black peppercorns,
  coarsely crushed

1 tablespoon roughly chopped thyme

1 tablespoon sea salt flakes

Salt and freshly ground black pepper

FOR THE STUFFING:

A good pinch of saffron

50 g (2 oz) can of anchovy fillets in oil, drained

1/2 *Preserved Lemon* (see p. 237), cut into
  thin slices

1 red pepper, roasted (see p. 238) and torn into
  wide strips

4–5 sun-dried tomatoes in oil, drained and
  thinly sliced

2 tablespoons olive oil

FOR THE SAUCE:

175 ml (6 fl oz) *Fish Stock* (see p. 232)

2 tablespoons extra virgin olive oil

15 g (1/2 oz) butter

Juice of 1/2 small lemon

1 tablespoon chopped flat-leaf parsley

1 tablespoon capers in brine, drained
  and rinsed

method

If your fishmonger has not already done so, you will need to bone the monkfish. You'll notice that the bone sticks out a bit more on one side of the tail. Cut the bone out from this side by carefully slicing either side of it, trying to keep the fish fillets attached to one another where you can, and then trim away the membrane from the outside of the fillets.

Pre-heat the oven to 200°C/400°F/Gas Mark 6.

Mix the saffron for the stuffing with 2 teaspoons of warm water and set to one side. Season the cavity of the fish from which the bone was removed with a little salt and pepper. Lay the anchovy fillets at regular intervals along the cut face of each fillet, followed by the slices of preserved lemon, pieces of roasted red pepper and finally the sun-dried tomatoes. Sprinkle over the saffron water and a little of the olive oil and then bring the sides up together so that you trap all the stuffing in place. Tie it at 2.5 cm (1 inch) intervals along its length with fine string.

Sprinkle the crushed black peppercorns, thyme and sea salt over the base of a small roasting tin. Add the monkfish and turn it over in the mixture so that it takes on an even coating. Now turn it right side up again and sprinkle over the rest of the olive oil.

Roast the monkfish for 25 minutes, then remove from the oven and transfer to a carving plate. Slice it across, between the pieces of string, into slices 2.5 cm (1 inch) thick. Keep warm while you make the sauce.

Place the roasting tin over a medium heat and add the fish stock. Bring to the boil, scraping up all the bits and pieces from the bottom of the tin as you do so. Strain the juices into a small pan and add any juices from the carving plate, plus the extra virgin olive oil, butter and lemon juice. Bring to the boil and leave it to boil vigorously for about 4 minutes, until it has reduced slightly and emulsified. Remove from the heat and stir in the parsley, capers and ½ teaspoon of salt.

Spoon the sauce around the fish and serve with plenty of *Steamed Potatoes* (see p. 223).

alternative fish

Substitute two thick loin fillets from a large cod, stuff them in the same way and then tie them together gently with plenty of fine string, as you would a rolled joint of meat. It will not be as firm as the monkfish but will taste just as good. You will probably be able to break it apart with a fork to serve.

Cuscus con Pesce (Fish Couscous)

I've spent quite a lot of time holidaying in Sicily because I find the seafood cooking so exciting. There's a strong North African influence on Sicilian food, hence the couscous. I'm quite particular about the type I use – a brand called Sipa with a camel on the front of the box. It's the easy-cook variety; I'm not sufficiently knowledgeable about the cuisine of North Africa to cook couscous from scratch but I like it to have a dry, fluffy, almost al dente finish. I hate soggy, stodgy couscous – and so do the Moroccans. The couscous for this dish is particularly aromatic, flavoured with bay leaf and cinnamon fried gently in olive oil, and I hope you like the almonds in the sauce as much as I do.

serves 4

225 g (8 oz) unskinned cod fillet

225 g (8 oz) unskinned sea bass fillet

4 tablespoons olive oil

4 garlic cloves, finely chopped

50 g (2 oz) blanched almonds, toasted
   and chopped

350 g (12 oz) plum tomatoes, skinned
   and chopped

1 red finger chilli, seeded and finely chopped

120 ml (4 fl oz) dry white wine

450 g (1 lb) mussels, cleaned (see p. 26)

12 cooked crevettes (Mediterranean prawns)

2 tablespoons chopped flat-leaf parsley

Salt and freshly ground black pepper

FOR THE COUSCOUS:

350 ml (12 fl oz) *Fish Stock* (see p. 232)

350 g (12 oz) couscous

1 small onion, finely chopped

1 garlic clove, finely chopped

4 tablespoons olive oil

1 bay leaf

7.5 cm (3 inch) piece of cinnamon stick

method

Cut the cod fillet into slices 5 cm (2 inches) wide and cut each sea bass fillet into 3. Lay them on a plate and sprinkle well on both sides with plenty of salt and pepper. Set aside for 10 minutes to allow the salt to permeate the fish a little.

To make the couscous, bring the fish stock to the boil, then pour it over the couscous in a bowl, stir and leave for about 3 minutes to allow the grains to absorb all the stock and swell up. Meanwhile, fry the onion and garlic gently in the olive oil with the bay leaf and cinnamon stick. Stir in the couscous and keep stirring over a low heat for about 4 minutes, until it is dry and fluffy. Season with ¾ teaspoon of salt and some pepper. Keep warm.

Heat the oil in a large, deep frying pan or saucepan. Add the garlic, almonds, tomatoes and chilli and simmer for 5 minutes. Now stir in the wine and mussels and rest the pieces of cod on top. Cover the pan with a tight-fitting lid and simmer for 3 minutes. Uncover (the cod should be almost cooked), add the sea bass pieces and crevettes, cover the pan again and simmer for 3–4 minutes, until the sea bass is cooked.

To serve, pile the couscous into the centre of a warmed shallow serving bowl. Lift the fish and crevettes out of the sauce and put them around the edge of the bowl. Add the parsley to the sauce and check the seasoning. Spoon it over the fish.

alternative fish

> *As with all fish stews, it doesn't really matter what you use as long as you have a mixture of fish and shellfish. Try, for example, clams instead of mussels, red mullet instead of sea bass and hake instead of cod.*

Grilled Scallops with Tomato, Garlic and Basil

Thank goodness you can get fresh scallops in the shell quite easily these days. They're such a pleasure. This is really just a way of making a charming first course of simple grilled scallops and a few easily available ingredients.

serves 4

3 tomatoes, skinned, seeded and diced (see p. 238)

3 garlic cloves, very finely chopped

3 tablespoons finely shredded basil leaves

150 ml (5 fl oz) olive oil

3 small sun-dried tomatoes, drained and
   finely chopped

12 prepared scallops, left in the shell (see p. 26)

Salt and freshly ground black pepper

method

Pre-heat the grill to high. Mix together the tomatoes, garlic, basil, olive oil, sun-dried tomatoes, ¾ teaspoon of salt and some pepper. Spoon the mixture over the scallops and put them on a baking tray or the rack of the grill pan. Grill for 2–2½ minutes (depending on the size of the scallop), until they are just cooked through. Serve with some fresh crusty bread.

Cacciucco

We've just begun cooking this marvellous Italian fish stew for our bistro in Padstow. I feel a little bit self-conscious about producing my own version of an Italian dish that brings with it the same sort of arguments about authenticity as bouillabaisse. But it is astonishingly good, mainly because it contains so many powerful flavours: garlic, wine, chilli, tomato and lots of squid, unusual for fish stews. In addition the Italians are not faint-hearted about using strong herbs such as sage but what they do, which I think is so sensible, is fry the sage in olive oil first. This reduces its rather thickly aromatic flavour to something much more subtle. Some recipes for cacciucco include the ink sacs from squid and cuttlefish, others don't. I think it's a good idea to put a certain amount in. You can consider it more as painting than flavouring. A certain amount of squid or cuttlefish ink with the tomato gives the stew a beautiful deep, reddish-brown colour.

serves 8

1 ciabatta loaf, cut into slices 1 cm (½ inch) thick

150 ml (5 fl oz) olive oil

5 garlic cloves, peeled

1 × 900 g (2 lb) John Dory, filleted

1 × 1.5 kg (3 lb) gurnard, filleted

900 g (2 lb) unskinned cod fillet

225 g (8 oz) prepared squid (see p. 27) – reserve one of the ink sacs if you prepare it yourself

1 cooked lobster, weighing about 450 g (1 lb)

1 large onion, chopped

1 large carrot, finely chopped

2 celery sticks, finely chopped

300 ml (10 fl oz) red wine

400 g (14 oz) can of chopped tomatoes

2 bay leaves

2–3 red finger chillies, slit open

2.25 litres (4 pints) water

6 sage leaves

900 g (2 lb) mussels, cleaned (see p. 26)

method

Pre-heat the oven to 200°C/400°F/Gas Mark 6. Put the ciabatta slices on a shallow baking tray and drizzle them with about 2 tablespoons of the olive oil. Bake for about 20 minutes, until crisp and golden. Now rub one of the peeled garlic cloves over both sides of each slice of bread. Thinly slice the remaining garlic.

Cut the fish fillets into slices 4 cm (1½ inches) thick. Slice the squid pouches across into rings and separate the tentacles. Remove the meat from the lobster (see p. 27) and reserve the shell.

Heat half the remaining olive oil in a large pan. Add the onion, carrot and celery and fry for about 8 minutes, until just beginning to brown. Add the red wine, the lobster shell, tomatoes, bay leaves, red chillies and water. If you have an ink sac, mash it with a little water to release the ink and add some to the pan. Bring everything to the boil and leave to simmer for 45 minutes. Pour into a sieve set over another large pan and press the debris against the sides of the sieve with a ladle to extract as much flavour and liquid as possible. You will need about 1.2 litres (2 pints) of well-flavoured stock. If there is more than this, bring it back to the boil and boil rapidly for a few minutes until reduced to roughly the required amount.

Heat the remaining olive oil in the cleaned pan, add the sage leaves and sliced garlic and fry for 1 minute. Add the squid and fry for 2 minutes or until lightly browned, then remove the squid from the pan. Put the mussels in a separate large pan with a splash of water or wine, cover and cook over a high heat for about 3 minutes, until they have opened. Discard any that have remained closed.

Add the reduced stock, mussel cooking liquor and the fish fillets to the pan in which you fried the squid, bring to the boil and simmer for 2 minutes. Add the lobster meat, squid and mussels and simmer for 1 minute.

To serve, bring the pan to the table with the crisp ciabatta. Tell everyone to lay 2 slices of bread in their soup plates and then to ladle the stew on top.

alternative fish

As the point of this stew is to get as much variety as possible with the fish and shellfish, even at its simplest you must have either squid or cuttlefish, one mollusc like mussels or clams, one crustacean such as prawn or lobster and one fish. So as long as you have at least four elements, the choice is up to you, but be sure to avoid oily fish.

Gremolata Prawns

Gremolata is what I call the Italian equivalent to the French persillade, *which is parsley finely chopped with garlic. I included a recipe in my book* Taste of the Sea *for deep-fried whitebait with* persillade *and now it's the turn of the prawn, with just a pinch of cayenne pepper to liven things up. I love eating seafood with my fingers, which is why I've left the shells on the prawns. As you split open the shells, the gremolata will flavour the flesh.*

serves 4

1 large lemon

2 tablespoons olive oil

20 unpeeled large raw prawns

Cayenne pepper (optional)

3 garlic cloves, very finely chopped

4 tablespoons chopped flat-leaf parsley

Coarse sea salt and freshly ground black pepper

method

Peel the zest off the lemon with a potato peeler, pile the pieces up a few at a time and then cut them across into short, thin strips. Heat the oil in a large frying pan. Add the prawns and toss them over a high heat for 4–5 minutes, seasoning them with some cayenne pepper or black pepper and sea salt as you do so.

Cut the lemon in half and squeeze the juice from one half over the prawns. Continue to cook until the juice has almost evaporated – the prawns should be quite dry. Take the pan off the heat and leave for about 1 minute to cool very slightly. Then sprinkle over the lemon zest, chopped garlic, parsley and ¼ teaspoon of salt and toss together well. Pile the prawns into a large serving dish and serve with some finger bowls and plenty of napkins.

alternative fish

This dish needs no alternatives as everyone can get hold of good-quality prawns these days. However, they must be in the shell.

Cozze con Fagioli (Mussels with Cannellini Beans)

I am a part of all that I have met; yet all experience is an arch wherethro' gleams that untravell'd world, whose margin fades for ever and for ever when I move.
'Ulysses' Alfred, Lord Tennyson.

The exciting thing about travelling and looking for new dishes is that occasionally, even in a country where you think you've read pretty much everything about its food, something new will crop up, an everyday dish that you've never seen before. This simple dish of mussels and cannellini beans was just that. This is pure excitement for me.

serves 4

225 g (8 oz) dried cannellini beans

1 bay leaf

1 sprig of thyme

4 garlic cloves, peeled

1 kg (2¼ lb) mussels, cleaned (see p. 26)

50 ml (2 fl oz) dry white wine

120 ml (4 fl oz) extra virgin olive oil

2 large plum tomatoes, roughly chopped

2 tablespoons chopped flat-leaf parsley

Salt and freshly ground black pepper

method

Cover the beans with plenty of cold water and leave them to soak overnight. The next day drain the beans and tip them into a pan. Pour in enough fresh water to cover them by about 5 cm (2 inches), then add the bay leaf, thyme and 2 of the peeled garlic cloves. Bring to the boil, skimming any scum from the surface as it appears, then lower the heat and simmer for about 1 hour or until the beans are very soft. Now increase the heat and boil rapidly until most of the liquid has disappeared. Discard the thyme stalk and bay leaf.

Put the mussels into a pan with the wine. Cover and cook over a high heat for 3–4 minutes, until they have opened. Strain them through a colander set over a bowl to catch the cooking liquor. When they are cool enough to handle, remove about three-quarters of the mussels from their shells (discard any that have remained closed).

Slice the rest of the garlic into a large pan and add the olive oil. Slowly heat the oil, then as soon as the garlic begins to sizzle, add the tomatoes and simmer for 2–3 minutes. Add the cooked beans and 150 ml (5 fl oz) of the mussel cooking liquor. Simmer for 5 minutes, until the liquid has reduced to a rich creamy sauce. Season with pepper and a little salt if necessary (you probably won't need any because mussels are quite salty). Add the mussels and simmer for 1–2 minutes, until they have heated through. Stir in the chopped parsley and spoon into 4 warmed soup plates to serve.

alternative fish

There's no reason why you couldn't make this dish with cockles or clams instead of mussels.

Chargrilled Tuna with Salsa Verde

I'm always amazed how quickly tuna cooks. It's because it has such an open texture and so the heat penetrates very quickly. The steaks in this recipe need literally just one minute on either side if your barbecue or ridged cast iron griddle is at the correct temperature. This is a dish of classic simplicity: one of the best sauces in the world combined with one of the best fish for cooking on a barbecue. A perfect summer dish, served with either a mixture of baby vegetables or a bowl of chips and some salad.

serves 4

4 × 175–225 g (6–8 oz) thick tuna loin steaks
A little olive oil
Salt and freshly ground black pepper

FOR THE SALSA VERDE:

3 tablespoons flat-leaf parsley leaves
1 tablespoon mint leaves
3 tablespoons capers, drained
6 anchovy fillets in oil, drained
1 garlic clove
1 teaspoon Dijon mustard
Juice of ½ lemon
120 ml (4 fl oz) extra virgin olive oil

method

You can make the salsa verde some time in advance. I like to hand chop all the ingredients on a board so that the sauce has plenty of rugged texture. By all means use a food processor if you prefer but don't turn it on for too long. Chop the parsley, mint, capers, anchovy fillets and garlic together. Scoop them into a bowl and stir in the mustard, lemon juice, olive oil and ½ teaspoon of salt.

If you are going to cook the tuna on a barbecue, make sure that you light it a good 40 minutes before cooking them. Brush the tuna steaks on both sides with some oil and season well with salt and pepper. If you are using a ridged cast iron griddle, place it over a high heat and leave it to get smoking hot, then drizzle it with a little oil. Now cook the tuna steaks for 1 minute on either side until nicely striped from the griddle on both sides but still pink and juicy in the centre.

Put the tuna on 4 warmed plates and spoon some salsa verde on top. Serve with either *A Melange of Early Summer Vegetables* (see p. 222) or a bowl of *Roughly Cut Chips* (see p. 224).

alternative fish

The salsa verde also goes particularly well with monkfish. Try chargrilling whole small monkfish tails weighing about 275–350 g (10–12 oz) each.

Risotto Nero

We're planning a Total Eclipse Dinner at the restaurant for August 1999. Cornwall will go dark for 20 minutes and about three million people are expected to come and see it. Our rooms have been booked for about three years already. I thought I would put on a menu of black food with black-labelled wines, then a pudding of strawberries from Trevone Farm with Cornish clotted cream to symbolize the return to light and colour. The star of the dinner will be Risotto Nero. The glistening blackness of the rice can only be perfectly achieved with cuttlefish ink.

serves 4

450 g (1 lb) uncleaned small cuttlefish
1.2 litres (2 pints) *Fish Stock* (see p. 232)
25 g (1 oz) butter
3 tablespoons olive oil
2 large shallots, finely chopped
3 garlic cloves, finely chopped

350 g (12 oz) Carnaroli or Arborio rice
150 ml (5 fl oz) dry white wine
3 tablespoons chopped flat-leaf parsley
1 tablespoon finely grated fresh
   Parmesan cheese
Salt and freshly ground black pepper

method

Prepare the cuttlefish as on p. 27, carefully removing the little pearly-white ink sacs without bursting them. Squeeze out the ink into the fish stock, then slit open the sacs and rinse them out in the stock to remove as much of the ink as you can. Bring the stock to the boil in a pan and keep it hot over a low heat. Cut the cuttlefish bodies into very thin strips and slice the tentacles into 4 cm (1½ inch) pieces.

Heat the butter and 1 tablespoon of the oil in a heavy-based saucepan. Add the shallots and garlic and cook gently until soft but not browned. Stir in the rice so that all the grains get well coated in the oil and butter. Add the wine and simmer over a low heat for a few minutes until it has almost disappeared. Add a ladleful of stock and simmer, stirring frequently, until it has all been absorbed. Continue to add the stock a ladleful at a time, stirring, until it has all been used and the rice is creamy and tender but still with a little bit of a bite – *al dente*. This should take about 20–25 minutes.

Heat the rest of the oil in a large frying pan. Add the cuttlefish and fry it over a high heat for 1½ minutes. Remove from the heat and stir in the chopped parsley and Parmesan cheese. Season with salt and pepper. Spoon it into 4 warmed bowls and pile the cuttlefish into the centre. Serve straight away.

alternative fish

Squid would be a good substitute but there's not enough ink in squid to make this dish satisfactorily. However, you can buy little sachets of ink from your fishmonger. You'll need about 4 for this dish.

Mussels with Chilli, Tomato and Parsley

This recipe pays homage to Nigel Slater. His three books, Real Fast Food, Real Fast Puddings *and* The 30 Minute Cook, *took the unprecedented view that recipes should actually reflect the way we live. They contained a few easy-to-get-hold-of ingredients and were all intended to be cooked in under half an hour. Since their publication, there have been lots more books like them but the demand for fast cooking is still there. This dish is so easy, but I know it's just the sort of dish that people will cook because, to be honest, it's the sort of thing I cook between getting home from the restaurant after lunch and whizzing out again for the evening service.*

serves 4

2 tablespoons olive oil

4 garlic cloves, finely chopped

1 large red finger chilli, seeded and
    finely chopped

½ teaspoon dried chilli flakes

3 vine-ripened tomatoes, skinned
    and chopped

1.75 kg (4 lb) mussels, cleaned
    (see p. 26)

50 ml (2 fl oz) dry white wine

4 tablespoons chopped flat-leaf parsley

Salt and freshly ground black pepper

method

Heat the olive oil in a large pan, add the garlic, chilli and chilli flakes and cook over a medium high heat for about 2 minutes, until softened. Add the tomatoes, mussels and wine, cover and cook over a high heat for 3–4 minutes, shaking the pan every now and then, until all the mussels have opened. Discard any that have remained closed. Add the parsley and some seasoning to taste and turn the mixture over once or twice. Spoon into large soup plates and serve with plenty of crusty bread.

alternative fish

This would also work well with any other small bivalves, such as clams or cockles.

Pasta con le Sarde

Although I've got all the right ingredients in this dish, it's very much my own recipe but, having recently eaten Pasta con le Sarde in Taormina in Sicily about seven times, I'm happy to report that none of them tasted the same and not all of them tasted nice. The best ones seemed to have amalgamated everything at the last minute so that you could pick out all the ingredients, like pine kernels, sultanas and fennel; the worst had definitely been cooked for some time so that the sardines and everything else had become a rather dehydrated paste.

serves 4

8 sardines, cleaned (see p. 26)

25 g (1 oz) sultanas

150 ml (5 fl oz) olive oil

2 fennel bulbs, roughly chopped into 1 cm
($\frac{1}{2}$ inch) pieces

50 g (2 oz) can of anchovy fillets in oil, drained
and finely chopped

A pinch of fennel seeds

2 garlic cloves, finely chopped

50 ml (2 fl oz) dry white wine

25 g (1 oz) pine kernels, toasted

350 g (12 oz) bucatini or spaghetti

1 tablespoon lemon juice

2 tablespoons chopped fennel herb (or the
frondy tops from the fennel bulbs)

Salt and freshly ground black pepper

method

Open out each sardine in turn and place it belly-side down on a chopping board. Gently but firmly press along the backbone with your thumb so that you gradually flatten out the fish. Turn the fish over and carefully pull out the backbone. Remove any small bones left behind with tweezers, then cut the fish across into strips 2.5 cm (1 inch) wide.

Cover the sultanas with 4 tablespoons of hot water and leave them to soak.

Meanwhile, heat 50 ml (2 fl oz) of the olive oil in a pan, add the chopped fennel, anchovies, fennel seeds and garlic and cook gently for about 2 minutes. Add the wine, cover and simmer for 8 minutes. Add the sultanas, their soaking liquid and the pine kernels and leave to simmer gently.

Bring 3.4 litres (6 pints) of water to the boil in a large pan with 2 tablespoons of salt. Add the pasta, bring back to the boil and cook for 7 minutes or until *al dente*.

Meanwhile, heat the rest of the oil in a frying pan. Add the sardine pieces and fry for 3 minutes, turning them over half-way through. Tip them into the sultana sauce and simmer for 2–3 minutes. Add the lemon juice, fennel herb and some salt and pepper to taste.

Drain the pasta well and return it to the pasta pan. Add the sauce and toss gently together. Spoon into 4 warmed bowls and serve.

alternative fish

Any oily fish such as herring or mackerel, or even less oily fish like red mullet or snapper, would work equally well in this dish.

Marinated Anchovies

This simple antipasto *dish seems like the most natural thing to do with a pound or two of fresh anchovies, which you can pick up in most Mediterranean countries for a few pence. I'd be quite happy to serve this as a starter with plenty of crusty unbleached bread and quite a rugged Italian red wine, such as a Salice Salentino.*

serves 4

450 g (1 lb) anchovies

Juice of 1 lemon

1 teaspoon finely chopped red chilli

1 garlic clove, finely chopped

1 tablespoon chopped flat-leaf parsley

50 ml (2 fl oz) extra virgin olive oil

Salt and freshly ground black pepper

method

To prepare the anchovies, pinch off the heads and pull them off; the guts should come out with them. Then pinch along the top edge of each fish and pull out the spine – it should come away quite easily because the flesh is soft. You will then be left with lots of little double fillets. Lay these skin-side down in a large shallow dish and pour over the lemon juice. Leave for 20 minutes, during which time the flesh will go slightly opaque and firm – it's a bit like making the Latin American *ceviche*, where fish fillets are 'cooked' by marinating them in pure citrus juice.

Drain off the excess lemon juice and then sprinkle over the chilli, garlic, parsley and some salt and pepper. Pour over the oil, cover and leave for 24 hours in the fridge to allow all the flavours to permeate the fish.

alternative fish

Fresh anchovies are hard to come by in the UK but this would also be good made with sprats, sardines or small mackerel.

Linguine ai Frutti di Mare (Linguine with Mixed Seafood)

In the '60s and '70s pasta with seafood usually meant a thin, watery tomato sauce flavoured with dried marjoram and containing tiny little pieces of rubber which were the clams, mussels and prawns. Here, fresh tomatoes, garlic and parsley are cooked in the best olive oil for a short time, then some just-cooked fresh seafood is tossed in and the sauce is poured over some perfectly cooked pasta whose centre still has a definite bite to it. The secret of all good pasta and seafood dishes lies in making sure that the sauce is what I would call 'tight' when it hits the pasta – i.e. not runny, so that everything clings to the pasta nicely.

serves 4

1 kg (2¼ lb) mixed shellfish, such as carpetshell clams, *tellines* or venus shell clams, mussels, *cigarela* or langoustine, and small, unpeeled raw prawns

50 ml (2 fl oz) dry white wine

450 g (1 lb) cherry tomatoes or small vine-ripened tomatoes

450 g (1 lb) dried linguine

120 ml (4 fl oz) olive oil

5 garlic cloves, thinly sliced

A pinch of dried chilli flakes

3 tablespoons chopped flat-leaf parsley

Salt and freshly ground black pepper

method

Clean the clams and mussels (see p. 26). Put them in a large pan with the wine, cover and cook over a high heat for 3–4 minutes, until they have opened (discard any that remain closed). Set aside. Squeeze the tomatoes to remove most of the seeds and juice, then coarsely chop them.

Bring 3.4 litres (6 pints) of water to the boil in a large pan with 2 tablespoons of salt. Add the linguine, bring back to the boil and cook for about 9 minutes or until *al dente*.

Meanwhile, put the olive oil and garlic into a large pan and heat slowly until the garlic begins to sizzle. Add the chilli flakes and tomatoes and simmer for 5 minutes. Strain in all but the last tablespoon or two of the cooking liquor from the clams and mussels. Bring back to the boil and simmer until the mixture has reduced to a sauce-like consistency. Stir the *cigarela* or langoustine into the sauce and turn them over until they go pink. Add the prawns and simmer for 2–3 minutes, until they are cooked. Stir in the cooked shellfish and the parsley and turn them over a few times until heated through. Season if necessary with a little salt and some pepper.

Drain the pasta well and tip it into a large warmed serving dish. Pour over the seafood sauce and toss together well.

alternative fish

You could use any mixture of shellfish in this dish. Use any combination of the above, plus maybe some scallops or squid.

Tonno con Fagioli (Tuna and Cannellini Beans)

This is often made with little more than the contents of two cans – tuna and beans. But if you use dried cannellini beans simmered with a bay leaf, shallot, garlic and thyme, and tuna slow-cooked with olive oil and herbs, you will produce something quite spectacularly better. This warm salad is finished with sliced red onion, parsley and extra virgin olive oil.

serves 4

225 g (8 oz) dried cannellini beans

1 bay leaf

1 shallot, thinly sliced

2 sprigs of thyme

1 garlic clove, peeled but left whole,
   plus 1 small garlic clove, crushed

85 ml (3 fl oz) extra virgin olive oil,
   plus a little extra to serve

3 tablespoons lemon juice

1 small red onion, thinly sliced

3 tablespoons chopped flat-leaf parsley,
   plus extra to garnish

Salt and freshly ground black pepper

FOR THE TUNA CONFIT:

275 g (10 oz) thick tuna loin steak

About 300 ml (10 fl oz) inexpensive olive oil

1 onion, thinly sliced

2 garlic cloves, sliced

2 fresh or dried bay leaves

$\frac{1}{4}$ small lemon, sliced

1 large sprig of thyme

method

Cover the beans with plenty of cold water and leave to soak overnight.

Make the tuna confit (if possible, do this the day before as well, so you can leave it for 24 hours to allow all the flavours to permeate the fish): sprinkle a thin layer of salt in a shallow dish, lay the tuna on top and cover it with another layer of salt. Set aside for 10 minutes. Now brush most of the salt off the fish and rinse it under cold water. Dry on kitchen paper, then cut it, if necessary, into pieces that will fit neatly in a single layer in a small saucepan. Heat 3 tablespoons of the oil in the pan, add the onion and garlic and fry gently for 5 minutes, until soft but not coloured. Add the bay leaves, lemon slices and thyme, put the tuna on top and then pour over the rest of the oil. If the oil does not cover the fish, add a little more. Place the pan over a low heat and slowly bring the temperature of the oil up to 100°C/220°F. Remove the pan from the heat and leave the tuna to cool.

Drain the beans, tip them into a large pan and add enough fresh water to cover them by about 2.5 cm (1 inch). Bring to the boil and add the bay leaf, shallot, thyme sprigs and the whole clove of garlic. Simmer for about 45 minutes or until tender, topping them up with boiling water if necessary to make sure that they stay just covered.

Just as the beans are ready, return the tuna to a low heat and bring back up to 100°C/220°F.

Drain the beans, discard the bay leaf, thyme and garlic and tip the beans into a bowl. Toss with the extra virgin olive oil, crushed garlic, lemon juice, some salt and plenty of freshly ground black pepper. Leave to cool slightly.

As soon as the tuna is back up to temperature, lift it out of the pan and allow the excess oil to drain away. Break the fish into chunky pieces and season them with ½ teaspoon of salt and some pepper.

Toss the red onion and parsley into the beans and then carefully stir in the tuna so that you don't break up the flakes too much. Spoon into a large serving bowl, drizzle over a little extra olive oil and sprinkle with chopped parsley. Serve with plenty of crusty fresh bread.

alternative fish

Bonito works quite well in a confit like this, as would salmon.

robust, honest and eurthy • *The majority of recipes in this chapter come from two visits I made last year to Galicia in northern Spain. Galicia is a bit like my home Cornwall, only warmer and emptier. The Galicians have a freshness and innocence about them, possibly because tourism is in its infancy, and they are also mad about an entirely unprepossessing little thing called a percebe (gooseneck barnacle) – a strange brown barnacle a bit shorter and stumpier than your little finger, which looks a bit like the foot of a tortoise – so mad, in fact, that they honour it every summer with a festival.*

Percebes fetch big money in Spain because fishing for them is very dangerous. The fishermen, called mariscadores, prise them off the rocks at low tide and often risk being swept away by an extra-large wave. On festival day you sit at long tables out on the harbour with ice-cold bottles of the excellent local white wine Albariño, which tastes of apples, and you eat platters of percebes, boiled with new potatoes. There is octopus, too, in a big black cauldron. You queue up and they hook them out deep red and long-boiled and, taking a pair of shears snip slices

Spain

off on to your wooden platter which they sprinkle with dark-green olive oil, cayenne pepper, paprika and sea salt. You queue again for rings of incredibly crusty bread and finally go back to your table to eat, while a lively band with two drummers (one with a whole kit mounted on what looks like a giant zimmer frame) promenades around the tents. Everyone tucks into percebes, breaking off the little claw-like ends and peeling off the hard leathery skins. The small meat you are left with tastes a bit like octopus, a bit like lobster, a bit like mussels – salty and fresh – and the potatoes have the same tang, and with the octopus and crusty bread, and the apple-like wine, the music and the sunny day, you're in a world of simplicity, robustness and honesty.

Almejas a la Marinera (Clams with Onion, Wine and Paprika)

Most menus in restaurants along the Galician coast just list the shellfish and fish that they have, without any reference to how they are cooked. This is normally because they only cook it in one way: with clams it's always a la marinera *(in a mariner's style), while with fish it's always* a la Gallego *(in Galician style). This doesn't necessarily mean it's going to come out the same every time, and you never know quite what to expect, but that makes it all the more fun!*

serves 4

50 ml (2 fl oz) extra virgin olive oil

1 onion, very finely chopped

1 teaspoon paprika

150 ml (5 fl oz) passata (sieved tomatoes)

1 bay leaf, cut into very fine strips

¼ teaspoon dried chilli flakes

50 ml (2 fl oz) dry white wine, such as Albariño

1.75 kg (4 lb) carpetshell clams, cleaned
 (see p. 26)

1 tablespoon *Beurre Manié* (see p. 239)

1 tablespoon chopped flat-leaf parsley

Salt and freshly ground black pepper

method Heat the olive oil in a large, deep pan, add the onion and paprika and cook gently until soft but not browned. Add the passata, bay leaf, chilli flakes and white wine and simmer for a minute or two. Now add the clams, cover and cook over a high heat, shaking the pan every now and then, for 3–4 minutes, until the clams have opened.

Stir in the beurre manié and simmer for about 1 minute until the sauce has thickened slightly. Stir in the parsley, adjust the seasoning if necessary and serve with plenty of crusty bread.

alternative fish

Mussels work fine cooked in this way.

Merluza a la Gallega (Hake with Chorizo, Potatoes and Tiny Green Peppers)

I think this dish is a bit like those local wines you find in places such as Provence, Sicily and Portugal, wines like Vinho Verde. You know, the ones where you say, 'I must take some of these home – I've never tasted wine like this before', and then you get them back and, well, they're just rather dull. But Albariño, the white wine of Galicia, is stunning, a perfect balance of acidity and beautifully appley fruit. So, actually, is this version of this classic Galician dish, which I found in Malpica on the Costa de la Muerte, the Coast of Death – so named because of the incredible number of shipwrecks that have happened along this rugged coastline, which ends at the 'end of the earth', Finisterre.

serves 4

50 ml (2 fl oz) olive oil
2 onions, thinly sliced
6 garlic cloves, sliced
2 teaspoons paprika
1 × 15 cm (6 inch) chorizo sausage, sliced
100 g (4 oz) pimientos de Padrón or
   other tiny green peppers (or 1 large green
   pepper, diced)

900 g (2 lb) floury new potatoes, scraped and
   halved lengthways
85 ml (3 fl oz) dry white wine, such as Albariño
300 ml (10 fl oz) water
8 × 100 g (4 oz) or 4 × 225 g (8 oz) hake steaks
Salt and freshly ground black pepper

method

Heat the olive oil in a terracotta *cazuela* or a shallow flameproof casserole. Add the onions and garlic and cook gently until soft. Add the paprika and fry for 2–3 minutes, then add the chorizo sausage and green peppers and fry for another 3–4 minutes. Stir in the potatoes, then pour in the wine and water, season with some salt and pepper and simmer for about 10 minutes, until the potatoes are just tender and the liquid has reduced a little.

Season the hake steaks well on both sides. Put them on top of the potatoes, cover and simmer for 8–10 minutes, until the hake is cooked through.

alternative fish

You could try making this with cod or haddock steaks instead but hake is best and the Spanish love it. Why the British don't, I'll never understand.

Pulpo a la Feria (Fairground Octopus)

This is the way they cook octopus everywhere in Galicia – served up, as a first course, on a round pine board, sprinkled with the best olive oil, sweet paprika and coarse sea salt. The oil is always hot and I'm convinced that this brings out a slight piney flavour from the board. When cooked in this way, the octopus is as soft and gelatinous as slow-cooked pig's trotters and when I first tasted it in a bar in Santiago de Compostela with a glass of Estrella, a local Galician beer served ice-cold in a glass straight from the freezer, I was filled with overexcited thoughts about the simple things in life being the best.

Octopus, completely rejected by us in the UK, is the star of seafood cookery in Galicia. The instructions for tenderizing it in this recipe are far more effective and agreeable than the Greek habit of bashing it against rocks. Most instructions for cooking octopus say that it should be dipped three times in boiling water before being simmered slowly. I've tried it and it didn't make a scrap of difference. What counts is a long freeze and then long, slow simmering.

serves 4

1 octopus, weighing about 750 g (1½ lb)
1 onion, peeled
4 bay leaves
½ teaspoon paprika

A good pinch of cayenne pepper
50 ml (2 fl oz) good olive oil
½–1 teaspoon sea salt flakes

method

You will need to start the preparation for this dish well in advance. Seal the octopus in a plastic bag and leave it in the freezer for 2 weeks (this helps to tenderize it). Then transfer it to the fridge the day before you want to cook it to allow it to thaw gently for 24 hours.

The next day, clean the octopus by turning the body inside out and pulling away the entrails and bone-like strips sticking to the sides. Locate the stomach sac, which is about the size of an avocado stone, and cut it away. Wash the octopus well inside and out and then turn the body right side out again. Press the beak and the soft surround out from the centre of the tentacles, cut out and discard.

Simmer the octopus for at least 1 hour in plenty of water to which you've added the onion and bay leaves. Test after half an hour and cook for a further 30 minutes if it is still a bit tough. Don't cook any longer than that, though, as it loses its fresh taste with long cooking.

Lift the octopus out of the pan and drain away all the excess water. Put it on a board, cut off the tentacles and thinly slice each one on the diagonal. Cut the body into similar-sized pieces, place them on 4 small pine boards or one large warmed serving plate and sprinkle with the paprika and the cayenne. Heat the olive oil in a small pan until it is sizzling. Drizzle it over the octopus and then finally sprinkle with the sea salt. Serve with plenty of crusty fresh bread.

Zarzuela

As I've said in other fish stew recipes, the secret of a brilliant stew lies in cooking the fish separately from the rest of the ingredients and bringing them together at the last minute for a final intermingling of flavours. What sets this famous Catalonian stew apart is the picada – *a fried bread, toasted almond and garlic paste which is stirred into the stew at the last minute to give it a good bang!* Zarzuela *also refers to the Spanish version of a Gilbert and Sullivan type of opera, which seems to sum up this bells and whistles sort of dish.*

serves 8

2 × 350 g (12 oz) red mullet,
ungutted if possible

4 × 75–100 g (3–4 oz) monkfish fillets

350 g (12 oz) prepared squid (see p. 27)

900 ml (1½ pints) *Fish Stock* (see p. 232)

4 tablespoons olive oil

1 large onion, finely chopped

6 garlic cloves, thinly sliced

½ red finger chilli, seeded and finely chopped

750 g (1½ lb) small, ripe beef tomatoes,
skinned and finely chopped

A large pinch of saffron

150 ml (5 fl oz) dry white wine

24 mussels, cleaned (see p. 26)

1 teaspoon paprika

16 cooked crevettes (Mediterranean prawns)

Salt and freshly ground black pepper

FOR THE PICADA:

5 blanched almonds

2 tablespoons extra virgin olive oil

1 slice of day-old white bread, crusts removed

2 large garlic cloves, chopped

2 tablespoons chopped parsley

1 tablespoon Pernod

method

Clean and gut the red mullet if necessary (see p. 26), saving the liver from one of the fish. Fillet the fish (see p. 26) and cut each fillet diagonally in half. Cut each monkfish fillet across into 3 pieces and each squid pouch across into strips 2.5 cm (1 inch) wide. Put the fish stock into a large pan and boil rapidly until reduced by half.

Make the *picada*: toast the almonds under the grill until golden. Heat the olive oil in a frying pan, add the slice of bread and fry gently on both sides until golden. Leave to cool slightly and then break it into the food processor and add the almonds, garlic, parsley, Pernod, the red mullet liver, if using, and 2 tablespoons of the reduced stock. Reduce to a smooth paste.

Heat half the olive oil in a large, heavy-based casserole. Add the onion, garlic and chilli and cook gently until they are soft and just beginning to colour slightly. Add the tomatoes and simmer until they have reduced to a thick sauce. Add the saffron,

120 ml (4 fl oz) of the wine and the rest of the reduced fish stock and bring to the boil. Lower the heat and leave to simmer while you cook the fish.

Pre-heat the grill to high. Put the mussels into a large pan with the rest of the wine, cover and cook over a high heat for 3–4 minutes to open them. Strain most of the mussel liquor into the simmering casserole. Discard any mussels that have remained closed and keep the rest warm.

Put the pieces of red mullet, monkfish and squid on one or two lightly greased baking trays and sprinkle lightly with the remaining olive oil, the paprika and some salt and pepper. Grill for just 4 minutes, adding the crevettes to the trays 1 minute before the end. Pour off the cooking juices into the stew. Keep the fish warm.

Take a good ladleful of the sauce from the casserole and add it to the *picada* paste in the food processor. Give it a quick whizz, then scrape the mixture into the casserole and simmer for 2 minutes. Season with salt and pepper.

Put the cooked mussels, crevettes, fish and squid on 8 warmed plates. Spoon the sauce over the seafood and serve with plenty of crusty bread to mop it up.

alternative fish

I'm assuming that you will be able to get some of the above fish but here are a few others you can use: try John Dory, cuttlefish, sea bass, grey mullet, clams, lobster, crab and tiger prawns.

Tortilla of Salt Cod with Sweet Onions and Potatoes

Salt cod is one of my favourite foods. I like commercially prepared cod, which is incredibly salty and needs at least 24 hours' soaking before you can use it, but I must admit it's a bit of an acquired taste. My home-salted cod has the advantage of being quick to make and is much moister and fresher tasting. To me, salt cod never tastes better than when it is set in contrast to some sweet-flavoured new potatoes. This traditional Spanish omelette is one of the great simple dishes of the world that I'm always searching for.

serves 6

350 g (12 oz) thick piece of unskinned cod fillet

85 ml (3 fl oz) extra virgin olive oil

1 large onion, thinly sliced

450 g (1 lb) potatoes, peeled and cut into
   chunky matchsticks

8 eggs

3 tablespoons chopped flat-leaf parsley

Salt and freshly ground black pepper

method

Salt the cod overnight (see p. 238). Rinse off the excess salt, put it in a pan of boiling water and simmer for about 6–8 minutes or until just cooked. Lift out and, when cool enough to handle, flake the fish, discarding the skin and any bones.

Heat the oil in a deep 23 cm (9 inch) well-seasoned or non-stick frying pan. Add the onion and cook over a medium heat for 3–4 minutes. Add the potatoes and cook, stirring now and then, for 15 minutes or until just tender. Add the flaked fish and a little seasoning and turn everything over once or twice to distribute the ingredients evenly. Beat the eggs with the parsley and a little salt and pepper. Pour them into the pan and cook over a very low heat for about 15 minutes, until almost set.

Pre-heat the grill to high. Put the pan under the grill for 2–3 minutes, until the tortilla is lightly browned on top. Cut it into wedges and serve warm with the *Little Gem Salad with a Garlic and Sherry Vinegar Dressing* (see p. 229).

alternative fish

See the suggestions under Chickpea, Parsley and Salt Cod Stew on p. 100.

Stir-fried Squid with Chorizo, Chilli, Red Pepper and Potatoes

This dish is designed for use with rather less than perfect squid. It's very good with perfect squid too, but I feel there's no point in being unrealistic about an endless supply of glistening seafood in the UK. Things are getting better, but even I come home with the odd pound of squid from the supermarket that I wouldn't sauté with just some olive oil and garlic. The strong flavours of chorizo and garlic more than compensate for any loss of flavour in the squid. For more information on chorizo, see p. 243.

serves 4

225 g (8 oz) prepared squid (see p. 27)
3 tablespoons extra virgin olive oil
50 g (2 oz) fresh chorizo sausage, thinly sliced
2 garlic cloves, crushed
1 red pepper, roasted (see p. 238) and diced
350 g (12 oz) small new potatoes, cooked and
    thinly sliced
1 red finger chilli, seeded and finely chopped
½ teaspoon chilli powder
1 plum tomato, skinned, seeded and diced
    (see p. 238)
Salt and freshly ground black pepper

method

Slice the squid pouches across into rings and halve or separate the tentacles, depending on how large they are.

Heat the oil in a large, heavy-based frying pan, add the squid and stir-fry over a high heat for 2 minutes, until well browned. Add the chorizo and garlic and stir-fry for 2 minutes. Add the red pepper, potatoes, chilli and chilli powder and stir-fry for a further 1–2 minutes, until the potatoes have heated through. Add the diced tomato and some salt and pepper and cook for 1 minute. Serve immediately, with chunks of French bread.

alternative fish

You could use cuttlefish instead of squid but I have also made this dish with some cooked and shredded skate meat from a wing, folded into the fried chorizo and potatoes at the last minute just to heat through.

Baked Scallops with Paprika, Serrano Ham and Crisp Garlic and Olive Oil Crumbs

I've got great affection for the seafood of Galicia in northern Spain. Galicia is a bit of a 'Lost World' – very few tourists from outside Spain seem to go there and yet it's so beautiful. It's quite like Cornwall but 10°C hotter. The seafood, when simply cooked, is probably the best in the world.

For this dish either buy the scallops in the shell and clean them yourself so you'll have them to use as little baking dishes, or ask your fishmonger for prepared scallops and 8 cleaned shells instead.

serves 4

4 tablespoons olive oil

1 onion, finely chopped

1 red pepper, finely chopped

100 g (4 oz) thinly sliced Serrano ham, finely chopped

5 tablespoons chopped flat-leaf parsley

1 teaspoon paprika

50 ml (2 fl oz) dry white wine

16 prepared scallops (see p. 26)

1 garlic clove, crushed

50 g (2 oz) fresh white breadcrumbs (made from day-old bread)

Salt and freshly ground black pepper

method

Pre-heat the oven to 190°C/375°F/Gas Mark 5.

Heat 2 tablespoons of the oil in a pan, add the onion and red pepper and cook gently for 25 minutes, stirring now and then. The object is to make them so soft they're almost melting. Stir in the ham, 4 tablespoons of the parsley, the paprika and wine and simmer for a few minutes until most of the liquid has been absorbed. Season to taste with salt and pepper.

Rest 8 cleaned scallop shells in a shallow baking tray. Place 2 scallops in each shell and spoon the ham mixture on top.

Heat the rest of the oil in a frying pan. Add the garlic, allow it to sizzle for a few seconds and then stir in the breadcrumbs and fry them, stirring all the time, for a few minutes until they are crisp and golden. Take the pan off the heat and stir in some seasoning and the rest of the parsley. Spoon the crumbs over the scallops and bake for 10 minutes. Serve immediately.

alternative fish

This is a classic Galician dish and it's really got to be made with scallops.

Razor Clams a la Plancha

A la plancha is perhaps the most popular way of cooking seafood in Spain. The seafood is simply dropped on to a very hot flat iron griddle and cooked on both sides with just a brush of oil. It comes to the table with no accompaniment other than perhaps a wedge of lemon, but the Spanish say that the freshest of fish doesn't need even that. Most of us don't have flat-topped griddles so use a large, heavy-based frying pan instead. The other way to cook this starter is to brush the clams with olive oil and put them under a hot grill for about 5 minutes.

serves 4   **24 razor clams, cleaned**
Good olive oil
Lemon wedges, to serve (optional)

method   Wash the clams well in plenty of cold water. Heat your largest heavy-based frying pan or a griddle pan over a high heat until very hot. Add a little olive oil and a single layer of the clams, hinge-side down. As soon as they have opened right up, turn them over so that the meats come into contact with the base of the pan and cook for about 1 minute, until lightly browned.

Turn the clams back over, drizzle over a little more olive oil and put them on a warmed serving plate. Serve with a lemon wedge or two, if you wish, and any juices from the pan. Repeat the process with any remaining clams if necessary.

alternative fish

You can do this with large carpetshell clams, too.

Fried Bream with Romesco Sauce

This is the Spanish way of frying fish, neither shallow nor deep, but in about half an inch of olive oil. The classic romesco pepper and hazelnut sauce, used in this starter, comes from Catalonia and is one of those terrific piquant sauces for fish like salsa verde, aïoli or charmoula. You could replace it with any one of these, if you like. The Andalucíans use a special, fairly coarse unbleached flour called harina de freir pescado *for frying fish but semolina produces almost as good results.*

serves 4

4 × 450 g (1 lb) bream, cleaned (see p. 26)
Olive oil for frying
50 g (2 oz) semolina or *harina de freir pescado*
Salt and freshly ground black pepper

FOR THE ROMESCO SAUCE:

1 dried choricero or ñora pepper (see p. 242)
225 g (8 oz) vine-ripened tomatoes
4 garlic cloves, peeled
15 g (½ oz) blanched hazelnuts
15 g (½ oz) slice of day-old white bread,
    crusts removed
120 ml (4 fl oz) olive oil
A pinch of dried chilli flakes
1 tablespoon sherry vinegar

method

For the romesco sauce, cover the dried pepper with warm water, weight it down with a saucer to keep it submerged and leave to soak overnight. The next day, drain and slit it open and remove the stalk and seeds. Chop it up roughly.

Pre-heat the oven to 200°C/400°F/Gas Mark 6.

Put the tomatoes and 3 cloves of garlic into a small roasting tin and bake for 10 minutes. Sprinkle over the nuts and bake for 15 minutes or until the nuts are golden brown. Remove from the oven and leave to cool. Remove the skins from the tomatoes.

Rub the slice of bread on both sides with the remaining clove of garlic. Heat a little of the oil in a frying pan, add the bread and fry it until richly golden on both sides. Leave to cool a little and then break it up. Put it in a liquidizer with the tomato, nut and garlic mixture, the red pepper, chilli flakes, sherry vinegar, ½ teaspoon of salt and some black pepper. Blend until smooth, then, with the motor still running, gradually pour in the rest of the oil to produce a mayonnaise-like sauce. Scrape the mixture into a serving bowl and set to one side.

Trim the tails from the bream and season on both sides with salt and pepper. Pour a good layer of olive oil into a frying pan that is large enough to hold 2 of the fish and heat it to 180°C/350°F. Dip 2 of the fish into the semolina or flour and fry for 3 minutes on each side until crisp, golden and cooked through. Lift out, drain briefly on kitchen paper and place on a large serving plate. Keep them warm in a low oven while you cook the remaining fish. Serve with the romesco sauce and the *Little Gem Salad with a Garlic and Sherry Vinegar Dressing* (see p. 229).

alternative fish

If you can't get bream for this dish, small farmed sea bass, red mullet, gurnard, grey mullet, small whiting or John Dory would be fine.

Seared Scallops with Ibérico Ham

Ibérico ham is the best cured ham in Spain. It is taken from the Ibérico negro pig, which is allowed to run free in the oak forests, getting plenty of exercise and therefore staying lean. It is very similar to the Italian Parma or French Bayonne ham but it has its own distinctive, and very fine flavour. However, you can use any cured or air-dried ham in its place if you wish. The salad for this dish should be the hearts of frisée or curly endive lettuce. What I mean by that is the lovely, crisp blanched leaves from the centre of the lettuce that haven't turned green because of exposure to the light. It's a pity that British supermarkets only seem to sell them in bags of washed salad leaves. I love those massive heads of bitter, chicory-type leaves like frisée de ruffec, escarole *or* cornet de Bordeaux *in France and similar whole salads in Italian and Spanish markets.*

serves 4

50 g (2 oz) chilled unsalted butter

12 prepared scallops (see p. 26)

3 tablespoons sherry vinegar

1 tablespoon chopped parsley

8 thin slices of Ibérico ham or a similar
   cured ham

Leaves from 1 frisée lettuce heart and a
   handful of other bitter salad leaves

Salt and freshly ground black pepper

method

Rub the base of a large non-stick frying pan well with the block of butter and cut the remainder into small pieces. Set the pan over a high heat and as soon as the butter starts to smoke, add the scallops and sear for 2 minutes on each side, seasoning them with a little salt and pepper as they cook. Transfer the scallops to a warmed baking tray and keep warm while you make the dressing.

Remove the pan from the heat, add the sherry vinegar and stir to scrape up any residue from the bottom of the pan. Return the pan to the heat and whisk in the butter, a few pieces at a time, then add the parsley and season with a little salt and pepper. Arrange the ham and a pile of the salad leaves on 4 plates. Arrange the scallops over the ham, spoon the dressing over the leaves and serve at once.

alternative fish

Much as I hate to admit this, because I always find the concept of 'surf 'n' turf' a bit vulgar, slices of cooked lobster or prawns would go very well with the Ibérico ham. However, simply toss them in a little melted butter and some seasoning to heat through instead of searing them.

Basque Salt Cod, Leek and Potato Soup

I love these rustic, rugged soups. I also particularly like salt cod, and I was just thinking the other day that though some purists claim that only the taste of reconstituted commercially salted and dried cod will do, I must own up to preferring fresh cod that has been salted overnight and rinsed off the next day. I use salt cod almost as I would bacon or salt pork, as a way of enhancing the flavour of ingredients such as eggs, potatoes or pulses like lentils or chickpeas (see Chickpea, Parsley and Salt Cod Stew on p. 100).

serves 4

350 g (12 oz) thick piece of unskinned cod fillet

2 tablespoons olive oil

4 garlic cloves, thinly sliced

1 small onion, thinly sliced

2 large leeks, thinly sliced

50 ml (2 fl oz) dry white vermouth

25 g (1 oz) butter

450 g (1 lb) potatoes, peeled and thinly sliced

1.2 litres (2 pints) *Fish Stock* (see p. 232)

A handful of chopped parsley

Salt and freshly ground black pepper

method

Salt the cod overnight (see p. 238).

The next day, heat the olive oil in a large pan, add the garlic, onion and leeks and cook over a gentle heat for about 10 minutes, until softened. Add the dry vermouth and simmer a little more vigorously until it has reduced by half. Add the butter and when it has melted add the potatoes and stock. Cover and simmer for 20 minutes.

Meanwhile, put the cod into a large pan of boiling water and simmer for about 6–8 minutes. Drain and, when it is cool enough to handle, flake the flesh, discarding the skin and any bones. Stir the flaked cod into the soup and simmer for another 5 minutes. Stir in the chopped parsley and season liberally with pepper. Check for salt but you probably won't need any because of the cod.

alternative fish

See the suggestions under Chickpea, Parsley and Salt Cod Stew *on p. 100.*

Cuttlefish with Broad Beans

This is a classic dish from Andalucía in southern Spain, recreated here as a starter. A lot of the fish cookery there uses sherry and in this recipe the slightly nutty flavour of dry manzanilla or fino adds an extra dimension. This is designed for young broad beans and some recipes call for the sliced pods to be added as well if they are young enough. But you can use young frozen broad beans here, too.

serves 4

450 g (1 lb) prepared small cuttlefish (see p. 27)

3 tablespoons olive oil

1 teaspoon paprika

2 garlic cloves, finely chopped

120 ml (4 fl oz) dry sherry such as manzanilla or fino

120 ml (4 fl oz) water

450 g (1 lb) shelled young broad beans

1 bay leaf, very finely shredded

2 tablespoons chopped flat-leaf parsley

Salt and freshly ground black pepper

method

Cut the cuttlefish bodies across into thin strips and separate the tentacles into similar-sized pieces.

Heat the oil in a large, heavy-based frying pan. Add the cuttlefish and paprika, season well with salt and pepper and stir-fry over a high heat for 1 minute. Add the garlic and cook for 30 seconds. Add the sherry, water, broad beans and shredded bay leaf, cover and simmer for 5–6 minutes, until the beans are tender.

Uncover the pan, increase the heat a little and simmer a little more quickly until the liquid has reduced to a well-flavoured sauce. Sprinkle over the chopped parsley and serve with some crusty white bread.

alternative fish

The obvious alternative would be squid but this dish is also excellent with skinned firm fish fillets such as monkfish, Dover sole or John Dory.

some classics and some French influences • *The ferry that goes from Plymouth, England, to Roscoff in Brittany is called the Quiberon. It is a small boat, and not the newest, but I like it. I like the lorry drivers, with broad arms, tattoos and white T-shirts, in the early morning in the canteen, and I even like the coffee and croissants. Though neither is particularly good, somehow they seem different from the ones you get in England. The voyage is usually rough (it is affectionately called 'the rough cross'), but I never fail to get just a little bit of a shiver down my spine when I see the coast of Brittany low on the horizon. We sail through little outcrops of rock into Roscoff harbour, reverse, then dock and drive out of the exhaust-filled clatter of the car decks into the low countryside of St-Pol-de-Léon with its clock-tower church. We veer left, through fields of artichokes that seem to go on for ever, past the scruffy war museum, and out towards Quimper and Concarneau.*

France

Days spent in Brittany are still among the happiest in my life. Le Conquet is where Jill and I had our first plateau de fruits de mer about 18 years ago and where I was so overwhelmed by its simplicity and the scent of the sea that I took the idea straight back to Padstow and probably changed the whole direction of my cooking with just that one dish. It's still on the menu at the Seafood Restaurant. And so are most of the recipes in this chapter on France: La Mouclade, Marmite Dieppoise, Steamed Fillet of Brill with Poached Oysters. My style of cooking, my influences, my enthusiasm owe more to France than to any other country, and I go back there to relive my happy memories as often as I can.

Whole Salmon Baked en Papillote
with Tarragon, served with Beurre Blanc

I wrote this recipe for the supermarket chain Tesco, with whom I work, mainly looking for ways of improving their wet fish counters. I find them refreshingly open to criticism and willing to take on new suggestions. They have a very good supply of farmed salmon which they asked me to show off at its best, and I'm really pleased with this.

serves 4

50 g (2 oz) butter, melted
1 × 1.5 kg (3 lb) salmon
A small bunch of tarragon, roughly chopped
120 ml (4 fl oz) dry white wine
Juice of ½ lemon
Salt and freshly ground black pepper

FOR THE BEURRE BLANC:

50 g (2 oz) shallots, very finely chopped
2 tablespoons white wine vinegar
4 tablespoons dry white wine
6 tablespoons water or *Fish Stock* (see p. 232)
2 tablespoons double cream
175 g (6 oz) chilled butter, diced

method

Pre-heat the oven to 220°C/425°F/Gas Mark 7.

Brush the centre of a large sheet of foil with some of the melted butter. Place the salmon in the centre and bring the edges of the foil up around the fish slightly. Put the open parcel on to a large baking sheet.

Mix the tarragon with the rest of the melted butter, plus the wine, lemon juice, salt and pepper. Spoon the mixture into the cavity of the fish and over the top. Bring the sides of the foil up over the fish and pinch together, folding over the edges a few times to make a loose, airtight parcel. Bake for 30 minutes.

Meanwhile, make the *beurre blanc*: put the shallots, vinegar, wine and water or stock into a small pan, bring to the boil and simmer until nearly all the liquid has evaporated. Add the cream and simmer until slightly thickened. Remove from the heat and whisk in the butter, a small piece at a time, to make a smooth sauce.

Remove the fish from the oven and open up the parcel. If you wish, remove the skin as follows: cut through the skin just behind the head and above the tail and lift it off. Carefully turn the fish over and repeat on the other side. Lift it on to a warmed serving dish. Serve with the *beurre blanc*, together with some *Boiled Potatoes* (see p. 223) and perhaps some cooked sliced green beans.

alternative fish

You could use a large bass or snapper, or any large trout such as sea trout or Atlantic trout from Australia.

Braised Sea Trout Fillets
with White Wine and Basil

The idea for this dish came from a very early exploration of Michelin-starred restaurants in France. At the Moulin de Mougins near Lorient in Brittany I remember being particularly impressed by the use of basil in a butter sauce. It's easy to forget just how recently basil has become a common herb in the UK. Sometimes I wish it wasn't so easy to get everything from everywhere. I'll never be bowled over again by the fragrance of basil in a sauce – except perhaps the basil from my garden, which has so much more flavour than most of the shop-bought stuff.

serves 4

75 g (3 oz) butter
75 g (3 oz) carrots, very thinly sliced
75 g (3 oz) celery, very thinly sliced
75 g (3 oz) leeks, very thinly sliced
85 ml (3 fl oz) dry white wine
600 ml (1 pint) *Chicken Stock* (see p. 232)

4 × 150 g (5 oz) skinned sea trout fillets
A handful of very finely shredded basil leaves,
    plus sprigs of basil to garnish
1 teaspoon lemon juice
Salt and freshly ground black pepper

method

Melt 50 g (2 oz) of the butter in a shallow pan large enough to hold the fish in one layer. Stir in the carrots, celery and leeks, cover and sweat over a medium heat for about 3 minutes. Add the wine and stock and simmer, uncovered, until almost all the liquid has evaporated but the vegetables are still moist. Lay the fish fillets on top, season with some salt and pepper and sprinkle over half the basil. Cover and simmer very gently for 8–10 minutes, until the fish is just cooked through.

Put the fish on 4 warmed plates and keep warm. If there is a little too much liquid left in the pan, boil rapidly until the juices have reduced and the sauce is glistening. Stir in the rest of the butter, the lemon juice and the rest of the basil and adjust the seasoning if necessary. Spoon the sauce over the fish and garnish with basil sprigs.

alternative fish

Salmon or king trout fillets.

Tarte aux Moules

I first saw this in a traiteur's *shop in Dieppe. The idea of a* traiteur *is beginning to take off in the UK, a shop filled with cooked food to take home. I remember looking through the window at blackened baking trays of pastry tarts as big as the tray – pissaladière, quiche Lorraine, pâté en croûte and seafood tarts. (I should also mention those delicious tartes au pommes Normandes made with local apples like Calville Blanc, almonds and crème pâtissière.) This is my version of one of those seafood tarts, made with local mussels, cream and butter encased in crisp, brown, buttery pastry.*

serves 8

900 g (2 lb) mussels, cleaned (see p. 26)

50 ml (2 fl oz) dry white wine

3 tablespoons chopped parsley (keep the stalks)

25 g (1 oz) butter

5–6 shallots, finely chopped

5 garlic cloves, finely chopped

3 eggs, beaten

300 ml (10 fl oz) double cream

Salt and freshly ground black pepper

FOR THE PASTRY:

225 g (8 oz) plain flour

1/2 teaspoon salt

65 g (2 1/2 oz) chilled butter, cut into pieces

65 g (2 1/2 oz) chilled lard, cut into pieces

1 1/2–2 tablespoons water

1 egg white

method

Pre-heat the oven to 200°C/400°F/Gas Mark 6.

For the pastry, sift the flour and salt into a food processor or a mixing bowl, add the chilled butter and lard and work together until the mixture looks like fine breadcrumbs. Stir in the water with a table knife until it comes together into a ball. Turn out on to a lightly floured work surface and knead briefly until smooth. Roll out and use to line a 25 cm (10 inch) loose-bottomed flan tin, 4 cm (1 1/2 inches) deep. Prick the base here and there with a fork and chill for 20 minutes.

Line the pastry case with a sheet of crumpled greaseproof paper, fill with baking beans and bake blind for 15 minutes. Remove the paper and beans and return the pastry to the oven for 5 minutes. Remove once more and brush the base with the unbeaten egg white. Return to the oven for 1 minute. Remove and lower the oven temperature to 190°C/375°F/Gas Mark 5.

Put the mussels into a large pan with the wine and parsley stalks. Cover and cook over a high heat for 3–4 minutes, shaking the pan every now and then, until the mussels have opened. Tip them into a colander set over a bowl to collect all the cooking liquor. Leave to cool slightly and then remove the mussels from their shells, discarding any that have not opened.

continued overleaf

Melt the butter in a pan, add the shallots and garlic and cook gently for about 7 minutes, until very soft. Add all but the last tablespoon or two of the mussel cooking liquor and simmer rapidly until it has evaporated. Scrape the mixture into a bowl and leave to cool. Then stir in the eggs, cream and parsley and season to taste with pepper and a little salt if necessary.

Scatter the mussels over the base of the pastry case and pour in the egg mixture. Bake for 25–30 minutes, until just set and lightly browned. Remove and leave to cool slightly before serving with the *Soft Green Lettuce Salad with Olive Oil Dressing* (see p. 228).

alternative fish

This delicate tart can be made equally successfully with small clams such as carpetshell, Venus or butter clams.

Carpetshell Clams with Cider, Cream and Parsley

I bought a couple of kilos of carpetshell clams (or palourdes, as they are known in France) the other day, steamed them open and ate them with no accompaniments. They were so sweet and tender that I thought only a very uncomplicated way of cooking them would do them justice. And here it is — they're just steamed open with some Normandy cider and shallots and finished off with parsley and cream.

serves 4

1.75 kg (4 lb) carpetshell clams, cleaned
    (see p. 26)
3 shallots, finely chopped
4 tablespoons chopped flat-leaf parsley
300 ml (10 fl oz) dry Normandy cider
150 ml (5 fl oz) extra-thick double cream
Salt

method

Put the clams into a large pan with the shallots, a quarter of the parsley and the cider. Cover and cook over a high heat, shaking the pan every now and then, until the clams have opened — about 3–4 minutes. Add the cream and simmer, uncovered, for 1 minute. Add the rest of the parsley, adjust the seasoning and spoon into warmed soup plates, leaving behind the last 2–3 tablespoons of sauce in case it contains a bit of sand. Serve with plenty of crusty white bread for mopping up the juices.

alternative fish

Carpetshell clams are the best-flavoured clams in the world but littleneck clams from America are pretty good, as are pipis, which come from Australia. Small, tender clams or cockles are the ones to use here, not those great big quahogs, which are best used in chowders.

Grilled Cod with Lettuce Hearts and a Rich Chicken and Tarragon Dressing

I am addicted to warm fish salads and this is essentially that. I love the soft taste of white flakes of cod against crisp lettuce and al dente asparagus. The salad is finished with a dressing made with some good chicken stock that has been reduced with tarragon and garlic until it is beautifully concentrated.

serves 4

550 g (1¼ lb) piece of skinned thick cod fillet
Coarse sea salt
1.2 litres (2 pints) *Chicken Stock* (see p. 232)
A few tarragon stalks
2 garlic cloves, peeled but left whole
2 tablespoons extra virgin olive oil
100 g (4 oz) asparagus tips

4 soft round lettuces
12 very thin slices of pancetta
1 teaspoon chopped chives
1 teaspoon chopped tarragon sprigs
1½ teaspoons white wine vinegar
Salt and freshly ground black pepper

method

Place the cod in a dish, cover with coarse salt and leave for 20 minutes. Wash the salt off and pat dry. Meanwhile, put the chicken stock, tarragon stalks and garlic cloves into a large pan and boil until reduced to about 85 ml (3 fl oz) and nicely concentrated in flavour. Strain into a small, clean pan and keep warm.

Brush the cod fillet with a little of the olive oil, season with some pepper and place on a lightly oiled baking tray.

Cook the asparagus tips in boiling salted water until just tender. Drain, refresh and keep warm. Remove the outside leaves from each lettuce until you get down to the hearts. Cut each one into quarters.

Pre-heat the grill to high, then grill the cod for about 10–12 minutes. Put the slices of pancetta over the fish and grill for 1–2 minutes, until it is crisp and lightly golden.

Put the quartered lettuce hearts in the centre of 4 warmed plates. Break the pancetta into small pieces and the cod into chunky flakes. Arrange the cod around the lettuce with the pancetta and asparagus. Sprinkle over the chives and tarragon. Spoon the warm chicken stock over the lettuce and a little over the rest of the plate. Whisk the remaining olive oil, vinegar and some seasoning together, drizzle over the plate and serve straight away.

alternative fish

I particularly like thick fillets of flaky fish for this. Haddock would be a good alternative, of course, but salmon would work well, too.

Marmite Dieppoise

On the cover of my very first cookery book, English Seafood Cookery, *there's a watercolour of the big, deep, round, red-enamelled iron pot that I use for all my fish stews. It's not quite a marmite (which has straight sides) but it's pretty close. There's something so welcoming about a much-loved cooking pot, filled with a warm, creamy, lightly curry-flavoured fish stew like this, with glimpses of mussels in their shells, bright green parsley, the pink of prawns and the gleaming white of fresh cod. Like most of my fish stews, I prefer to cook the fish separately then combine fish and stew at the last moment. I think it tastes so much better this way. The suggested ways of serving the stew are either in a pot or carefully arranged on 4 warm plates.*

serves 8

100 g (4 oz) butter

2 leeks, sliced

2 fennel bulbs, thinly sliced

2 onions, thinly sliced

1 teaspoon fennel seeds, lightly crushed

2 teaspoons good-quality medium
   curry powder

175 ml (6 fl oz) medium-dry white wine,
   such as Chenin Blanc or a Chardonnay from
   the Languedoc

2 plum tomatoes, skinned and roughly chopped

40 g (1½ oz) plain flour

1.2 litres (2 pints) *Fish Stock* (see p. 232)

900 g (2 lb) mussels, cleaned (see p. 26)

225 g (8 oz) monkfish fillet

450 g (1 lb) skinned cod fillet

225 g (8 oz) skinned lemon sole fillets

12 prepared scallops (see p. 26), each cut in
   half horizontally

450 g (1 lb) cooked langoustine

150 ml (5 fl oz) double cream

2 teaspoons lemon juice

½ teaspoon paprika

Salt and freshly ground black pepper

method

Melt 75 g (3 oz) of the butter in a large casserole, add the leeks, fennel, onions, fennel seeds and curry powder and cook gently for 10 minutes, until soft. Add 120 ml (4 fl oz) of the wine and the tomatoes and simmer until almost all the liquid has evaporated. Stir in the flour and cook for 1 minute. Gradually stir in the fish stock and then simmer gently for 15 minutes.

Meanwhile, put the mussels into a large pan with the rest of the white wine, cover and cook over a high heat for 3–4 minutes, until they have opened (discard any that remain closed). Tip them into a colander set over a bowl to collect the cooking liquor. Keep the mussels warm.

Now strain the sauce through a conical sieve, pressing out as much liquid as you can, return it to the pan and add all the mussel cooking liquor except the last 2 tablespoons (as this might be a bit gritty), plus 1 teaspoon of salt. Bring back to a rapid boil and boil until reduced to 750 ml (1¼ pints).

Meanwhile, pre-heat the grill to high. Melt the rest of the butter. Cut the monkfish into slices 1 cm (½ inch) thick and cut the cod and lemon sole fillets diagonally across into strips 2.5 cm (1 inch) wide. Put the monkfish and cod pieces on a greased baking tray and the sole and scallop pieces on a second one. Brush on both sides with the melted butter and season well with salt and pepper.

Cook the monkfish and cod under the grill for 4–5 minutes. Keep warm while you cook the lemon sole and scallop slices for about 2 minutes. Meanwhile, stir the langoustines, cream and lemon juice into the sauce and adjust the seasoning if necessary. Simmer for 1 minute, until they have heated through, then stir in the mussels and take the pan off the heat.

You can serve this dish up in one of two ways. For an elegant dinner-party type of serving, where you do all the work, arrange the pieces of grilled fish in the centre of 6 or 8 warmed plates and put a few of the langoustine and mussels in amongst them. Spoon over the sauce, sprinkle with the paprika and serve. Or you can simply add the pieces of grilled fish to the pot, carefully mix them in so that they don't break up too much, then sprinkle the stew with the paprika. Take the pot to the table and leave people to help themselves. Either way, you've still got all the beautiful flavours of the fish and shellfish cooked separately.

alternative fish

Here are a few other fish that will go well in a marmite: Dover sole, hake, flounder, raw prawns, unpeeled North Atlantic prawns, clams and lobster.

Merlan Frit en Colère (Deep-fried Whiting)

I've always liked the name of this dish, which means something like 'whiting in a bad temper'. The whiting's tail is twisted round and secured in its mouth before being breaded and deep-fried. I have an image here of my dog Chalky turning around to bite a flea on his tail. Whiting is perhaps not the best-flavoured fish in the world but a small, perfectly fresh one cooked in this way is quite charming.

serves 4

4 × 350 g (12 oz) whiting, cleaned (see p. 26)

Sunflower oil for deep-frying

75 g (3 oz) plain flour

2 eggs, beaten

175 g (6 oz) fresh white breadcrumbs, made from day-old bread

Salt and freshly ground black pepper

FOR THE TOMATO TARTARE SAUCE:

3 tablespoons white wine vinegar

6 black peppercorns, coarsely crushed

½ shallot, finely chopped

A few tarragon stalks, broken into small pieces

2 plum tomatoes, skinned, seeded and finely chopped (see p. 238)

15 g (½ oz) each finely chopped green olives, gherkins and capers

2 teaspoons each chopped tarragon, parsley and chives

100 g (4 oz) *Mustard Mayonnaise* (see p. 235)

method

For the tomato tartare sauce, put the vinegar, peppercorns, shallot and tarragon stalks into a small pan and boil until the vinegar is reduced to 1 teaspoon. Cool slightly and then strain into a bowl. Mix in the rest of the ingredients and some salt and pepper to taste.

To prepare the whiting, twist each one around and push its tail into its mouth. Secure it in place by pushing a cocktail stick up through the soft part of the under-mouth, the tail and head.

Heat some oil for deep-frying to 160°C/320°F. Season the flour with ½ teaspoon of salt and some pepper. Season each fish with a little salt, then coat them one at a time in the flour, followed by the beaten egg and then the breadcrumbs. Deep-fry one at a time for 5 minutes or until crisp, golden and cooked through. Transfer to a baking tray lined with kitchen paper and keep warm in a low oven while you coat and cook the rest of the fish in the same way. Serve with a bowlful of the tomato tartare sauce on a pile of *Roughly Cut Chips* (see p. 224).

alternative fish

If you're lucky enough to live in Australia, a sand whiting would transform this from one of life's pleasurable dishes into something quite spectacular. Alternative European fish, however, are small hake (pin hake) or codling.

Steamed Fillet of Brill with Poached Oysters

I wouldn't say that cooking is an art form because it's a bit too basic for that, but I find recipe writing a pleasingly creative activity. It's a way of expressing how a particular place fills my senses. Every time I cook this recipe I think of those estuaries in Brittany filled with oyster beds and dotted with little fishing ports, where beautifully fresh brill is unloaded in the salty spring air.

serves 4

2 × 550 g (1¼ lb) brill
300 ml (10 fl oz) *Fish Stock* (see p. 232)
50 g (2 oz) butter
1 shallot, finely chopped
50 ml (2 fl oz) dry white wine

16 oysters
2 tablespoons double cream
1 tablespoon chopped chives
Salt and freshly ground black pepper

method

For this dish you need to fillet the brill into two large, topside and underside fillets. They are called cross-cut fillets by fishmongers and are the standard way that they fillet flat fish. Simply make a cut around the back of the head and across the tail, but not down the centre of the fish. Then cut the fish away from the bones in the same way as described on p. 26, so that you end up with 2 double fillets from each fish instead of 4 thinner fillets.

Put the fish stock into a small pan and boil it rapidly to reduce to about 120 ml (4 fl oz).

Melt a knob of the butter in a medium-sized pan. Cut the rest into small pieces. Add the shallot to the pan and cook gently for 5 minutes, until soft. Add the wine and simmer until reduced to about 2 tablespoons. Add the reduced fish stock and keep warm.

Open the oysters as described on p. 27. Clean 4 of the deeper shells for serving.

Season the fish fillets on both sides with a little salt and lay them on a heatproof plate. Place a trivet or an upturned plate in a large pan and pour in about 2.5 cm (1 inch) of water. Bring to a vigorous simmer, then put the plate on the trivet, cover the pan and steam for 4 minutes. Lift the fish out of the steamer and pour the juices from the plate into the sauce. Cover the fish and keep it warm. Bring the sauce to a gentle simmer, add the oysters and any juices and poach for 2 minutes. Lift them out with a slotted spoon and keep them warm with the brill.

Add the cream to the sauce and simmer vigorously for 3 minutes. Then whisk in the butter, a few pieces at a time, to form an emulsified sauce. Stir in the chives and season with black pepper and a little salt if necessary.

To serve, place the fish fillets skin-side down on 4 warmed plates. Rest one of the oyster shells alongside the fish. Put a poached oyster in each shell and arrange the rest over and around the fish. Pour the sauce over and serve.

alternative fish

This is a dish where only a few fish will do – turbot, lemon sole, American flounder or John Dory.

Éclade (Mussels Cooked on the Beach)

I got this idea from an excellent cookery book which I've had for years called Cuisine de Terroir. *It's full of real country recipes from France, some of which I've never seen in any other book. This recipe comes from the west Atlantic coastline of France, near Bordeaux, where there are miles and miles of sandy beaches backed by thick pine forests. They build up enormous wheels of mussels on old pine boards, pile pine needles on top and set them alight. We don't have pine-backed beaches near Padstow but we do have fields of hay and straw which work just as well, particularly on a sunny day in late September, when the harvest is over and the beaches are less crowded.*

serves 4

1.75–2.75 kg (4–6 lb) mussels, cleaned (see p. 26)
Plenty of crusty French bread
Chilled white wine, such as Muscadet, to serve

YOU WILL ALSO NEED:
A large piece of wood (pine if possible) about 1 metre (3 feet) square
4 large nails and a hammer
A large sackful of hay, straw or dry pine needles
A box of matches
A bucket of seawater

method

Soak the wood in water for about an hour. Then rest it on some stones if necessary so that it lies flat. Knock the tips of the nails into the centre of the wood in a 2.5 cm (1 inch) square and then rest one mussel between each pair of nails, convex side towards you and hinge pointing upwards. Now rest another 4 mussels in between these ones and continue to work your way outwards to create a massive rosette, using the larger mussels first and leaving the smaller ones until last. This will require a little patience but it does work.

Carefully cover the mussels completely with a layer of the hay, straw or pine needles about 26 cm (10 inches) thick. Set light to this here and there and leave to burn until the flames die down; it should burn quite hot for about 5 minutes. Now just fan away the ash, throw a bucket of seawater over them to get rid of the last of it and discard any mussels that haven't opened. Transfer to plates and eat with lots of French bread and plenty of chilled Muscadet.

La Mouclade

The curry in this classic mussel dish from La Rochelle was probably introduced into the Charentes-Maritime by Dutch spice traders on their way to and from India in the sixteenth century. This fact in not that important except that it is an indication of how long the French have been bringing flavours from other countries into their cooking. At the moment some chefs in France feel that French cuisine should be preserved, almost by law, like you would a monument in danger. I can sympathize with this sentiment as it's almost as if cooks in most countries are busy copying each other to such an extent that we will all end up cooking the same dishes in time. But a country's cooking is like its language and new flavours and words keep creeping in. This brilliantly creamy, rich dish is full of delicate traces of saffron and spice and is a testimony to the ability of the French to take a foreign flavour and make it seem as though it has been French forever.

serves 4

a good pinch of saffron

1.75 kg (4 lb) mussels, cleaned (see p. 26)

120 ml (4 fl oz) dry white wine

25 g (1 oz) butter

1 small onion, finely chopped

2 garlic cloves, finely chopped

½ teaspoon good-quality medium curry powder

2 tablespoons cognac

2 teaspoons plain flour

200 ml (7 fl oz) crème fraîche

3 tablespoons chopped parsley

Salt and freshly ground black pepper

method

Put the saffron into a small bowl and moisten it with 1 tablespoon of warm water. Place the mussels and wine in a large pan, cover and cook over a high heat for 3–4 minutes, shaking the pan now and then, until the mussels have opened. Tip them into a colander set over a bowl to catch all the cooking liquor and discard any that haven't opened. Transfer the mussels to a large serving bowl and keep warm.

Melt the butter in a pan, add the onion, garlic and curry powder and cook gently without browning for 2–3 minutes. Add the cognac and cook until it has almost all evaporated, then stir in the flour and cook for 1 minute. Gradually stir in the saffron liquid and all but the last tablespoon or two of the mussel cooking liquor, which might contain some grit. Bring the sauce to a simmer and cook for 2–3 minutes. Add the cream and simmer for a further 3 minutes, until slightly reduced. Season to taste, stir in the parsley and then pour the sauce over the mussels. Stir them together gently and serve with plenty of French bread.

alternative fish

This is a dish where you have to have good-quality live mussels, and nothing else will do.

Filets de Sole Joinville

This is a classic sautéed dish from the Normandy town of Joinville. It would once have been made with Dover sole fillets but I am loath to do anything with Dover sole other than cook it whole, grilled or à la meunière – the latter being the whole fish cooked just as in this recipe but without the mushrooms and shrimps.

Lemon sole is very easy to buy ready-filleted and has a really good flavour. The only slight drawback is that it tends to be a bit delicate and therefore you need to be careful when turning the fillets during cooking. Ideally this starter should be made with those little brown shrimps but I have also given the right quantity of North Atlantic prawns bought in the shell, which are so much better-flavoured than those prepared ones that you get in sandwiches.

serves 4

8 large unskinned lemon sole fillets

50 g (2 oz) well-seasoned flour

50 g (2 oz) *Clarified Butter* (see p. 239)

225 g (8 oz) small button mushrooms, thinly sliced

75 g (3 oz) peeled cooked brown shrimps or 24 peeled cooked North Atlantic prawns

100 g (4 oz) unsalted butter

Juice of 1 lemon

3 tablespoons chopped parsley

Salt and freshly ground white pepper

method

Season the lemon sole fillets on both sides with a little salt and pepper. Dip them in the seasoned flour so that they are well coated on both sides, then dust off the excess.

Heat the clarified butter in a heavy-based frying pan and fry the fish fillets in a couple of batches for 1 minute on each side. Add the mushrooms and fry, then add the shrimps or prawns at the last minute just to warm through. Arrange the fish fillets, mushrooms and shrimps on a warm serving plate.

Wipe out the pan and heat the unsalted butter until it begins to brown and smell nutty. Add the lemon juice, parsley and a good pinch of salt and pour over the fish. Serve with *Sautéed Potatoes* (see p. 225) and a *Soft Green Lettuce Salad with Olive Oil Dressing* (see p. 228).

alternative fish

Well, if you've got the money, use Dover sole; otherwise small brill or very fresh plaice fillets.

Truite au Bleu with Mousseline Sauce

Last summer, in the Pyrenees, we stayed at the Hotel Arcé in St Etienne de Baïgorry. Of course my boys took real delight in pronouncing its name wrongly. It was one of those family-run hotels where the family seem to do everything. Reception was a hatch between the restaurant and the kitchen and the chef (also the owner) would hand us our room key, deliver messages or take a booking. He also caught the trout for his truite au bleu, in the stream in front of the restaurant. We would watch him wade through the shallow water and hook them out, one after the other. With this performance before dinner, we were sure not to be disappointed when we sat down to eat, and we weren't. The trout must be dropped into the simmering vinegary court bouillon very soon after they are killed so that their natural slime sets to give them a delicate slate blue tinge.

serves 4

750 g (1½ lb) tiny new potatoes, scrubbed

4 × 275–350 g (10–12 oz) trout, bought live if
possible or killed within the last hour

1 tablespoon finely chopped parsley

Salt

1 celery stick, sliced

A handful of parsley sprigs

6 black peppercorns, lightly cracked

3.4 litres (6 pints) water

6 tablespoons salt

FOR THE COURT BOUILLON:

120 ml (4 fl oz) good-quality white wine vinegar

1 small onion, thinly sliced

1 carrot, sliced

FOR THE MOUSSELINE SAUCE:

½ quantity of *Hollandaise Sauce* or *Quick
Hollandaise Sauce* (see p. 234)

25 ml (1 fl oz) double cream

method

For the court bouillon, put all the ingredients into a shallow pan or casserole dish large enough to hold the trout in one layer. Bring to the boil and simmer for 10 minutes.

Bring a pan of boiling salted water to the boil, allowing 1 teaspoon of salt for every pint of water. Add the potatoes and cook them for 15 minutes or until tender.

When the potatoes are about half-way through cooking, bring the court bouillon back to the boil, then turn off the heat and when the bubbles have subsided slip in the trout. Leave them to poach for 7–8 minutes.

Meanwhile, make the hollandaise sauce according to the instructions on p. 234. Whip the cream until it just begins to form soft peaks. Gently fold it into the hollandaise sauce.

Drain the potatoes and toss them with the chopped parsley. Carefully lift the trout out of the pan, drain well and serve with the potatoes and the mousseline sauce. For complete perfection this should also be accompanied by some freshly boiled young asparagus.

alternative fish

This is a classic dish, only made with trout so there's no real alternative. However, it might be interesting to cook freshwater fish such as smelt or small zander (pike or perch) in the same way.

Provençal Seafood Salad with Aïoli Dressing

This is a great favourite at our delicatessen. We've had the deli for about 12 years and gradually we've made more and more products for it ourselves because that seems to be what everyone wants. Nothing sells better than seafood, however. We sell loads of fish and crab cakes, fish pasties, fish pies and terrines and seafood salads like this one, which I think people find refreshingly unusual.

serves 4

350 g (12 oz) piece of unskinned thick
   cod fillet

100 g (4 oz) prepared squid (see p. 27)

1 tablespoon olive oil

450 g (1 lb) new potatoes

3 eggs

1 fennel bulb

75 g (3 oz) French beans, halved

100 g (4 oz) peeled large cooked prawns,
   cut in half

450 g (1 lb) cooked butterbeans or drained
   and rinsed canned ones

2–3 tablespoons chopped flat-leaf parsley

Salt and cayenne pepper

FOR THE AÏOLI DRESSING:

½ tablespoon white wine vinegar

½ teaspoon Dijon mustard

2 tablespoons olive oil

2 heaped tablespoons *Aïoli* (see p. 236)

Freshly ground black pepper

method

Salt the cod overnight (see p. 238). The next day, put the cod in a pan of boiling water and simmer for about 6–8 minutes. Drain and, when cool enough to handle, break the fish into large flakes, discarding the skin and any bones.

Cut the squid pouches across into thin rings and separate the tentacles. Heat the olive oil in a frying pan. Add the squid, season well with some salt and cayenne pepper and stir-fry over a high heat for 1½–2 minutes, until lightly browned. Transfer to a plate and leave to go cold.

Cook the potatoes in well-salted boiling water (see p. 223) for 20 minutes or until just tender, then drain. Leave to cool and slice thickly. Hard-boil the eggs for 8 minutes, then drain, cover with cold water and leave to cool.

Cut the fennel bulb in half through the root and then across into 2 cm (¾ inch) slices. Cook in boiling salted water for 2 minutes, then lift out with a slotted spoon and refresh under cold water. Leave to drain while you cook the French beans for 2 minutes in the same water. Drain and refresh as before.

Mix the flaked salt cod, squid, prawns, potatoes, fennel, French beans, butterbeans and parsley together in a large bowl.

For the dressing, whisk the vinegar and mustard together and then gradually whisk in the oil, followed by the aïoli to make a slightly creamy dressing. Season to taste with salt and pepper and then gently stir it into the salad.

Peel the hard-boiled eggs and cut them into quarters. Pile the salad into a serving dish and garnish with the eggs. Sprinkle with a little more parsley if you wish and serve with lots of crusty French bread.

alternative fish

See the suggestions under Chickpea, Parsley and Salt Cod Stew *on p. 100.*

Gratin of Seafood

Last time I was in France I chose a seafood gratin from a menu in a seaside town in the south, not because I was enthusiastic about the idea but because there was nothing much else on the menu. I had forgotten just how fantastic seafood with cream and cheese can be.

serves 4

450 g (1 lb) unpeeled cooked North
   Atlantic prawns
½ onion, roughly chopped
65 g (2½ oz) butter
1 tablespoon cognac
600 ml (1 pint) *Fish Stock* (see p. 232)
50 ml (2 fl oz) white wine
2 tomatoes, roughly chopped
900 g (2 lb) mussels, cleaned (see p. 26)
2 shallots, finely chopped
20 g (¾ oz) plain flour
150 ml (5 fl oz) double cream

1 tablespoon chopped parsley
Juice of ½ lemon
8 prepared scallops (see p. 26)
175 g (6 oz) skinned haddock fillet, cut into
   small chunks
100 g (4 oz) button mushrooms, sliced
100 g (4 oz) fresh white crab meat
100 g (4 oz) Gruyère, Emmenthal, fontina or
   Jarlsberg cheese, coarsely grated
¼ teaspoon paprika
A pinch of cayenne pepper
Salt and freshly ground black pepper

method

Peel the prawns, reserving the heads and shells. Fry the onion in 15 g (½ oz) of the butter until soft. Add the prawn heads and shells and cognac and fry for 1–2 minutes. Add the fish stock, wine and tomatoes, bring to the boil and simmer for 20 minutes.

Add the mussels to the pan, cover and cook over a high heat for 3–4 minutes. Strain through a large sieve set over a bowl. If there is any less than 600 ml (1 pint) of stock, make it up with a little fish stock; any more and you need to boil it once more until it is reduced to the required amount. Remove the mussels from their shells (discarding any that have not opened) and set aside with the peeled prawns. Discard everything else in the sieve.

Fry the shallots in another 25 g (1 oz) of the butter until soft. Add the flour and cook for 1 minute, stirring. Gradually stir in the stock, bring to the boil, while stirring, and then stir in the cream and simmer very gently for 10 minutes, until the sauce coats the back of a wooden spoon. Add the parsley and season with some lemon juice, salt and pepper.

Pre-heat the grill to high. Melt the remaining butter. Scatter the scallops, haddock and mushrooms into a large gratin dish, brush with melted butter, season and grill for 2 minutes. Turn the scallops and grill for a further 2 minutes. Add the prawns, mussels and crab meat to the dish and spoon over the sauce. Sprinkle with the cheese, dust with paprika and cayenne pepper and grill for another 1–2 minutes, until golden and bubbling.

alternative fish

Try a selection of seafood: cooked lobster, monkfish, cod and queen scallops.

Anguilles au Vert

This recipe for eel from the north of France and Belgium is very popular there. Much as I love it, I've always found it a little bit too rich. Tastes have changed but there's no reason for losing a good recipe — all you need to do is serve it as a starter and cut some of the fat out of it, as I've done here. Let's call it restoring an Old Master.

serves 4

300 ml (10 fl oz) *Fish Stock (see p. 232)*

15 g (½ oz) butter

2 large shallots, very finely chopped

½ garlic clove, crushed

1 small sprig of thyme

1 small bay leaf

50 ml (2 fl oz) dry vermouth, such as Noilly Prat

25 g (1 oz) spinach leaves, shredded

25 g (1 oz) watercress leaves (stalks removed)

1 tablespoon each chopped tarragon, parsley, chervil and chives, plus extra to garnish

25 g (1 oz) sorrel leaves, shredded

¼ loaf of French bread

50 ml (2 fl oz) *Clarified Butter (see p. 239)*

350 g (12 oz) eel fillets, skinned (ask your fishmonger to do this) and cut into pieces about 10 cm (4 inches) long

175 ml (6 fl oz) double cream

3 egg yolks

Lemon juice

Salt and freshly ground black pepper

method

For the sauce, boil the fish stock rapidly until reduced to about 4 tablespoons. Melt the butter in another pan, add the shallots, garlic, thyme and bay leaf and cook gently until soft but not coloured. Add the fish stock and the vermouth and boil until reduced by about three-quarters. Discard the thyme and bay leaf. Add the spinach, watercress and chopped herbs and cook for 2 minutes. Add the sorrel and just allow it to wilt into the sauce, then tip into a liquidizer and whizz until smooth. Return the sauce to the pan.

Cut the bread on the diagonal into four long slices, no more than 1 cm (½ inch) thick. Fry the bread pieces in half the clarified butter for a couple of minutes on each side, until crisp and lightly golden. Keep warm (but don't let them dry out).

Pre-heat the grill to high. Brush the eel with the rest of the clarified butter and season. Lay on a grilling tray and grill for 1–1½ minutes. Mix the cream and egg yolks together until smooth, then stir them into the sauce. Cook over a low heat until lightly thickened, but take care not to get it too hot or it will scramble. Season with a little lemon juice, salt and pepper to taste and whisk to make it slightly frothy.

To serve, put the fried bread on 4 warmed plates and top with the eel. Spoon over the sauce and garnish with a very small bunch of tarragon, parsley, chervil and chives.

alternative fish

This is a classic eel dish, so eel it's got to be … or has it? I have a feeling it would work well with thin fillets of any white fish like plaice, lemon sole or whiting.

and the Seafood Restaurant • *After travelling all over the world, we finished filming the Seafood Odyssey series in Suffolk and Essex in England. We came home to cook a cod dish in a Suffolk pub and to eat cockles in Leigh-on-Sea. I've never had much time for the British way with cockles before, served up as they are by the pint with malt vinegar and white pepper. But it was the height of the cockle season when we made our visit and, fresh from the sea, they were undeniably good. We sat outside the Crooked Billet pub looking over the estuary flats, tinged with pale-green weed, to the flat horizon of Kent and watched the ships plying up and down the Thames. I fell into conversation with a tough ex-Marine, the sort of man who looked as if he'd seen some bitter times behind enemy lines and come out smiling, and who you could be sure would get you through a force-ten storm at sea. He spoke eloquently about his love of simple British seafood like cockles, jellied eels and whelks, and as I sat there listening I began to see the similarities between this man and the gumbo fanatics in South Carolina, the percebes-lovers in Galicia in Spain, the passionate Italians adoring their pasta with tomatoes and 'sea fruits', and my homesick friend Rui missing his Indian vindaloos and dhals when he visited us in Cornwall. It occurred to me that, despite having the world on a plate, we often end up loving food from home best. After all my adventurous wanderings and exotic eating, that Cod with Beer, Bacon and Cabbage I had eaten in that Suffolk pub, with a pint of beer, had seemed to me like Odysseus's homecoming to Ithaca. And that's what the recipes in this chapter are all about … home.*

Britain

Hake with a Fondue of Carrot and Coriander

In the '80s I used to go to a small, sadly departed, restaurant in Islington, north London, called Mr Fish. Actually it wasn't the best restaurant in the world but my sister, Henrietta, and her friends went there lots and I used to go there a bit too when I was in London. You just get used to some places as long as the food is good and honest, and I think those sorts of local restaurants are sometimes better loved than the big and impressive ones. In the trade we're all so obsessed with ever-improved standards of food and service that it's actually rather nice to go to a place where you can wander past the kitchen and tell them to get a move on with your lobster penne and know that they're not going to regard it as a massive indictment of the whole operation, because they know and you know you'll be back next week.

Anyway carrot and coriander soup finished with a squeeze of fresh orange juice was big in those days, though it's pretty run of the mill these days, and I thought I'd take those flavours and use them as the basis for a slow-cooked vegetable fondue. The hake is sprinkled with a chiffonnade of orange zest and coriander and baked in the oven – a memory of the '80s.

serves 4

350 g (12 oz) large carrots, peeled
1 small orange
150 g (5 oz) unsalted butter
1 onion, finely chopped
2 garlic cloves, crushed
2.5 cm (1 inch) fresh root ginger, finely grated
1 teaspoon ground coriander
600 ml (1 pint) *Chicken Stock* (see p. 232)

50 ml (2 fl oz) medium-dry white wine, such as Vouvray
Juice of $\frac{1}{2}$ lemon
4 × 175–225 g (6–8 oz) hake steaks
A few coriander leaves, plus 1 tablespoon chopped coriander
Sea salt flakes and coarsely crushed black pepper

method

Cut the carrots lengthways into slices 5 mm (¼ inch) thick, then across into short, stubby batons. Pare the zest from half the orange with a potato peeler, taking care not to remove any of the bitter white pith. Cut each piece lengthways into fine shreds. Finely grate the zest off the rest of the orange.

Melt 50 g (2 oz) of the butter in an ovenproof frying pan, add the carrots, onion, garlic, ginger, ground coriander and finely grated orange zest and cook gently for a few minutes until the onion has softened. Add 450 ml (15 fl oz) of the chicken stock, plus the wine and lemon juice and cook gently for a further 30 minutes, until the carrots are soft and the mixture has reduced and thickened. Season with some salt and pepper to taste.

Pre-heat the oven to 220°C/425°F/Gas Mark 7.

Melt 25 g (1 oz) of the remaining butter. Season the fish steaks well on both sides with salt and pepper and place on top of the carrot fondue. Sprinkle the strips of orange zest, the coriander leaves, some coarsely crushed black pepper and some sea salt flakes on top of the fish and then drizzle over the melted butter. Put the frying pan into the oven and bake for 20 minutes. Take out, lift the fish off on to a serving dish and keep warm. Return the pan to the heat (careful with the hot handle) and stir in the remaining stock and the butter. Let it reduce to a thick, buttery fondue then spoon it round the fish. Sprinkle the unctuous sauce with the chopped coriander and serve. A glass of Gewürztraminer with this would be an added pleasure.

alternative fish

This fondue goes really well not only with haddock and cod but also with salmon, sea trout, sea bass, jewfish or mahi mahi.

Fish Pie

The older I get the keener I am to keep ingredients out of recipes instead of adding them. This is as simple a recipe for fish pie as you can imagine but if the fish is good (and that includes the smoked fish, which must be of the best quality), there is no better fish dish in the world than a British fish pie.

serves 4

1 small onion, thickly sliced

2 cloves

1 bay leaf

600 ml (1 pint) milk

300 ml (10 fl oz) double cream

450 g (1 lb) unskinned cod fillet

225 g (8 oz) undyed smoked cod fillet

4 eggs

100 g (4 oz) butter

45 g (1¾ oz) plain flour

5 tablespoons chopped flat-leaf parsley

Freshly grated nutmeg

1.25 kg (2½ lb) peeled floury potatoes such as
   Maris Piper or King Edward

1 egg yolk

Salt and freshly ground white pepper

method

Stud a couple of the onion slices with the cloves. Put the onion slices in a large pan with the bay leaf, 450 ml (15 fl oz) of the milk, the cream, cod and smoked cod. Bring just to the boil and simmer for 8 minutes. Lift the fish out on to a plate and strain the cooking liquor into a jug. When the fish is cool enough to handle, break it into large flakes, discarding the skin and bones. Sprinkle it over the base of a shallow 1.75 litre (3 pint) ovenproof dish.

Hard-boil the eggs for just 8 minutes, then drain and leave to cool. Peel and cut them into chunky slices and arrange on top of the fish.

Melt 50 g (2 oz) of the butter in a pan, add the flour and cook for 1 minute. Take the pan off the heat and gradually stir in the reserved cooking liquor. Return it to the heat and bring slowly to the boil, stirring all the time. Leave it to simmer gently for 10 minutes to cook out the flour. Remove from the heat once more, stir in the parsley and season with nutmeg, salt and white pepper. Pour the sauce over the fish and leave to cool. Chill in the fridge for 1 hour.

Boil the potatoes for 15–20 minutes. Drain, mash and add the rest of the butter and the egg yolk. Season with salt and freshly ground white pepper. Beat in enough of the remaining milk to form a soft, spreadable mash.

Pre-heat the oven to 200°C/400°F/Gas Mark 6. Spoon the potato over the filling and mark the surface with a fork. Bake for 35–40 minutes, until piping hot and golden brown.

alternative fish

Try making this with haddock and smoked haddock or, if you live in Australia, substitute flat-head for the unsmoked fish.

Clear Crab and Prawn Soup with Tarragon and Tomato

I love consommés — beautifully clear, intensely flavoured soups. However, they require a lot of ingredients and a lot of work so I've kept this as easy as possible, but it still produces a lovely soup through which you can see the bottom of the plate quite easily. The tomatoes should be a well-flavoured English summer variety, i.e. pleasingly acidic, so that the soup is not too sweet, and the tarragon leaves dropped in at the end should not be chopped.

serves 4

750 g (1½ lb) cooked brown crab

750 g (1½ lb) unpeeled cooked North
   Atlantic prawns

450 g (1 lb) salad tomatoes

25 g (1 oz) butter

2 carrots, finely chopped

1 large onion, finely chopped

2 celery sticks, finely chopped

85 ml (3 fl oz) dry white wine

1.75 litres (3 pints) *Fish Stock* or *Chicken Stock*
   (see p. 232)

100 g (4 oz) skinned white fish fillet such as
   coley or ling, finely chopped

2 egg whites

½ teaspoon salt

1 tablespoon tarragon leaves

method

Break the legs off the crab. Prise off the back shell by forcing a large-bladed knife just behind the mouth and giving it a twist. Scrape out the brown meat from the back shell. Discard the shell. Cut the body into small pieces. Break up the legs and crack the shells with a hammer.

Shell a third of the prawns, reserving the shells, and roughly chop the remainder. Skin and seed one tomato (see p. 238) and cut the flesh into thin, crescent-shaped strips. Set aside with the prawns. Roughly chop the rest of the tomatoes.

Melt the butter in a large pan, add the carrots, onion and celery and cook until lightly browned and beginning to smell sweet. Add the crab pieces, brown crab meat, prawn shells, chopped prawns, wine and chopped tomatoes. Cook for 1–2 minutes. Add the stock, bring to the boil and simmer gently for 30 minutes. Strain through a fine sieve into another pan and leave to cool.

To clarify the soup, set the pan over a medium heat, add the chopped white fish and the egg whites and whisk steadily until the mixture boils. The fish and egg white will set and rise to the surface, trapping all the little bits and pieces from the liquid. Stop whisking immediately, turn off the heat and leave it to cool a little. Then part the crust, carefully ladle out the clear liquid from underneath and pour through a muslin-lined sieve into a clean pan. Add salt to the soup and bring back to the boil. Put the peeled prawns, tomato strips and tarragon leaves into 4 warmed soup bowls, ladle over the soup and serve.

alternative fish

For the soup base, any type of crab will do, e.g. spider crab, blue crab, mud crab and those little green shore crabs from Cornwall.

Kedgeree of Arbroath Smokies

About 10 years ago I appeared in a series for Yorkshire Television called Farmhouse Kitchen *with Grace Mulligan. I got on very well with her and she taught me a lot about cooking on the box. She also introduced me to Arbroath smokies, which was just as valuable. A true Scottish delicacy, these are small haddock or sometimes whiting that are brined and then heavily smoked on the bone, which keeps the fillet moist and sweet.*

serves 4

25 g (1 oz) butter

1 small onion, chopped

2 green cardamom pods, split open

¼ teaspoon turmeric powder

2.5 cm (1 in) piece of cinnamon stick

1 bay leaf, very finely shredded

350 g (12 oz) basmati rice

600 ml (1 pint) *Chicken Stock* (see p. 232) or *Vegetable Nage* (see p. 233)

2 eggs

450 g (1 lb) Arbroath smokies

2 tablespoons chopped flat-leaf parsley, plus a few sprigs to garnish

Salt and freshly ground black pepper

method

Melt the butter in a large pan, add the onion and cook over a medium heat for 5 minutes, until soft but not browned. Add the cardamom pods, turmeric, cinnamon stick and shredded bay leaf and cook, stirring, for 1 minute. Add the rice and stir it around for about 1 minute, until all the grains are thoroughly coated in the spicy butter. Add the stock and ½ teaspoon of salt and bring to the boil. Cover the pan with a close-fitting lid, lower the heat and leave it to cook very gently for 15 minutes.

Meanwhile, hard-boil the eggs for 8 minutes, then drain. When just cool enough to handle, peel them and cut into small pieces. Flake the Arbroath smokies into small chunky pieces, discarding the skin and bones.

Uncover the rice and gently fork in the fish and chopped eggs. Re-cover and return to the heat for 5 minutes or until the fish has heated through. Then gently stir in the chopped parsley and season with a little more salt and black pepper to taste. Serve garnished with sprigs of parsley.

alternative fish

Use any smoked fish like Finnan haddock, smoked cod or good kippers, such as those from Whitby or Seahouses in Northumberland instead. This dish also works really well with flaked poached salmon.

Seared Swordfish with Mushroom Gravy and Garlic and Olive Oil Mash

The idea of fish with gravy sounded very appealing to me, but how do you make a dark, well-flavoured gravy without using overpowering flavours like, say, beef or caramelized onions? I hit on the idea of simmering dried mushrooms in a good chicken stock. This produces a beautifully coloured and flavoured liquid which goes fantastically well with a good steak of meaty fish like swordfish.

serves 4

4 × 175–225 g (6–8 oz) swordfish steaks
Olive oil
1 teaspoon chopped thyme
Salt and freshly ground black pepper
Coarsely chopped parsley, to garnish

FOR THE MUSHROOM GRAVY:
25 g (1 oz) butter
1 celery stick, finely chopped
50 ml (2 fl oz) dry white wine
600 ml (1 pint) *Chicken Stock* (see p. 232)
7 g (¼ oz) dried porcini mushrooms

A pinch of dried chilli flakes
1 teaspoon *Beurre Manié* (see p. 239)

FOR THE GARLIC AND OLIVE OIL MASH:
1.25 kg (2½ lb) floury potatoes, such as Maris Piper or King Edward, peeled and cut into chunks
1 garlic clove, crushed
50 ml (2 fl oz) good olive oil
A little milk
Freshly ground white pepper

method

Boil the potatoes for 15–20 minutes. Drain, mash and beat in the garlic, olive oil and a little milk to form a soft mash. Season with salt and freshly ground white pepper. Keep warm.

For the mushroom gravy, melt the butter in a small pan, add the celery and cook for 5 minutes, until softened but not browned. Add the wine and boil until it has almost evaporated. Add the chicken stock, dried mushrooms and chilli flakes and boil until reduced by half. Strain to remove the flavouring ingredients, then return to the pan and whisk in the beurre manié. Season with a little salt if necessary and keep hot.

Brush the swordfish steaks on both sides with plenty of olive oil and sprinkle with the chopped thyme and some salt and pepper. Place a heavy-based frying pan over a high heat. Brush the pan with a little oil and sear the steaks for 2 minutes on each side, then serve with the mash and the mushroom gravy, sprinkled with a little coarsely chopped parsley.

alternative fish

I wanted good, thick, meaty fish for this so tuna, shark or kingfish would be great alternatives.

Crab and Basil Timbales with a Sweet and Sharp Tomato Dressing

A timbale is simply a particular type of round dish that we use at the restaurant to mould the crab and then turn it out in a pleasing shape on the plate, but a ramekin will do just as well. The crab is served with a dressing which I'm particularly fond of. You make a really rich thick tomato sauce, let it go cold and then mix in the tart sherry vinegar and your best olive oil just before serving.

serves 4

350 g (12 oz) fresh white crab meat

10 basil leaves, very finely shredded,
   plus sprigs of basil to garnish

2 tablespoons extra virgin olive oil

1 tablespoon lemon juice

Salt and freshly ground black pepper

Small salad leaves, to serve

FOR THE TOMATO AND BASIL DRESSING:

1 small onion, chopped

1 small garlic clove, chopped

6 tablespoons olive oil

200 g (7 oz) can of chopped tomatoes

50 ml (2 fl oz) red wine vinegar

2 teaspoons sugar

1 tablespoon sherry vinegar

method

For the dressing, fry the onion and garlic in 1 tablespoon of the olive oil until soft. Add the chopped tomatoes and simmer for 30 minutes until very thick; you should be able to draw a spoon across the base of the pan without the mixture running back, a bit like the parting of the Red Sea. Put the vinegar and sugar into a small pan and boil down to about 1 teaspoon. Add to the tomato sauce and leave to cool. Season with salt and pepper.

Mix the crab meat, basil, olive oil and lemon juice together in a bowl, then season with salt and pepper. Line 4 lightly oiled timbales or ramekins with a sheet of clingfilm, spoon the crab mixture into each one and lightly press it down.

Put the remaining oil for the dressing into a bowl with the sherry vinegar and whisk together. Stir in the tomato sauce and adjust the seasoning if necessary. Turn out the timbales on to 4 plates and, using a teaspoon, spoon little pools of the dressing around each one. Place a pile of small leaves alongside and serve garnished with basil.

alternative fish

You can make this with all kinds of seafood, prawns, lobster, scallops and even skate or firm fish like John Dory or sole.

Poached Whole Sea Bass with Dill and Potato Salad and Dressed Herbs

A sea bass served cold or just warm is delightful and yet for most people the idea of cold poached fish doesn't stretch beyond salmon. You can, of course, use salmon for this dish but why not treat yourself to a nice 1.5 kg (3 lb) sea bass, or even two or three smaller sea bass if you can't get one big one?

serves 4

2 tablespoons salt
3.4 litres (6 pints) water
1 × 1.5 kg (3 lb) sea bass, cleaned (see p. 26)

FOR THE DILL AND POTATO SALAD:
750 g (1½ lb) waxy new potatoes, such as
   Jersey Royals, Charlotte or Pink Fir Apple,
   scraped and cut into matchsticks 5 mm
   (¼ inch) thick
75 g (3 oz) *Mustard Mayonnaise* (see p. 235)
1 shallot, finely chopped
2 tablespoons chopped dill
Salt and freshly ground black pepper

FOR THE DRESSED HERBS:
A small bunch each of tarragon, chives,
   flat-leaf parsley and chervil sprigs
A few drops of extra virgin olive oil

method   Put the salt and water into a fish kettle and bring to the boil. Slip in the fish, allow the water to bubble twice, then take the kettle off the heat, cover and leave for 15 minutes. Meanwhile, cook the potatoes in a pan of boiling salted water for 3–4 minutes, until just tender. Drain and leave to cool.

Lift the fish out of the water on to a serving dish and leave to cool.

Mix the mayonnaise with the shallot, dill and some salt and pepper, then gently fold in the potatoes. Spoon into a shallow serving bowl. Place the herb sprigs in another bowl and toss with the olive oil and a little seasoning.

Take the sea bass to the table together with the 2 bowls of salad. To serve the fish, run a knife lengthways down the centre between the two fillets and gently ease the flesh away from the bones. Once you can get a palette knife under the fillets, lift them off on to 2 plates. Then turn the fish over and repeat on the other side.

alternative fish

A good-sized salmon, not a farmed one, would be the most obvious choice but a whole snapper or even a barramundi would be ideal.

Tronçon of Turbot with an Olive Oil Sauce Vierge

I approach the subject of accompaniments to turbot with some reservation, because actually a grilled piece of turbot with a little salt, a lick of butter and a few new potatoes is about as close to heaven as one can get with food. But this sauce vierge with a tronçon of turbot has the same sort of understated appeal to me as long as you don't put too much of it on the plate. This means you get lots of turbot and a few little emphasis points of olive oil, olives, tomatoes, garlic and anchovies. The chopped herbs and oil used to coat the fish before cooking are not overpowering either, and make the grilled fish look very attractive.

serves 4

85 ml (3 fl oz) extra virgin olive oil,
   plus extra for brushing
1 teaspoon chopped rosemary
1 teaspoon chopped thyme
1 bay leaf, very finely chopped
$\frac{1}{2}$ teaspoon crushed fennel seeds
1 teaspoon coarsely crushed black peppercorns
Sea salt flakes
4 × 175–225 g (6–8 oz) tronçons of turbot

FOR THE SAUCE:

85 ml (3 fl oz) extra virgin olive oil
2 tablespoons lemon juice
1 plum tomato, seeded and cut into small dice
8 black olives, pitted and cut into fine strips
2 small anchovy fillets in oil, drained and diced
1 garlic clove, finely chopped
1 heaped teaspoon coarsely chopped parsley
Salt and coarsely ground black pepper

method

Pre-heat the grill to high. Mix together the olive oil, chopped herbs, fennel seeds, crushed peppercorns and 1 teaspoon of sea salt in a shallow dish. Add the pieces of turbot and turn them over in the mixture so that they are well coated. Place on an oiled baking tray, skin-side up, and grill for 7–8 minutes.

Meanwhile, for the sauce, put everything except the chopped parsley and seasoning into a small pan. Just as the fish is ready, place over a very low heat just to warm through.

To serve, lift the pieces of fish into the centre of 4 warmed plates. Stir the parsley and seasoning into the sauce and spoon it around the fish. Brush the top of each piece of fish with a little more oil and sprinkle with a few sea salt flakes.

alternative fish

Thick fillets of brill, John Dory or sea bass or fillets of flaky fish such as cod, haddock or hake.

Grilled Lemon Sole with Lemongrass Butter

Here's a paean to lemon sole. A couple of years ago I was asked to meet some buyers from Tesco's supermarket at Plymouth fish market, to look at the quality of the fish there. They were exploring an idea about supplementing the centrally bought fish from Grimsby, sold at their fish counters, with good local fish in season; an idea which has now, I'm pleased to say, become reality. It was early March when we visited the market – during a spell of spring high pressure, calm seas and good fishing. There was a lot of fish, all caught-that-day fresh: red mullet glistening pink with flashes of yellow and eyes so clear you could gaze to the bottom of the sea through them; and lemon sole, bright of eye and stiff and slimy. I felt so proud of our local fish. You wouldn't see better in a market anywhere in the world. I can think of no better way to cook beautifully fresh lemon sole than by simply grilling it. Here it's served with a typically British flavoured butter, but I've added a modern spin to it with a few Thai ingredients.

serves 4

4 × 350–450 g (12 oz–1 lb) lemon sole
15 g (½ oz) butter, melted
Salt and freshly ground black pepper

FOR THE LEMONGRASS BUTTER:

1 lemongrass stalk, outer leaves removed and
　the core very finely chopped
Finely grated zest of ½ lime
2 teaspoons lime juice
1 cm (½ inch) fresh root ginger,
　very finely chopped
2 tablespoons chopped parsley
100 g (4 oz) slightly salted butter, softened
1 tablespoon Thai fish sauce (*nam pla*)

method

First make the lemongrass butter: put everything into a food processor and season well with black pepper. Blend until smooth, then spoon the mixture into the centre of a large sheet of clingfilm, shape into a roll 4 cm (1½ inches) thick, wrap and chill in the fridge or freezer until firm.

When the butter is firm, pre-heat the grill to high. Trim the fins and tails of the fish with kitchen scissors. Brush the fish on both sides with the melted butter and season with a little salt and pepper. Depending on the size of your grill, cook them 1 or 2 at a time, dark side up, on a buttered baking tray or the rack of a grill pan for 7 to 8 minutes or until the flesh is firm and white at the thickest part, just behind the head. Keep warm while you cook the rest.

Unwrap the lemongrass butter and slice into thin rounds and serve on top of the fish.

alternative fish

Plaice, flounder, small brill and chicken (small) turbot would also work well.

Scandinavian Herring Fish Cakes

This is my idea of a recipe from Scandinavia, although I've never actually been there. In a way, the cooking of Scandinavia is an imaginative ice palace for me. I think of all those beautiful fish in ice-cold waters, firm herrings and giant cod, dill and aquavit, caraway seeds, lovely dark rye bread and all kinds of pickles, and I almost don't want to go there in case it shatters my illusions.

serves 4

900 g (2 lb) well-flavoured new potatoes, such
   as Jersey Royal or Pink Fir Apple, scraped
450 g (1 lb) fresh herrings, cleaned (see p. 26)
8 tablespoons *Mustard Mayonnaise* (see p. 235)
2 tablespoons chopped dill, plus extra
   to garnish
4 tablespoons finely chopped shallots
Salt and freshly ground black pepper

FOR THE SOURED CREAM SAUCE:
1.2 litres (2 pints) *Chicken Stock* (see p. 232)
4 tablespoons soured cream
1 teaspoon lemon juice

method

Boil the potatoes in well-salted water until tender.

For the sauce, put the chicken stock into a large pan and boil rapidly until it has reduced to 85 ml (3 fl oz). Transfer it to a small pan.

Pre-heat the grill to high. Season the herrings with salt and pepper and grill them for about 4 minutes on each side. Remove the heads, skin and bones while still hot.

Cut up the potatoes while still warm and mix in a bowl with the mustard mayonnaise, dill and shallot, together with some salt and pepper to taste. Gently stir in the herrings.

Place a 10 cm (4 inch) pastry cutter in the centre of each of 4 warmed plates and spoon the mixture into them. Lightly level the tops and then carefully lift away the cutters.

Reheat the reduced chicken stock, stir in the soured cream, lemon juice and a little salt to taste and gently warm it through. Drizzle some around each fish cake, sprinkle with a little more chopped dill and serve.

alternative fish

I find oily fish very satisfactory in fish cakes and I would suggest mackerel or trout as suitable alternatives.

Hake en Papillote
with Oven-roasted Tomatoes and Tapenade

Cooking fish en papillote – in a paper parcel – works really well for two reasons: first, all the flavours are trapped inside and, second, it's an ideal dinner-party dish because all the tricky bits are done some time beforehand. The number of times I have had friends around to dinner and have let myself down by leaving everything until the last minute I would be reluctant to analyse. The only drawback, I feel, is that after your guests have marvelled at the aromas coming out of the freshly slit paper there is a slight feeling of anticlimax half-way through eating the dish. You feel you need something else, so I've added a nice piquant tapenade sauce to live up to everyone's expectations.

serves 4

Olive oil for brushing
1 quantity of *Oven-roasted Tomatoes* made with
   1 teaspoon thyme leaves (see p. 237)
2 tablespoons finely shredded basil leaves

4 × 175–225 g (6–8 oz) pieces of unskinned
   hake fillet
4 tablespoons *Tapenade* (see p. 236)
Salt and freshly ground black pepper

method   Pre-heat the oven to 240°C/475°F/Gas Mark 9. To prepare the parcels, cut out four 38 cm (15 inch) squares of greaseproof paper. Brush them with plenty of olive oil, put the tomatoes slightly off-centre on each one and sprinkle over the basil. Season the pieces of hake on both sides with salt and pepper and put them on top of the tomatoes.

Bring the other side of the paper over the fish so that the edges meet. Start to fold over about 1 cm (½ inch) of the edge, doing about 5 cm (2 inches) at a time, working around it to form a semi-circular parcel. Now go around again to make an even tighter seam and then give the edge a good bash with a rolling pin. Place the parcels on a baking sheet and bake for 10 minutes if the fillets are thin or 15 minutes if they are thick.

Serve the parcels on a splendid large plate and make a lot of fuss of slitting them open and placing the contents on 4 warmed plates, drizzling them with the cooking juices. Spoon some of the tapenade around and accompany with plenty of *Garlic and Olive Oil Mash* (see the recipe for *Seared Swordfish* on p. 172).

alternative fish

Any thick fillets of good-sized fish such as cod, haddock, salmon and even large sea bass or other grouper-type fish would work well cooked in this way.

Steamed Haddock on Buttered Leeks
with Grain Mustard Sauce

Recently I discovered that my book Taste of the Sea *had been given a Health Which?*
magazine consumer test. They were quite complimentary about the taste and appearance of
most of the dishes, and indeed said that some of them were healthy, but they had a right old
go at me about my use of butter and cream in others. I must confess to a shred, just a shred
of irritation with this point of view. The food police are on to me again. I mean, you're not
going to cook this sort of dish every day – it's not exactly staple food – but when you do
indulge once in a while, isn't it wonderful? Now in this dish you take three pounds of butter ...
only joking.

serves 4

900 g (2 lb) large leeks, trimmed and washed

175 g (6 oz) unsalted butter

50 ml (2 fl oz) dry white wine

4 × 175–225 g (6–8 oz) pieces of unskinned
   haddock fillet

2 tablespoons white wine vinegar

2 shallots, roughly chopped

1 tablespoon double cream

1 teaspoon wholegrain mustard

2 tablespoons chopped parsley

Salt and freshly ground black pepper

method

Cut the leeks in half lengthways, then across into pieces 5 cm (2 inches) long. Melt 50 g (2 oz) of the butter in a heavy-based pan, add the leeks and cook gently for 3 minutes. Add the wine, 1 teaspoon of salt and some pepper, then cover and cook for 10 minutes, until the leeks are really soft. Keep warm.

Place a trivet or an upturned plate in a large saucepan. Add about 2.5 cm (1 inch) of water and bring to the boil. Place the haddock on a heatproof plate, rest it on the trivet, cover and steam for 8 minutes.

Meanwhile, for the sauce, put the vinegar and shallots into a small pan. Cover and simmer gently for 5 minutes, then take off the lid and boil until almost all the liquid has evaporated. Add the cream, turn the heat down to low and whisk in the remaining butter, a few pieces at a time, until amalgamated into a sauce. Strain through a sieve into a clean pan, stir in the mustard and season to taste with a little salt.

Uncover the leeks and cook over a high heat for a minute or two to drive off all the remaining liquid. Stir in the parsley and then spoon on to 4 warmed plates. Lift the haddock out of the steamer and remove the skin. Put the haddock on top of the leeks, spoon the sauce around and serve.

alternative fish

Use thick fillets from any of the fish in the Flaky Fish section on pages 10–11.

Spiced Mackerel Fillets

I developed this recipe for our deli as a superior alternative to pickled herring. Although it appears to be a very straightforward, simple dish, it took a long time to get it right. I wanted to add a little bit of sweetness but not that overpowering sickliness you get with a lot of commercial marinades. You can also use this marinade in all kinds of Scandinavian preserved herring dishes.

serves 4

8 × 100 g (4 oz) unskinned mackerel fillets
65 g (2½ oz) salt
40 g (1½ oz) caster sugar
600 ml (1 pint) hot water

FOR THE MARINADE:

150 ml (5 fl oz) white wine vinegar
150 ml (5 fl oz) water
25 g (1 oz) caster sugar
¼ teaspoon black peppercorns
1 carrot, very thinly sliced
½ small onion, very thinly sliced

method

Lay the mackerel fillets in a large, shallow, non-metallic dish. Stir the salt and sugar into the hot water until dissolved, then leave to cool. Pour the water over the fish and leave for 3–4 hours.

Meanwhile, put all the marinade ingredients into a pan, bring to the boil and simmer for 3–4 minutes. Leave to cool.

Drain the brine off the mackerel and pour over the marinade. Cover and leave for at least 24 hours.

To serve, lift the fillets out of the marinade and drain off the excess liquid. Arrange the fillets on 4 serving plates and scatter around a few pieces of onion and carrot from the marinade. Serve with brown bread and butter.

alternative fish

Herrings, trout and sardine fillets.

North Atlantic Prawn Pilaf

Like a number of recipes in this book, this uses ingredients you can get from any fishmonger or supermarket. I really want this book to be used every day. This is a nice, gentle dish, ideal for supper with a glass of New Zealand Chardonnay.

serves 4

800 g (1lb 12 oz) unpeeled cooked North Atlantic prawns

50 g (2 oz) butter

1 small onion, chopped

1 small carrot, roughly chopped

½ teaspoon tomato purée

900 ml (1½ pints) *Chicken Stock* (see p. 232)

2 shallots, finely chopped

1 garlic clove, very finely chopped

3 cloves

3 green cardamom pods

1 cinnamon stick, broken into 4

¼ teaspoon turmeric powder

275 g (10 oz) basmati rice

3 tablespoons chopped coriander

3 plum tomatoes, skinned, seeded and diced (see p. 238)

Salt and freshly ground black pepper

method

Peel the prawns but keep the heads and shells. Put the prawns on a plate and set aside. Heat 25 g (1 oz) of the butter in a large pan, add the onion and carrot and fry over a medium heat for 6–7 minutes, until lightly browned. Add the prawn heads and shells and continue to fry for 3–4 minutes. Add the tomato purée and chicken stock, bring to the boil and simmer for 15 minutes. Strain into a measuring jug; if there is more than 600 ml (1 pint), return it to the pan and boil rapidly until reduced to this amount.

Melt the rest of the butter in a saucepan and add the shallots, garlic, cloves, cardamom pods, cinnamon stick and turmeric and fry gently for 5 minutes. Add the rice and stir well to coat the rice with the spicy butter. Add the stock to the pan, season with salt and bring to the boil, then turn the heat right down to the slightest simmer, put a lid on the pan and leave to simmer for 15 minutes. Don't lift the lid during this time.

Uncover and gently stir in the peeled prawns, coriander, diced tomatoes and some seasoning to taste. Re-cover and leave for 5 minutes to warm through. Then spoon into a warmed serving dish and serve.

alternative fish

Everyone should be able to get prawns of some sort, but if you can't get hold of unshelled prawns, use frozen peeled prawns instead – you just won't have the shells for the stock.

A Ragout of Seafood with Lemon and Saffron

Everyone loves delicate, fragrant, first-course seafood dishes where great care is taken with the precise cooking of exquisite morsels of prime shellfish. This sauce is so intense in its saffron and lemon flavour, it's almost unbearable until you spoon it over. Then the dish is perfect.

serves 4

½ lemon

Ingredients for 1 quantity of *Vegetable Nage*
  (see p. 233)

A good pinch of saffron

8 unpeeled large raw prawns

2 × 50–75 g (2–3 oz) skinned lemon sole fillets

8 baby carrots, scraped and trimmed

8 very small broccoli florets

8 French beans, trimmed and halved

8 mussels, cleaned (see p. 26)

4 prepared scallops (see p. 26)

100 g (4 oz) chilled unsalted butter, diced

Salt and freshly ground black pepper

Sea salt flakes, to garnish

method

The nage is best made 24 hours in advance. I find the flavour intensifies if it is left in the fridge unstrained with all the aromatic vegetables and herbs. Pare the zest off the piece of lemon and then cut away and discard all the bitter white pith. Cut the fruit across into slices. Make the nage according to the instructions on p. 233, adding the lemon zest and flesh to the pan with the vegetables. The next day strain the stock and put 1.2 litres (2 pints) into a pan (save or freeze the rest for later use). Add the saffron and boil rapidly until it has reduced to 120 ml (4 fl oz).

Peel the prawns, leaving the tail segment in place. Cut each lemon sole fillet diagonally across into 4 pieces.

Drop the vegetables in boiling salted water, bring back to the boil, drain and then plunge into cold water to set their colour. To complete the dish you need to find a couple of plates that will fit in a steamer and put all the blanched vegetables on one and the prawns, lemon sole, mussels and scallops on the other. Steam the vegetables for 3 minutes and then steam the fish for 3–4 minutes. Keep everything warm while you make the sauce.

Drain all the cooking juices from the plate of fish into the reduced stock. Bring this to a gentle simmer and then whisk in the butter, a few pieces at a time, until you have a smooth, thickened sauce. Season to taste with some salt and pepper.

Arrange the seafood and vegetables on 4 warmed plates. Spoon over the lemon and saffron sauce and serve sprinkled with some sea salt flakes.

alternative fish

Here is another occasion for using expensive seafood like lobster, oysters and langoustine. Freshwater crayfish wouldn't be out of place either.

Crab and Parmesan Soufflés

One of the most gratifying things about cooking is to take something like a whole crab and turn it into an exquisite first course, full of warmth and the scents of the sea. One crab alone won't serve six people but by using it to produce six beautiful, light creations like these, everyone will remember the meal. These won't rise like sweet soufflés because of the weight of the crab meat but they are still very fluffy and, together with the sauce made with the brown meat, which is poured into the centre just before serving, you get right to the heart of the matter.

serves 6

1 × 750 g (1½ lb) cooked brown crab

50 g (2 oz) butter

1 carrot, finely chopped

1 celery stick, finely chopped

1 onion, finely chopped

4 tomatoes, chopped

85 ml (3 fl oz) dry white wine

600 ml (1 pint) *Fish Stock* (see p. 232)

25 g (1 oz) plain flour

150 ml (5 fl oz) milk

3 eggs, separated

1 tablespoon finely grated fresh
   Parmesan cheese

A pinch of cayenne pepper

50 ml (2 fl oz) double cream

1 teaspoon tomato ketchup

Salt and freshly ground black pepper

method

Remove the meat from the crab as described on p. 27. If the outside of the brown meat is quite hard, peel it away and discard it. You only need the soft brown meat for the sauce. Reserve all the pieces of shell except the back shell.

Melt half the butter in a pan, add the carrot, celery and onion and cook gently for 5 minutes without browning. Stir in the pieces of crab shell, then add the tomatoes, white wine and stock and simmer for 35 minutes. Strain the mixture through a fine sieve into another pan and take out 150 ml (5 fl oz) for making the soufflés. Boil the rest until reduced to 85 ml (3 fl oz).

Place a baking sheet in the oven and pre-heat the oven to 220°C/425°F/Gas Mark 7. Grease six 200 ml (7 fl oz) ramekins with butter and dust with a little plain flour.

Melt the remaining butter in a pan, add the flour and cook gently for 1 minute. Take the pan off the heat and gradually stir in the reserved crab stock and the milk. Return the pan to the heat and bring to the boil, stirring. Simmer for 2–3 minutes to cook out the flour and then leave to cool slightly. Stir in the egg yolks, Parmesan cheese, cayenne pepper, 150 g (5 oz) of white crab meat and some seasoning to taste.

Whisk the egg whites in a large bowl until they form soft peaks. Fold a large spoonful of the egg whites into the mixture to loosen it a little, then carefully fold in the rest. Spoon it into the prepared ramekins, put them on the hot baking tray and bake for 12–15 minutes until risen and golden brown.

Meanwhile, blend the brown crab meat, reduced stock, cream and tomato ketchup in a liquidizer until smooth. Pour into a pan and leave over a gentle heat to warm through. Serve without delay by parting each soufflé and pouring in the hot, creamy sauce.

alternative fish

You can make a very similar soufflé with lobster, using all the brown meat in the head part and the coral.

Cockle Cream with Bacon, Tomatoes and Potatoes

We once filmed at the cockle and jellied eel stalls in Leigh-on-Sea because I was fascinated to find out why it is that boiled cockles served with malt vinegar and white pepper get the people from all over Essex and Kent so excited. I eventually came to like them too, but this delightful English cockle soup, which comes from a cookery writer who I really admire, Lindsey Bareham, is slightly more 'my cup of tea'.

serves 4

2.4 litres (4 pints) cleaned cockles (see p. 26)
900 ml (1½ pints) water
25g (1 oz) butter
50g (2 oz) lean bacon, diced
1 leek, cleaned and finely sliced
1 stick celery, finely chopped

2 plum tomatoes, skinned and thinly sliced
2 potatoes (about 350 g/12 oz), peeled and diced
Juice of 1 small lemon
2 eggs
2 tablespoons chopped fresh parsley
Salt and freshly ground black pepper

method

Place the cockles in a large pan with 150 ml (5 fl oz) of the water. Cook over a high heat, occasionally shaking the pan, until they have opened. Tip into a colander set over a bowl to collect the liquid and leave them to cool a little. Melt the butter in a large pan, add the bacon and cook until it is just beginning to brown. Add the leek, celery and tomatoes and cook until the mixture 'begins to flop'. Meanwhile, remove the cockle meats from the shells.

Pour all but the last tablespoon or two of the cockle liquor into the pan, add the rest of the water and the potatoes and leave the soup to simmer until the potatoes are soft – about 10 minutes.

Add the shelled cockles and taste the soup for seasoning. Whisk the lemon juice with the eggs in a bowl. Pour on a ladle full of the hot soup, whisk together and then stir the liaison into the soup. Stir it over a low heat to thicken slightly but don't let the soup boil. Stir in the parsley and serve.

Grilled Salted Cod with Beer, Bacon and Cabbage

This recipe comes from a chef who has sadly left us to run a pub and restaurant in the Home Counties. His name is Jason Fretwell and he was a very inventive chef who was keen on British food. This was one of his best dishes. He also had a great recipe for a steamed fish pudding, which I must get from him some time.

serves 4

4 × 175 g (6 oz) pieces of unskinned thick
    cod fillet
50 g (2 oz) butter
1 small Savoy cabbage, weighing about 750 g
    (1½ lb), cored and thinly sliced
2 tablespoons sunflower oil
75 g (3 oz) rindless smoked streaky bacon, cut
    into thin strips

1 onion, finely chopped
1 garlic clove, very finely chopped
300 ml (10 fl oz) *Chicken Stock* (see p. 232)
300 ml (10 fl oz) pale ale
2 tablespoons chopped parsley, plus extra
    to garnish
Salt and freshly ground black pepper
Sea salt flakes, to serve

method

Place the cod skin-side down on a plate and sprinkle heavily with some salt. Leave for 20 minutes, then rinse the salt off and dry on kitchen paper. Melt 25 g (1 oz) of the butter. Brush the cod with a little of the butter and sprinkle the skin with salt and pepper.

Put the cabbage into a large pan of boiling salted water and bring back to the boil. Drain and refresh under cold running water.

Heat the oil in a large, heavy-based pan, add the bacon and fry over a high heat until crisp and lightly golden. Add the rest of the melted butter, onion and garlic and fry for 5 minutes, until the onion is soft and lightly browned. Add the chicken stock and beer to the pan and reduce the volume of liquid by three-quarters over a high heat. Add the cabbage and the rest of the butter and cook gently for a further 5 minutes till the cabbage is tender. Season to taste with salt and pepper, add the parsley and keep warm.

Pre-heat the grill to high. Grill the cod for 8 minutes on one side only, until the skin is crisp and the fish is cooked through. Put the cabbage in 4 large, warmed soup plates. Sprinkle the skin of the cod with a little sea salt, coarsely ground black pepper and chopped parsley, place on top of the cabbage and serve.

alternative fish

Use haddock or hake. It also works quite well with really thick fillets of plaice or lemon sole, folded over themselves to look like one thick fillet.

Cream of Shrimp Soup

Last August I went on a shrimp boat in the Thames estuary. They boil the shrimps in seawater on the boat and then scoop them on to a net stretched between two old wooden poles to cool off. They told me to pick the shrimps off the pile and eat them still warm. I sat there on a sunny summer afternoon with a handful of shrimps, eating them whole, looking over to Southend with container ships passing through on their way to London. I had my dog, Chalky, with me, who had taken an extreme liking to the shrimp boat's skipper, Ted. The shrimps were so good that at the time there was nothing else in the world I would rather have done than eat them on their own, and talk to Ted and Peter and think that when I was a boy, days were always like this. This velouté *soup's pretty good, though.*

serves 4

100 g (4 oz) butter
1 carrot, finely diced
1 onion, finely chopped
750 g (1½ lb) unpeeled raw or cooked shrimps
900 ml (1½ pints) *Fish Stock* (see p. 232)
1 bay leaf

150 ml (5 fl oz) dry white wine
25 g (1 oz) plain flour
300 ml (10 fl oz) milk
150 ml (5 fl oz) double cream
A pinch of cayenne pepper
Salt and freshly ground black pepper

method

Melt 25 g (1 oz) of the butter in a medium-sized pan. Add the carrot and onion and cook over a medium heat for 3–4 minutes. If you are using raw shrimps, add them to the pan and turn them over for 5 minutes, until they are just cooked and have all turned pink. Remove a third of the shrimps from the pan and, when they are cool enough to handle, shell them and return the shells to the pan. If you are using cooked shrimps, just shell a third of them and put the shells and the rest of the shrimps into the pan. Add the fish stock, bay leaf and white wine, bring to the boil and simmer for 20 minutes.

Liquidize the soup (in batches if necessary) for a few seconds until coarsely blended but not completely smooth. Pour into a conical sieve set over a clean pan and press out all the liquid with the back of a ladle.

Melt 40 g (1½ oz) of the remaining butter in another pan, stir in the flour and cook for 30 seconds. Gradually stir in the milk and then the strained soup and simmer over a low heat for 15 minutes, stirring occasionally. Whisk in the remaining butter, plus the cream and cayenne pepper and season with a little more black pepper and some salt.

Pour the soup into a warmed tureen and serve with a bowl of the peeled shrimps. Place a few of the shrimps into each soup bowl before ladling over the soup.

alternative fish

You can also make a very good soup with some cooked unpeeled North Atlantic prawns.

Grilled Sea Bass with Fennel, New Potatoes, Sorrel and Pernod

I haven't actually asked Fred Fisher if I can put this recipe in my book but I know he won't mind. He was a regional finalist in a cookery competition set by the Radio Times magazine called 'Impress Rick Stein with a fish dish' or some such title, and he certainly did. Fred's a policeman, who I first met when he won the round of Masterchef I was judging. He's a natural cook and spent a week of his hard-earned holiday cooking in my kitchen last summer, after which he said, 'I thought it was hard work in the police force until now!'.

serves 4

450 g (1 lb) new potatoes, scraped

1 large fennel bulb

600 ml (1 pint) *Fish Stock* (see p. 232)

1 star anise

1 shallot, chopped

250 ml (9 fl oz) dry white wine

25 g (1 oz) unsalted butter

A little sunflower oil for chargrilling

1 tablespoon Pernod

2 tablespoons crème fraîche

350 g (12 oz) fresh spinach,
   large stalks removed

Freshly grated nutmeg

2 × 550 g (1¼ lb) sea bass, filleted (see p. 26)

A handful of sorrel leaves (about 50 g/2 oz),
   finely chopped

Coarse sea salt

method

Cook the potatoes in boiling salted water until just tender. Drain and cool under cold running water. Cut in half lengthways.

Trim the fennel and cut it in half lengthways through the root. Slice each half into 6 wedges. Bring the fish stock to the boil, add the fennel and simmer for 20 minutes. Remove with a slotted spoon and set aside. Add the star anise to the stock, bring back to the boil and boil until reduced to about 300 ml (10 fl oz).

Put the shallot and wine into another pan and boil until reduced to about 1 tablespoon. Add the reduced fish stock and then pass through a sieve into a clean pan.

Heat a large frying pan over a medium heat. Add all but a knob of the butter and as soon as it stops foaming, add the potatoes, toss them in the butter and cook, turning now and then, until golden.

Meanwhile, heat a ridged cast iron griddle over a medium–high heat. Brush it lightly with some oil, then cook the fennel segments on it for about 5 minutes, until they are marked with brown ridges underneath. Turn over and repeat. Place on a baking tray and keep warm.

Bring the sauce up to a simmer. Add the Pernod and simmer for about 3 minutes to cook off the alcohol. Add 1 tablespoon of the crème fraîche and continue to simmer until the sauce is thick enough to coat the back of a spoon lightly. Keep warm.

Place a frying pan over a medium heat, add the remaining butter and the spinach and toss around for 3–4 minutes, until the spinach has wilted. Stir in the rest of the crème fraîche, a grating of nutmeg and a pinch of salt. Keep warm.

Pre-heat the grill to high. Lay the fillets of bass on a lightly oiled rack or baking tray, skin-side up, and sprinkle the skin with some coarse sea salt. Put the fish under the grill, a few inches away from the heat, and cook until the skin begins to turn golden brown and crisp – about 2 minutes. The flesh on the underside at this stage will be slightly underdone, but will continue to cook after you remove it from the heat.

Toss the sorrel leaves into the sauce and check the flavour, adding a little seasoning if necessary. It should be rich and aromatic, with a slight sourness from the crème fraîche and sorrel. To serve, place the fennel wedges on 4 warmed plates, interspersed with the spinach. Scatter around the potatoes and lay the fish neatly on top, skin-side up. Spoon the sauce around the edge.

alternative fish

As Fred said in his description of this recipe, 'Sea bass seems to take the flavours of fennel and Pernod very well'. Grey mullet works well too, as would snapper and the Australian jewfish.

Cod Niçoise

This is the second recipe in this book from a rather memorable competition set by the Radio Times *magazine, where readers were asked to impress me with their fish cookery. The finalists' recipes were indeed extremely impressive and Janine Lishman-Peat's recipe was one I might well have written myself except that she thought of it and I probably never would.*

serves 4

600 g (1 lb 6 oz) Charlotte potatoes (or other large, waxy new potatoes), scraped if very new

Olive oil for grilling

4 × 175–225 g (6–8 oz) pieces of unskinned thick cod fillet

4–6 tablespoons *Mayonnaise* made with half sunflower, half olive oil and lemon juice instead of vinegar (see p. 235)

50 g (2 oz) baby salad leaves

4 tablespoons *Tapenade* (see p. 236)

Salt

Parsley or basil sprigs, to garnish

FOR THE TOMATO SAUCE:

150 g (5 oz) cherry tomatoes

1 tablespoon sun-dried tomato paste

1 tablespoon tomato purée

2 teaspoons caster sugar

method

To make the tomato sauce, purée the tomatoes in a food processor until smooth, press through a sieve to remove the skin and seeds and then return to the cleaned food processor bowl with the sun-dried tomato paste, tomato purée, half the sugar and a pinch of salt. Blend once more and then taste. Add the remaining sugar if you need to, but this will depend on the sweetness and ripeness of the tomatoes. What you should aim for is a sweet and sour taste without any bitterness. Pour the sauce into a bowl.

Cook the potatoes in boiling salted water until tender, then drain and leave until just cool enough to handle.

Meanwhile, heat a ridged cast iron griddle or frying pan until it is very hot, then brush with a little oil. Rub a little salt into the skin of the cod and place it on the griddle, skin-side down. Cook for about 5 minutes until the skin is crisp. Turn over and cook for another 3–4 minutes or until just cooked through.

While the cod is cooking, peel the skins off the warm potatoes (if you haven't already scraped them) and slice them fairly thickly. Spread both sides of each slice with the mayonnaise. Arrange in the middle of each plate and top with the salad leaves. Rest the cod on top of the leaves. Drizzle a little of the tomato sauce around the edge and then spoon around a little of the tapenade. Garnish with a sprig of parsley or basil.

alternative fish

Really, any fish that doesn't have a particularly strong flavour, such as haddock, pollack or Australian flat-head, would work well with this dish.

Potted Shrimps

I often go back to the Cotswolds, where I lived till I was 18, and in particular to the town of Burford. The Bay Tree was the best hotel around. Its owner, Sylvia Grey, was a tremendous influence on how to run a good and hospitable restaurant with rooms. It's all to do with enthusiasm for making people happy.

The real treat at the Bay Tree was Hook Norton Ale out of pewter mugs in front of the fire in the bar, then dinner, which for me had to start with potted shrimps. Now that we get food from everywhere it's hard to remember how appealing this dish was in the '60s and '70s. The sweetness of those shrimps in mace-flavoured butter, spread on thin brown toast with, maybe, an exotic glass of Muscadet to go with them is a fond memory for me.

serves 6

100 g (4 oz) butter

2 blades of mace

A good pinch of cayenne pepper

Freshly grated nutmeg

600 ml (1 pint) peeled brown shrimps

6 tablespoons C*larified Butter* (see p. 239)

method

Put the butter, mace, cayenne pepper and a little grated nutmeg into a medium-sized pan and leave to melt over a gentle heat. Add the peeled shrimps and stir over the heat for a couple of minutes until they have heated through, but don't let the mixture boil. Remove the mace and divide the shrimps and butter between 6 small ramekins. Level the tops and then leave them to set in the fridge. Spoon over a thin layer of clarified butter and leave to set once more. Serve with plenty of brown toast or crusty brown bread.

alternative fish

You could also make this with peeled North Atlantic prawns, fresh white crab meat or chopped cooked lobster.

Panaché of Scallops, Squid and John Dory
with a Tomato, Tarragon and Chervil Dressing

I created this dish for a dinner that I cooked at Blenheim Palace in Oxfordshire. I had to spend the day talking to 30 chefs about my style of cooking and we also prepared and cooked a four-course dinner for about 150 guests. It was the second course in that dinner, but I have made it for use as a starter here. It was quite a memorable occasion because we had the film crew in and Chalky as well, who spent the day misbehaving and chasing pheasants around the grounds.

The squid and scallops are fried to colour them nicely and produce that irresistible flavour of caramelized seafood, while the John Dory is gently steamed to provide a contrast of flavour and texture. The seafood is then piled on to plates and surrounded by a light, fragrant virgin olive oil sauce flavoured with tomato, saffron, fresh tarragon and chervil, slightly enriched with a little clarified butter.

serves 4

225 g (8 oz) unskinned John Dory fillet

175 g (6 oz) prepared squid (see p. 27)

8 prepared scallops (see p. 26)

1 tablespoon olive oil

¹/₂ teaspoon paprika

15 g (¹/₂ oz) butter

15 g (¹/₂ oz) lamb's lettuce

1 teaspoon lemon olive oil or ordinary olive oil

Salt and freshly ground black pepper

FOR THE DRESSING:

300 ml (10 fl oz) *Fish Stock* (see p. 232)

4 tablespoons olive oil

1 tablespoon *Clarified Butter* (see p. 239)

1 plum tomato, skinned, seeded and diced
  (see p. 238)

1 small garlic clove, very finely chopped

1 teaspoon each chopped tarragon and chervil

¹/₄ small red finger chilli, seeded and very
  finely chopped

1 tablespoon white wine vinegar

A small pinch of saffron

¹/₂ teaspoon finely chopped anchovy fillets

method

Cut the John Dory fillet across into slices 2.5 cm (1 inch) wide. Cut the squid pouches across into thin rings and separate the tentacles. Cut each scallop horizontally in half.

For the dressing, put the fish stock into a pan and boil rapidly until it has reduced to about 2 tablespoons. Remove from the heat.

Bring about 1.2 litres (2 pints) of water to the boil in a large pan. Meanwhile, heat the oil in a large, heavy-based frying pan. Add the squid, sprinkle with the paprika and some seasoning and stir-fry for 2–3 minutes, until nicely browned. Transfer to a plate and keep warm. Heat the butter in the pan, add the scallops and some seasoning and cook for about 30 seconds on each side, until well browned. Set aside with the squid.

Place the pieces of John Dory on a heatproof plate and season with salt and pepper. Place a trivet or an upturned plate in the pan of boiling water, lower in the plate of John Dory so that it stays above the water, cover and steam for 3 minutes. Add all the other dressing ingredients to the pan containing the reduced fish stock and leave just to warm through over a low heat – but don't let it come anywhere near boiling.

Toss the lamb's lettuce leaves in the lemon oil with a little seasoning.

Pile the seafood on to 4 warmed plates. Spoon some of the dressing around the edge of the plate, pile the salad leaves next to the fish and serve.

alternative fish

This is an occasion for expensive seafood. You could substitute red mullet, snapper or gilthead bream for the John Dory, lobster for the scallops and perhaps small spiny lobster or big chunks of cooked blue crab meat for the squid, added at the very last minute just to heat through.

the place for comfortable seafood • _I like to think of a lot of American food as comfortable. I think this has a much nicer sound to it than 'comfort' food, which to me has a slightly neurotic feel about it. Comfortable, on the other hand, entirely describes food like Maryland Crab Cakes, Hangtown Fry and even my own Broiled Haddock Fillets with Succotash. Indeed a great deal of American food is just the sort of food we love to eat but which often leads to extended waistlines and bottoms if we eat too comfortably for too long._

I could almost go further and describe the food there as easy, available, friendly, welcoming. That's what America means to me, especially on the Eastern Seaboard. Many people view the United States as being too big, too brash and too influential, but meandering through the little inlets and islands of Chesapeake Bay or picking oysters in a muddy creek with a local oysterman with a French accent typical of the islanders of South Carolina and an evocative name, Goat Lafayette, doesn't make it feel like that to me at all. Neither does sitting with Jill

East-coast
America

eating a plate of deep-fried clams and mayonnaise, or cracking my way through a pile of freshly steamed crab with crab-boil seasoning and chatting to the most downhome and friendly waitress on a lazy Saturday lunchtime. East-coast America feels charming and local, with a cuisine that the people are crazy about. I learnt one very important thing in the States which we chefs in our trendy restaurants, trying to keep up with the latest fashions in food, tend to forget. Food is about where you come from. So many times on my travels I've picked up the intense emotions of people relating their cultural identity through food. To Americans, dishes like Charleston Seafood Gumbo and Shrimp and Grits are what they love, and it's food that reflects them well, because in America it's all about what you know, what you feel comfortable with.

Cod and Lobster Chowder

I can't resist slipping a chowder into each of my books – I love that subtle combination of salt pork, seafood and cream so much. This one is really special, made with lobster (but not a great deal) and using the soft parts of the lobster to thicken the broth.

serves 4

1 × 450–550 g (1–1¼ lb) lobster,
   freshly cooked

4 water biscuits

50 g (2 oz) butter, softened

100 g (4 oz) salt pork or rindless streaky bacon,
   in one piece

1 small onion, finely chopped

15 g (½ oz) plain flour

1.2 litres (2 pints) milk

2 medium potatoes (about 225 g/8 oz),
   peeled and diced

1 bay leaf

450 g (1 lb) skinned thick cod fillet

120 ml (4 fl oz) double cream

A pinch of cayenne pepper

2 tablespoons chopped parsley

Salt and freshly ground black pepper

method

First remove the meat from the cooked lobster as described on p. 27, cutting the meat from the tail section into thin slices and scraping all the white curd-like material out of the shells.

Put 2 of the water biscuits into a plastic bag and crush to very fine crumbs by rolling them with a rolling pin. Then mix with the tomalley, other soft material from the head and half the butter, or blend everything in a small food processor.

Cut the piece of salt pork or bacon into small dice. Heat the rest of the butter in a medium-sized pan, add the pork or bacon and fry over a medium heat until lightly golden. Add the onion and cook gently until softened. Stir in the flour and cook for 1 minute. Gradually stir in the milk, then the potatoes and bay leaf and simmer for 10 minutes or until the potatoes are just tender. Add the cod and simmer for 4–5 minutes, then break the fish apart into large flakes with a wooden spoon.

Stir in the water biscuit paste, lobster meat and cream and simmer for 1 minute. Season with the cayenne pepper, 1 teaspoon of salt and some black pepper. To serve, coarsely crush the 2 remaining water biscuits and sprinkle them over the soup with the chopped parsley.

alternative fish

Chowders can be made out of almost any seafood. Try this with clams, mussels and any flaky white fish such as those pictured on pages 10–11.

Frogmore Stew

There's no such place as Frogmore in South Carolina and this isn't a stew, but it tastes real good nevertheless. This recipe comes from Hoppin' John's Low Country Cooking. *The author, John Taylor, with whom I first tried this dish, says that Frogmore stew is usually served out of doors on paper plates on newspaper-covered picnic tables with plenty of ice-cold beer. I must say I used to think that beers like Budweiser and Rolling Rock were a bit lacking in flavour, but a cold Bud outdoors with Frogmore stew on a 38°C South Carolina day sure hits the spot. This dish is also known as a Seafood Boil and is commonly made with either prawns (called shrimp in the US) or lobster up and down the east coast of America. It uses a commercially prepared seasoning mix called Old Bay to flavour the cooking water, so if you go to the east coast, pick some up and substitute it for the mixture below.*

serves 4

6.75 litres (12 pints) water

900 g (2 lb) firm potatoes such as Wilja or Désirée, peeled and cut into large chunks

2 × 225 g (8 oz) smoked pork sausage rings, cut into pieces 5 cm (2 inches) long

4 ears of sweetcorn, cut into 4

900 g (2 lb) unpeeled raw prawns

FOR THE SHRIMP-BOIL SEASONING:

2 tablespoons yellow mustard seeds

1 tablespoon black peppercorns

1 tablespoon dried chilli flakes

3 dried bay leaves

½ tablespoon celery seeds

½ tablespoon coriander seeds

½ tablespoon ground ginger

2 blades of mace

4 tablespoons salt

method

To make the shrimp-boil seasoning, put everything except the salt into a spice grinder and grind to a fine powder. Add the salt and blend for 2–3 seconds.

Bring the water to the boil in a very large pan and add 8 tablespoons of the shrimp-boil seasoning. Add the potatoes and simmer for 5 minutes. Add the sausage and cook for 5 minutes. Then add the sweetcorn and cook for another 5 minutes. Finally, add the prawns and cook for 3 minutes (you don't wait for it to come back to the boil).

Drain immediately and, in true American style, serve on large paper plates with plenty of ice-cold beer and the remaining seasoning to sprinkle over if you wish.

alternative fish

It is quite common to add pieces of crab in the shell and clams to this dish. It can also be made just with lobsters, as they do in Maine, further north.

Eggs Benedict with Smoked Haddock

I'm not usually very keen on taking a well-established dish, replacing some of the ingredients with fish and then calling it something new. But I make the exception for my eggs Benedict because poached eggs and smoked haddock go so well together.

serves 4

½ **quantity of** *Hollandaise Sauce* **or** *Quick*
  Hollandaise Sauce **(see p. 234)**
4 × 100 g (4 oz) pieces of smoked haddock fillet
1 tablespoon white wine vinegar
4 eggs
2 English muffins
Coarsely crushed black peppercorns and a few
  chopped chives, to garnish

method

Make the hollandaise sauce and keep it warm, off the heat, over a pan of warm water. Bring about 5 cm (2 inches) of water to the boil in a shallow pan, add the pieces of smoked haddock, bring back to a simmer and cook for 4 minutes. Lift out on to a plate, peel off the skin and keep warm.

Bring about 5 cm (2 inches) of water to the boil in a medium-sized pan, add the vinegar and reduce it to a gentle simmer. Break the eggs into the pan one at a time and poach for 3 minutes. Meanwhile, slice the muffins in half and toast them until lightly browned. Lift the poached eggs out with a slotted spoon, shaking the spoon gently to remove any water.

To serve, place the toasted muffin halves on 4 warmed plates, top with the smoked haddock and then a poached egg. Spoon over the hollandaise sauce and garnish with a sprinkling of crushed black pepper and chopped chives.

alternative fish

Try using some lightly grilled slices of smoked salmon or a thicker piece of smoked cod fillet instead.

Shrimp and Grits

The success of good grits depends on what you add at the beginning – a good stock and plenty of salt. You can't get more Southern than this. Use polenta as an alternative to the grits, if you wish – it is quite similar in taste and texture but yellow rather than white.

serves 4

450 g (1 lb) unpeeled headless raw prawns

3 tablespoons olive oil

175 g (6 oz) smoked pork sausage,
   thickly sliced

1 onion, chopped

2 celery sticks, sliced

1 green pepper, chopped

2 garlic cloves, finely chopped

$\frac{1}{4}$ teaspoon cayenne pepper

Salt and freshly ground black pepper

FOR THE GRITS:

1.2 litres (2 pints) *Chicken Stock* (see p. 232)

25 g (1 oz) butter

175 g (6 oz) hominy grits

method

First cook the grits: put the chicken stock, butter and ¾ teaspoon of salt into a pan and bring to the boil. Pour in the grits in a slow, steady stream, stirring all the time. Bring back to the boil, then reduce to a very gentle simmer and cook for 25–30 minutes, stirring every now and then to prevent sticking.

Peel the prawns, leaving the last tail segment of each one in place – this makes them look more interesting. Heat the oil in a frying pan, add the sliced sausage and fry on both sides until nicely browned. Add the onion, celery and green pepper and fry gently for 10 minutes, until softened and lightly browned.

Add the prawns and stir-fry for 3 minutes, until just cooked. Sprinkle over the chopped garlic, cayenne pepper and some salt and pepper to taste and cook for another minute.

Serve the grits on a big warm serving plate with the 'shrimp' spooned down the middle.

Broiled Haddock Fillets with Succotash

The American word broiled simply means grilled. I've kept it in to add the right atmosphere to the dish. These things matter to me.

Until I went to the Southern states of America I had always thought that succotash was some kind of squash-type vegetable, but it's actually a down-home mix of beans, sweetcorn, bacon and cream, finished with chives. Once I'd made it I knew it was a dead certainty to go with a nice thick fillet of white fish such as haddock. American recipes for succotash normally call for lima beans. These are the same as butterbeans, one name referring to the capital of Peru, where they were first grown, and the other to their buttery, creamy texture.

serves 4

175 g (6 oz) dried butterbeans

100 g (4 oz) rindless smoked streaky bacon,
   in one piece

1 small onion, chopped

1 tablespoon sunflower oil, if needed

300 ml (10 fl oz) *Chicken Stock* (see p. 232)

3 ears of sweetcorn

50 ml (2 fl oz) double cream

4 × 175–225 g (6–8 oz) pieces of unskinned
   thick haddock fillet

15 g (½ oz) butter, melted

2 tablespoons chopped chives, plus a few extra
   to garnish

Salt and freshly ground black pepper

method

Put the dried beans into a pan and cover with plenty of water. Bring to the boil, then cover, remove from the heat and leave to soak for 2 hours.

Cut the bacon into 5 mm (¼ inch) dice, put it into a pan and cook over a low heat until the fat begins to melt. Increase the heat a little and allow it to fry in its own fat until crisp and golden. Add the onion (and the sunflower oil, if it looks a little dry) and cook for about 5 minutes, until soft.

Drain the beans and add them to the pan with the stock. Simmer gently until they are just tender and the stock is well reduced.

Stand the sweetcorn up on a chopping board and slice away all the kernels. Add the sweetcorn to the beans with the cream and simmer for 5 minutes.

Meanwhile, pre-heat the grill to high. Brush the pieces of haddock on both sides with the melted butter and season with salt and pepper. Place skin-side up on a lightly oiled baking sheet or the rack of the grill pan and grill for 7–8 minutes.

Stir the chives into the beans and season with salt and pepper. Spoon the mixture into 4 warmed soup plates and place the haddock on top. Scatter over a few more chives and serve.

alternative fish

We filmed this recipe using striped sea bass in America, so a fillet from a good-sized bass would be ideal, but you could also use cod, hake or kingfish.

Betsy Apple's Crab Salad with Basil, Parsley and Chives in a Lemon Vinaigrette

Betsy and Johnny Apple are friends of mine who have a weekend house just up the road from Gettysburg in Pennsylvania. Johnny is the chief political correspondent for the New York Times but, more important to me, is that between them he and Betsy know more about the best restaurants in the world than anyone I have met. They cooked Sunday lunch for Jill and me last May and I thought this was one of the best ways ever of serving up the fantastic meat of the American blue crab.

serves 4

450 g (1 lb) fresh white crab meat

2 tablespoons finely shredded basil

2 tablespoons each finely chopped flat-leaf
   parsley and chives

A few whole chives, with blossoms attached
   if possible

FOR THE LEMON VINAIGRETTE:

1 ¹/₂ tablespoons lemon juice

1 teaspoon Dijon mustard

4–5 tablespoons extra virgin olive oil

Salt and freshly ground black pepper

method

It's a good idea to pick over the crab meat to find any pieces of shell first, then place it in a pretty serving bowl.

For the vinaigrette, mix together the lemon juice and mustard and then gradually whisk in the oil, ½ teaspoon of salt and plenty of freshly ground black pepper. Stir it into the crab with the chopped herbs just before serving. Check the salad for seasoning and then garnish with a few whole chives. Serve with plenty of crusty French bread and chilled white wine.

alternative fish

There is no alternative to the crab meat but try to use white meat that is in largish chunks rather than lots of little pieces.

Barbecued Shrimp with Coleslaw

This is a pretty classic American recipe for cooking shrimp (as prawns are known in the US) with a barbecue flavour. You can cook it quite successfully under the grill or on a barbecue, but if using a barbecue, heat the remaining marinade in a small pan to the side of the rack to cook out any raw flavours from the marinated prawns. The coleslaw goes spectacularly well with them but it must be freshly made and crunchy. I can't stand that soft stuff you buy in tubs – make your own!

This recipe uses unshelled prawns because I like sitting and peeling them, and I'm not averse to eating the odd one or two with the shell still on, but do peel them before marinating if you prefer.

serves 4

150 ml (5 fl oz) olive oil

120 ml (4 fl oz) chilli sauce

3 tablespoons Worcestershire sauce

1 teaspoon salt

4 garlic cloves, crushed

1 tablespoon sweet chilli sauce (or clear honey)

$\frac{1}{2}$ teaspoon Tabasco sauce

900 g (2 lb) unpeeled raw prawns

FOR THE COLESLAW:

350 g (12 oz) white cabbage, cored and thinly sliced

2 celery sticks, thinly sliced

1 green pepper, thinly sliced

6 spring onions, thinly sliced

3 tablespoons chopped dill

2 teaspoons Dijon mustard

1 heaped teaspoon creamed horseradish

$\frac{1}{2}$ teaspoon Tabasco sauce

1 tablespoon red wine vinegar

2 tablespoons extra virgin olive oil

2 tablespoons *Mayonnaise* made with olive oil (see p. 235)

A pinch of cayenne pepper

Salt and freshly ground black pepper

method

Mix the olive oil, chilli sauce, Worcestershire sauce, salt, garlic, sweet chilli sauce and Tabasco sauce together in a large bowl. Stir in the prawns, cover and leave to marinate at room temperature for 2 hours, or overnight in the fridge.

Pre-heat your barbecue or grill. Meanwhile, make the coleslaw: mix the cabbage, celery, green pepper, spring onions and dill together in a bowl. Mix the rest of the ingredients together to make a dressing. Stir it into the vegetables at the last minute and spoon it into a large serving bowl.

If you are barbecuing the prawns, you might prefer to thread them on to large metal skewers first, which will make things easier when you come to turn them. Cook them for $\frac{1}{2}$–2 minutes on each side, basting them with some of the marinade. Pile them into a warmed serving bowl. Bring the remaining marinade to the boil in a small pan and pour it over the prawns. Serve them with the coleslaw and plenty of crusty French bread.

Poached Bonito with Warm Thyme and Tomato Potatoes

I got the idea of mixing mayonnaise with warm stock to make a lovely sauce from Mexico. I'm always looking for interesting ways of cooking bonito and in fact, it being an oily fish like salmon, with lots of flavour, I think poaching actually improves it.

I think you should try a good Californian wine with this, though maybe not a Chardonnay or a Sauvignon. There are one or two inventive winemakers in the Napa Valley who seem to be having a lot of success with grape varieties that are normally part of a blend in France. Look for Roussanne, Viognier or Marsanne, pay some decent money and have a good time.

serves 4

4 × 175 g (6 oz) pieces of thick bonito fillet, small bones removed

4 tablespoons *Mayonnaise* made with olive oil (see p. 235)

6 black olives, such as Kalamata, pitted and thinly sliced

Salt and freshly ground black pepper

4 parsley sprigs, to garnish

FOR THE POTATOES:

450 g (1 lb) firm potatoes, such as Désirée or Wilja, peeled and cut into 2 cm (³/₄ inch) pieces

25 g (1 oz) unsalted butter

1 large shallot, finely chopped

Leaves from 1 sprig of thyme

1 plum tomato, skinned, seeded and diced (see p. 238)

1 tablespoon chopped parsley

method

Cook the potatoes in boiling salted water until tender, then drain. Melt the butter in a medium-sized pan, add the shallot and thyme leaves and cook for about 4 minutes, until the shallot is soft but not browned. Add the potatoes and cook for 2 minutes, turning them over very gently every now and then so as not to break them up too much. Take the pan off the heat and stir in the tomato, parsley and some seasoning.

While the potatoes are cooking, bring 600 ml (1 pint) water and 1 tablespoon of salt to the boil in a large frying pan. Reduce to a simmer, add the bonito fillets and poach for 3 minutes, turning them over after 1½ minutes. Lift them out with a slotted spoon, cover and keep warm.

Take 40 ml (1½ fl oz) of the poaching liquor and stir into the mayonnaise with the black olives. Serve the bonito garnished with parsley sprigs. I like to put all the fish on one big plate with the potatoes beside and serve the sauce separately.

alternative fish

This dish can equally well be made with those beautiful, plump, big mackerel you get in winter in the UK. Try making it with sea trout, skipjack tuna or salmon, too.

Charleston Seafood Gumbo

The director of my cookery series Rick Stein's Seafood Odyssey, *insisted that I cooked gumbo while we were in America. I found it pretty nerve-racking trying to impress a bunch of locals with a dish that they'd been eating ever since they were children. But it worked – they really liked it, mainly, I'm sure, because I almost instinctively understood that the secret of a good gumbo lies in starting with a good stock.*

serves 4

40 g (1½ oz) bacon fat, lard or vegetable oil

40 g (1½ oz) plain flour

75 g (3 oz) rindless smoked streaky bacon, cut
    into strips

1 onion, chopped

1 large celery stick, sliced

1 green pepper, seeded and chopped

225 g (8 oz) okra, thickly sliced

450 g (1 lb) plum tomatoes, roughly chopped

1 green jalapeño chilli, thinly sliced

1 large sprig of thyme

2 bay leaves

225 g (8 oz) skinned boneless chicken, cut into
    5 cm (2 inch) pieces

20 small clams or mussels, cleaned (see p. 26)

100 g (4 oz) fresh white crab meat

2 spring onions, cut into 2.5 cm
    (1 inch) lengths

1 tablespoon chopped parsley

Salt and freshly ground black pepper

FOR THE STOCK:

450 g (1 lb) unpeeled large raw prawns

4 large chicken wings

1 carrot, sliced

1 large onion, sliced

1 celery stick, sliced

A handful of fresh herbs: parsley, thyme
    and oregano

1 bay leaf

1.75 litres (3 pints) water

method

First make the stock: peel the prawns but don't throw away the shells. Put the shells and the rest of the stock ingredients into a large pan and bring to the boil. Reduce the heat to a gentle simmer and cook for 1 hour to produce an aromatic, very well-flavoured stock. Strain through a colander into another pan.

For the gumbo, heat the fat in a large pan, add the flour and cook over a gentle heat, stirring continuously, until it has turned a golden biscuit brown. Add the bacon and continue to cook for 2 minutes. Gradually add the stock, stirring as you do. Now add the onion, celery and green pepper (they call these the Holy Trinity in the Southern States), plus the okra, tomatoes, jalapeño chilli, thyme and bay leaves. Leave everything to simmer for 25 minutes. The vegetables need to be very well cooked, almost blending into the now beautifully flavoured sauce. Add the chicken after 20 minutes and add the prawns and clams or mussels shortly after. Finally stir in the crab meat, spring onions, parsley, 1½ teaspoons of salt and some freshly ground black pepper. Serve ladled over some cooked long grain rice.

alternative fish

Use whatever is to hand. It's a bit like making a paella – just include whatever seafood you like. The locals sometimes make it with squirrel and alligator, too!

Hangtown Fry

This was apparently the last breakfast for a condemned prisoner in a Western frontier town, who dreamed it up as a dish containing all of his favourite things. The Americans are really good at hearty breakfasts, though personally I think this recipe is unlikely to have come from someone who was just about to die. It has all the enthusiasm of somebody enjoying themselves too much for that. Although primarily designed for breakfast, it is great for lunch too, with some sautéed potatoes and a simple green salad.

serves 4

8 large oysters

6 eggs

6 cream crackers or Saltines

4 tablespoons sunflower oil

4 tablespoons *Clarified Butter* (see p. 239)

3 tablespoons plain flour

15 g ($\frac{1}{2}$ oz) chilled butter

3 tablespoons double cream

2 tablespoons chopped parsley

15 g ($\frac{1}{2}$ oz) finely grated fresh
   Parmesan cheese

A little lemon juice

8 thin rashers of rindless streaky bacon

Salt and freshly ground black pepper

method

Remove the oysters from their shells (see p. 27). Beat the eggs and pour them into a shallow dish. Put the cream crackers in a plastic bag and crush them into fine crumbs with a rolling pin. Tip them into a dish.

Heat the oil and the clarified butter in a 20 cm (8 inch) non-stick frying pan. Dust the oysters in the flour, then dip them into the beaten egg and finally into the cracker crumbs. Fry for 1 minute on each side until golden brown, then remove from the pan, season with a little salt and keep warm. Drain away the cooking fat from the pan and wipe it out with some kitchen paper. Rub the base well with the chilled butter.

Add the cream, parsley, Parmesan cheese and some seasoning to the leftover beaten eggs. Return the oysters to the pan and squeeze over a little lemon juice. Pour the egg mixture around the oysters and cook over a low heat until just set – about 10–12 minutes. Meanwhile, grill the bacon until crisp and golden.

As soon as the 'fry' is set, put the pan under the grill until it is browned and puffed up. Lay the bacon rashers on top, take the pan to the table and serve.

alternative fish

You really can't reproduce this classic American dish using any other seafood. It simply works best with oysters.

Maryland Crab Cakes with Tarragon and Butter Sauce

Everywhere you go on the east coast of America you will find crab cakes. I've become a bit of a connoisseur of them now and as David McCullam, the owner of the Tilghman Island Inn in the Chesapeake Bay, said, the secret of a good crab cake is crab. The less you need to add to the crab meat the better. Another secret is to chill the cakes for at least an hour to firm up, so that they hold their shape when you cook them.

I've combined the crab cakes with a very simple tart tomato, tarragon and butter sauce, which seems to cut through the richness of the crab meat very satisfactorily.

serves 4

40 g (1½ oz) cream crackers or Saltines

450 g (1 lb) fresh white crab meat

2 tablespoons chopped parsley

1 egg, beaten

2 tablespoons *Mayonnaise* made with sunflower oil (see p. 235)

1 tablespoon English mustard powder

1 tablespoon lemon juice

A dash of Worcestershire sauce

4 tablespoons *Clarified Butter* (see p. 239)

Salt and freshly ground white pepper

FOR THE TARRAGON AND BUTTER SAUCE:

50 ml (2 fl oz) white wine vinegar

4 tablespoons *Clarified Butter* (see p. 239)

1 plum tomato, skinned, seeded and diced (see p. 238)

1 teaspoon chopped tarragon

method

Put the crackers into a plastic bag and crush into fine crumbs with a rolling pin. Put the crab meat into a bowl with the parsley and add just enough of the cracker crumbs to absorb any moisture from the crab. You may not need to add them all.

Break the egg into a small bowl and whisk in the mayonnaise, mustard, lemon juice, Worcestershire sauce and some seasoning. Fold this mixture into the crab meat but try not to break up the lumps of crab too much. Shape the mixture into eight 7.5 cm (3 inch) patties, put them on a plate, cover with clingfilm and chill for at least 1 hour.

Heat the clarified butter in a large frying pan. Add the crab cakes (in batches if necessary) and cook over a medium heat for 2–3 minutes on each side, until crisp and richly golden. Keep the first lot warm if you need to, while you cook the second batch.

Meanwhile, for the sauce, boil the vinegar in a small pan until reduced to about 2 tablespoons. Add the clarified butter, diced tomato, chopped tarragon and some salt and pepper to taste and gently warm through.

Serve the crab cakes immediately, with the sauce.

Chargrilled Snapper with a Mango, Prawn and Chilli Salsa

We filmed this in a field of spring flowers on Bowens Island just outside Charleston in South Carolina. I was trying to encapsulate some of the flavours of that part of the States in a modern way. It has nothing to do with the local cuisine but everything to do with what was available in the excellent fresh food sections of the supermarkets there. I'm not a great fan of fruit with meat or fish but if you can find an almost ripe mango that has plenty of acidity, it combines really well with the avocado, chilli, spring onions and coriander and creates a powerful combination of flavours.

serves 4

4 × 100 g (4 oz) unskinned snapper or red mullet fillets

Extra virgin olive oil

Salt and freshly ground black pepper

A bunch of coriander sprigs, to garnish

FOR THE SALSA:

2 large red finger chillies

100 g (4 oz) peeled cooked tiger prawns, thickly sliced

4 spring onions, thinly sliced

1 small garlic clove, finely chopped

1 ripe but firm avocado, peeled and cut into small dice

½ ripe but firm mango, peeled and cut into small dice

Juice of 1 lime

A pinch of salt

method

You can cook this dish over a chargrill, barbecue or under a conventional grill. Pre-heat whichever you are using to high. Meanwhile, for the salsa, cut the chillies in half lengthways and scrape out the seeds with the tip of a small knife but leave the ribs behind to give the salsa a little more heat. Cut them across into thin slices. Then simply mix all the ingredients together.

Brush the fish fillets on both sides with olive oil and season well with salt and pepper. Cut each one into 3, cutting slightly on the diagonal; it will look more elegant like this. Carefully slide a palette knife under each sliced fillet and place either skin-side down over the chargrill or barbecue or skin-side up on an oiled baking sheet to go under the grill. Cook for 3–4 minutes.

To serve, spoon the salsa on to 4 plates and arrange the grilled strips of fish on top. Drizzle a little oil around the edge and garnish with coriander sprigs.

alternative fish

Try sea bass, bream, John Dory or grey mullet.

A Feast of Mahi Mahi, Tortillas and Salsa de Tomate Verde

Probably my most favourite part of a meal in Mexico is the first course, when a pile of corn tortillas comes warm in a wicker basket, wrapped in a napkin. There is some fish or meat and piles of shredded lettuce, sliced avocados, coriander, chopped tomatoes and onions, and a bowl of tomatillo sauce called salsa de tomate verde. *Eating tortillas is a bit like eating Chinese crispy aromatic duck pancakes – you help yourself to whatever filling you want, then roll it up in a warm tortilla and wash it down with plenty of cold beer. The fish I've chosen for this recipe is entirely apt. Mahi mahi, or dolphin fish as it is also known, is firm of texture and sweet to taste, ideal for grilling, slicing and serving with this hot but very fresh jalapeño-flavoured salsa.*

serves 4

1 Romaine lettuce heart, thinly sliced across

2 avocados, halved, skinned and sliced

3 tomatoes, cut into small dice

1 onion, halved and very thinly sliced

8 fresh corn tortillas

4 × 175 g (6 oz) mahi mahi fillets or monkfish fillets, skinned

A little sunflower oil for tossing

Salt and freshly ground black pepper

FOR THE SALSA DE TOMATE VERDE:

2 tomatillos or green tomatoes

2 jalapeño or green finger chillies

1 garlic clove, roughly chopped

1 small onion, roughly chopped

1 tablespoon chopped coriander

A little freshly squeezed lime juice if you are using green tomatoes

method

For the salsa, peel the papery husks of the tomatillos if using. Drop them or the green tomatoes and the jalapeño chillies into a pan of boiling water. Simmer for 10 minutes, then strain and cool slightly. Tip them into a food processor and add the rest of the salsa ingredients, and a little lime juice if you have used green tomatoes instead of tomatillos. Pulse the mixture for a few seconds until you have a fairly smooth sauce with a little bit of texture. Season with salt and spoon into a serving bowl.

Put the shredded lettuce, avocado, coriander, tomato and onion into 5 other serving bowls.

To reheat the tortillas, either stack them on a plate, cover with a tea towel and cook in the microwave on high for about 30 seconds. Alternatively, heat a dry frying pan over a medium heat. Add a tortilla and leave it in the pan for a few seconds, then turn it over, adding a second tortilla on top of it. After a few seconds turn them over together and add a third one to the pan. Continue like this until all your tortillas are in the pan, then remove them and wrap them in a napkin. Keep warm while you cook the fish.

Pre-heat the grill to high. Cut the mahi mahi or monkfish fillets into short, chunky strips. Toss them with a little oil and plenty of seasoning and spread them out on a grilling tray. Cook them for about 2 minutes on one side only until just cooked through.

Lift the fish on to a serving plate and take it to the table with all the other bits and pieces. Let everyone fill their own tortillas with whatever they fancy.

alternative fish

Mahi mahi, which is found mostly in the Pacific and Indian Oceans, is difficult to get hold of in the UK. Apart from monkfish, sea bass would be an excellent substitute, as would John Dory fillets.

Po' Boys

I think we tend to dismiss American fast food as (a) bad for you, (b) made out of junk and (c) unsubtle. But because there's so much rubbish around, do we sometimes miss the real gems? Fast food like these po' boys, for example, in no way subtle and made out of good wholesome ingredients, go straight to the heart of what you sometimes want, just like a great rock 'n' roll song. When the Americans get fast food right, like this dish, nobody does it better! As the name might suggest, po' boys originated as food for the poor, or at least that's what most of the explanations of the name suggest. The most plausible to me is that it originated in New Orleans in the nineteenth century as an oyster sandwich which was given as charity to the poor. Though oysters were the original filling, po' boys are made with both shrimp and clams as well.

makes 6

2 baguettes

Sunflower oil for deep-frying

350 g (12 oz) peeled raw prawns

175 g (6 oz) *Mayonnaise* made with sunflower oil
   (see p. 235), plus extra to serve

2½ tablespoons milk

25 g (1 oz) plain flour

175 g (6 oz) fresh white breadcrumbs

1 small crisp green lettuce

Salt and cayenne pepper

method

Cut each baguette into three and then cut each piece in half lengthways. Pull out a little of the soft white crumb to make a very shallow dip in each half. Lay them on a baking tray, cut-side up, and toast very lightly under the grill. Remove and set aside.

Heat some oil for deep-frying to 190°C/375°F. Season the prawns well with salt and cayenne pepper. Whisk the mayonnaise and milk together in a bowl, put the flour into a second bowl and spread the breadcrumbs over a large plate. Dip the prawns into the flour, mayonnaise and then the breadcrumbs so that they take on an even coating. Treat them gently once they are done because the coating is quite delicate. Pick them up by their tails, drop them into the hot oil about 6 at a time, and fry for 1 minute, until crisp and golden. Transfer to a tray lined with kitchen paper and keep warm in a low oven while you cook the rest.

To serve, spread the bottom half of each piece of bread with a little more mayonnaise, then put some lettuce leaves on top. Pile on a few of the fried prawns, cover with the tops and eat straight away.

alternative fish

Po' boys are excellent made with oysters and even small goujons of fish such as lemon sole and plaice. I particularly like them made with clams, especially the soft-shell clams from the east coast of America, known locally as 'pissers' due to their disconcerting habit of squirting at you through their long necks, which don't look much like necks at all.

Sautéed Soft-shell Crabs with Garlic Butter

I first tried sautéed soft-shell crabs in St Michaels, a little town on the shores of the Chesapeake Bay in America. It was a bit early in the season but I went into a restaurant called The Crab Pot and asked if by any chance they might have some soft-shell crabs, and the waitress said, 'Go into the kitchen and ask Eric.' So I did, and he'd just got some in a box and had just had an order for two portions, the first of the season. I explained to him who I was and he said, 'Why don't you cook some?'. So I did.

serves 4

8–12 soft-shell crabs

100 g (4 oz) plain flour

1 tablespoon shrimp-boil seasoning (see p. 199)
   or Old Bay seasoning mix

3 tablespoons *Clarified Butter* (see p. 239)

100 g (4 oz) butter, at room temperature

3 garlic cloves, crushed

1 tablespoon lemon juice

2 tablespoons chopped parsley

Salt and freshly ground black pepper

method

To prepare the crabs, rinse them first in cold water. Cut off the eyes and mouth with scissors – cut straight across the face, about 5 mm (¼ inch) just behind the eyes. Push your finger into the opening and hook out the stomach, a small jelly-like sac. Then turn the crab over and lift up and pull off the little tail flap. Finally, lift up both sides of the soft top shell in turn and pull out the dead man's fingers (the gills).

Sift the flour, shrimp-boil seasoning, 1 teaspoon of salt and some pepper on to a plate. Dredge the crabs well in the flour, then pat off the excess.

Heat the clarified butter in a large frying pan. Fry the crabs in batches over a moderate heat for 2 minutes on each side, until lightly browned. Shake any excess butter off as you remove them from the pan. Keep warm while you fry the rest.

Add the rest of the butter and the crushed garlic to the pan and allow it to sizzle for a few seconds. Add the lemon juice, then throw in the parsley and some seasoning. Spoon the butter over the crabs and serve immediately.

Deep-fried Soft-shell Crabs in a Cornmeal Crust

This is a variation of the recipe opposite and just as good. It comes from my friend, Johnny Apple (see p. 204). He always uses buttermilk, which is now quite easy to get in the UK. It's slightly thicker than milk and has a slight tartness to it, which sure smelled good when he was mixing up the batter.

serves 4

8 soft-shell crabs

100 g (4 oz) coarse yellow cornmeal or polenta

50 g (2 oz) plain flour

300 ml (10 fl oz) buttermilk or milk

Corn or vegetable oil for deep-frying

Salt and freshly ground black pepper

method

Prepare the crabs as described in the recipe opposite and season on both sides with a little salt and pepper. Mix the cornmeal, flour and some salt and pepper together in a large shallow dish and pour the buttermilk or milk into a second dish.

Heat some oil for deep-frying to 180°C/350°F. Dip the crabs into the milk, then the cornmeal mixture and press it on to give a good, even coating. Lower them about 2 at a time into the hot oil and fry until crisp and golden brown. Lift them on to kitchen paper and keep warm while you cook the rest. Serve while they are still hot and crisp.

alternative fish

We now make these recipes in Padstow using the local shore crabs, which we collect when their shells are soft. They are just as good as the American ones, only quite a bit smaller.

Everyone should have a vegetable garden. Mine is a refuge from the vicissitudes of life. It's not very tidy but it's very relaxing. There are lots of herbs like fennel, parsley and rocket, a riot of fig trees against one wall and unusual plants like cardoons, lovage and angelica. It's a place where I can go to be quiet – a retreat 'to a green thought in a green shade' as the poet Andrew Marvel wrote about his own garden.

I love the variety of shape, colour, texture and flavour of vegetables. Take artichokes for example – I can't think of anything more beautiful. I've got a big bed of them in my garden, most of which are grown from a cutting taken during a visit to Brittany. I eat them dripping with butter, or warm from a blanc – where the water is acidulated with lemon juice and whisked with a little flour – and moist with a light olive oil dressing. Lately, I've taken to cutting my artichokes when they're tiny and adding them to a

Vegetables, rice and **salads**

whole mixture, or melange, of vegetables: young peas and the tender leaves of the same pea plant, early carrots with some of the green tops still on them, the smallest of early potatoes, waxy and white, some broad beans and even the broad bean pods if they're young enough, spinach, runner beans only two inches long, and lashings of herbs, chives, parsley, a little celery leaf and thyme.

This melange is just the sort of vegetable dish I like to eat with fish or shellfish. Vegetables like courgettes, fresh from the garden with their flowers still on, simply thinly sliced and gently stewed in butter with French tarragon and chives, or spinach, are always excellent, too. Any salad leaves, sorrel, rocket and lamb's lettuce, with sprays of parsley, chervil, and cress grown outside in my garden with a view of the bay, are a delight with simply grilled fish.

Vegetables

French Beans with Shallots

method   For 4 people, trim off the stalk ends of 350 g (12 oz) French beans. Cook them in a
pan of boiling salted water for about 2 minutes, until just tender. Drain and refresh
under cold water. Set aside while you fry 2 very finely chopped shallots in 25 g (1 oz)
of butter until soft but not browned. Toss in the beans and cook for about 1 minute to
drive off any excess moisture. Season with freshly ground black pepper and a little salt
if necessary and then serve.

Blanched French Beans with Tomatoes and Thyme

method   For 4 people, trim the stalk ends off 350g (12 oz) French beans and cook them in
boiling salted water for about 2 minutes until tender. Drain well. Return to the pan and
add 2 tablespoons of extra virgin olive oil, 2 seeded and diced tomatoes, 1 finely
chopped clove of garlic, ½ teaspoon of picked thyme leaves and some salt and pepper.
Turn them together gently to mix and serve warm.

Courgettes with Tarragon and Chives

method   If you can get hold of very small (and just-picked) courgettes all the better. For 4
people, slice 350 g (12 oz) young courgettes across into thin discs. Melt 25 g (1 oz)
butter in a large sauté pan. Add the courgettes and fry over a low heat until just
tender, sprinkling them with about 1 tablespoon each of chopped tarragon and chives
and a little salt and pepper about 1 minute after they have started cooking.

A Melange of Early Summer Vegetables

method   To serve 4, pour 50 ml (2 fl oz) extra virgin olive oil into a large sauté pan. Add 675 g
(1½ lb) of any combination of the following vegetables in order of how long they will
take to cook: young carrots, halved tiny artichokes, courgettes, peas, mangetout, pea
tops, spinach, haricots verts, just-cooked baby new potatoes, spring onions and a little
finely chopped garlic. Stir in a small bunch of flat-leaf parsley sprigs, halved chives and dill
sprigs. When they have just wilted down season with a little salt and pepper and serve.

Potatoes

Boiled Potatoes

This recipe should be subtitled 'teaching your grandmother to suck eggs' but I enjoy reading recipe books for dishes I could cook with my eyes shut. I find that a little nuance of detail in a very simple process can change everything. So this is how I boil potatoes.

method To serve 4 people, you will need about 675 g (1½ lb) of potatoes. First, the water. It needs to be well salted and by this I mean allow 1 teaspoon of salt to every 600 ml (1 pint) of water. This seems a lot but potatoes don't absorb as much as you might expect.

Next, the type of potatoes you choose. I like to use a waxy potato that won't break up in the water when cooking. Any potatoes freshly dug from the garden and boiled within minutes are a total delight – you can almost taste the tobacco scent of the leaves as you eat them – but when buying potatoes, there are some varieties that I particularly favour: La Ratte (also known as Cornichon or Asparges), Belle de Fontenay, Charlotte, Pink Fir Apple, a red-skinned potato called Roseval and Jersey Royals.

I'm not a great fan of potatoes boiled in their skins because of the oxalic taste caused by the acid present in the skins. I prefer to rub them or, if the skins are a little thicker, scrape them, so that only a little of the skin is left on. I'm always reminded of a poem by Robert Herrick called 'To Julia', and the two lines that say, 'A sweet disorder in the dress, kindles in clothes a wantonness'. I love wanton potatoes.

I always bring my roots and tubers up to the boil from cold and always add a good sprig of fresh mint to new potatoes. To check if they're cooked, pierce them with the tip of a knife and there should be no resistance. Drain them well and serve straight away.

Steamed Potatoes

One of the quiet delights I enjoy in France is a fillet of fish such as brill with beurre blanc or hollandaise sauce and a couple of steamed potatoes. Choose one of the varieties mentioned above – to serve 4, you will need about 675 g (1½ lb) of fairly large potatoes.

method Peel the potatoes, then cut each one lengthways into 6–8 chunky wedges. Pour 2.5 cm (1 inch) of water into a large pan and put a metal flower-petal steamer in it. Bring the water to a vigorous simmer, put the potatoes into the steamer and cover the pan with a tight-fitting lid. Steam for 10 minutes, until they are just tender. Season lightly with a few sea salt flakes and serve about 3 per person in a neat pile on each plate.

Crushed New Potatoes with Olive Oil and Basil

I got this idea from a chef friend of mine, Nick Nairn. It's such a simple idea but so fresh and exciting that you wonder why you've never come across it before.

method   For 4 people, rub or scrape most of the skin off about 675 g (1½ lb) well-flavoured new potatoes and cook them until just tender (see *Boiled Potatoes* on p. 223). Drain them well, tip them into a bowl or return them to the pan and add 85 ml (3 fl oz) good olive oil. Then gently crush each potato with the back of a fork against the sides of the bowl until it just bursts open. Season well with some sea salt and freshly ground black pepper and then gently fold in 3 tablespoons of finely shredded basil leaves and 25 g (1 oz) very thinly shaved Parmesan.

Roughly Cut Chips

method   Prepare the chips just before you are ready to cook them. To serve 4, take about 675 g (1½ lb) of medium-sized floury new potatoes, about 7.5 cm (3 inches) long, and lightly scrape them with a knife, the object being to leave some of the skin behind. Then cut each one lengthways into about 4 wedges. Quickly rinse them under cold water to remove the surface starch and dry them well on a tea towel.

Next, heat the oil. Usually the best oil to use for chips is groundnut because it is stable at high temperatures, but sunflower and vegetable oil are also fine. However, these chips, the idea for which came from Greece, are best fried in olive oil. Pour some oil into a large pan until it is about one-third full and heat it to 130°C/260°F. You'll need a chip basket here, too. Drop the chips into the basket and cook them for about 5 minutes, until tender when pierced with the tip of a knife. Lift them out and drain off the excess oil. You can do this stage in advance if you wish.

To finish, bring the oil up to 190°C/375°F and cook the chips in smaller batches for about 2 minutes, until they are crisp and golden. Lift them out of the pan and give them a good shake to remove the excess oil. Flick over some sea salt and serve straight away.

Sautéed Potatoes

The secret of a really good sautéed potato is to use only as much butter and olive oil as the potato can absorb. You then create a dry, sandy texture that is not at all greasy. The best potatoes to use are ones with a slightly floury texture, such as King Edward or Maris Piper. They have to be properly precooked, otherwise they will not absorb the buttery oil.

method   For 4 people, peel about 675 g (1½ lb) of potatoes. Cut them into 2.5 cm (1 inch) pieces and bring them to the boil in some well-salted water (see p. 223). Simmer until tender, then drain well and leave until the steam has died down and they have dried off a little.

    Heat equal quantities of butter and oil in a large, heavy-based frying pan. (Allow about 50 g (2 oz) of butter and 4 tablespoons of olive oil to 900 g (2 lb) peeled potatoes.) Toss them repeatedly over a medium heat for 10 minutes until they are crisp, dry, sandy and light-brown – the outside of the potatoes should break off a little as you sauté them to give them a nice crumbly, crunchy crust. Finish at the last minute with some freshly ground black pepper and a little salt.

Rice

It never ceases to amaze me how difficult it is to do the simplest cooking jobs in the kitchen – things like making omelettes, cooking vegetables and making gravy to go with roast beef. Cooking rice is another. The two main problems are the amount of liquid to add and the speed at which you cook it. By far the best piece of equipment for cooking rice is an electric rice cooker with a thermostat. Every Asian family I've ever met has one of these cookers, just as we have a kettle, and all of my ex-pat friends always come home to England with one. But it is a bit of a luxury and so I've worked out a pretty foolproof method for cooking rice without one.

The other little-discussed dilemma of rice cookery is whether to add salt. The Indians and Sri Lankans do add salt and, as Charmaine Solomon says in her excellent Encyclopaedia of Asian Food, *'Forgetting to add salt to the rice would be an unpardonable oversight for which the cook would surely be rebuked'. But in South-east Asia, China and Japan, salt is never added and this is simply because of the thoroughly satisfying contrast between the bland rice and salty additions such as soy, fish sauce and all the vast range of pickled and salted ingredients like pickled cabbage, salted black beans, shrimp paste and pickled ginger.*

Steamed Rice

serves 4
350 g (12 oz) basmati or Thai jasmine rice
600 ml (1 pint) boiling water
½ teaspoon salt

method
Tip the rice into a large saucepan and add the water and, if using basmati rice, the salt. Bring to the boil, cover with a tight-fitting lid, then reduce the heat to its lowest setting. Let it cook for 10 minutes, then take it off the heat and leave it undisturbed for a further 5 minutes. Uncover, fluff up the grains with a fork and the rice is ready to serve.

Salads

I'm a great enthusiast for fish with salads. There are a lot of recipes in this book which I have recommended eating with a salad. Here are a few of my favourites. By the way, if the salad you're making happens to have originated from another country where plum or beef tomatoes are the ones needed, I've come to the conclusion that in the UK you're better off buying the best-flavoured homegrown or vine-grown tomatoes. I've never bought a beef or plum tomato in the UK that matches anything you can get abroad.

Kachumber Salad

method   For 4 people, thinly slice 450 g (1 lb) of well-flavoured salad tomatoes. Cut 1 medium red onion into quarters lengthways and then thinly slice across. Layer in a shallow dish with 2 tablespoons of roughly chopped coriander, ¼ teaspoon of ground cumin, a good pinch of cayenne pepper, 1 tablespoon of white wine vinegar and ¼ teaspoon of salt. Serve straight away with any Indian-style dishes.

Tomato, Basil and Red Onion Salad

Having said what I have about not buying beef tomatoes, if you can get hold of a French variety called Marmande, *from Provence, you'll be well pleased with it. Otherwise, stick to vine-grown tomatoes for this salad.*

method   To serve 4, very thinly slice 450 g (1 lb) of large beef tomatoes and arrange them, slightly overlapping, in a large shallow dish. Sprinkle over 3 tablespoons of very finely chopped red onion or shallot and about 12 finely shredded basil leaves. Make a dressing by whisking together 1 teaspoon of white wine vinegar with 5 teaspoons of extra virgin olive oil, some salt and a little freshly ground black pepper. Drizzle this over the salad just before serving.

Tomato, Onion and Lime Salad

This salad idea comes from the Ronil Hotel, in Goa, India.

method   For 4 people, thinly slice 450 g (1 lb) ripe but firm tomatoes into slightly thicker slices and mix them in a shallow dish with 1 thinly sliced small red onion, separated into rings, 1 tablespoon of freshly squeezed lime juice and ¼ teaspoon of salt.

Italian Lemon and Mint Salad

Just occasionally in the UK you can get enormous lemons that come from southern Italy (I know because an enterprising Italian from Sicily supplied our deli with them for a year or so). They are about double the size of an ordinary lemon and have pith about 2.5 cm (1 inch) thick which is not at all bitter tasting, but rather surprisingly a bit like cucumber.

serves 4

2 large Italian lemons
A pinch of dried chilli flakes
½ garlic clove, finely chopped
A handful of mint leaves, coarsely chopped
50 ml (2 fl oz) extra virgin olive oil

method

Peel the zest off the lemons with a small sharp knife and discard (or use in another recipe). Cut each lemon into wedges and then cut each wedge across into chunky slices. Place in a large, shallow dish and sprinkle over the dried chilli flakes, garlic and some salt. Scatter over the mint leaves, then drizzle over the olive oil. Turn everything over gently until well mixed.

Soft Green Lettuce Salad with Olive Oil Dressing

During the '70s and '80s, soft, bog-standard corner-shop lettuces went out of favour and in came crisp American iceberg lettuces – then everyone woke up to the fact that the only notable feature of an iceberg lettuce was its crunch; flavour there was none. Thank goodness we can go back to those soft lettuces, which dressings like this one cling to so lovingly.

method

To serve 4, break about 225 g (8 oz) of any soft lettuce such as Tom Thumb, Little Gem or oak-leaf into leaves, wash them well and dry them off in a salad spinner. Just before serving, whisk together 1 tablespoon of white wine vinegar, 4 tablespoons of olive oil, ¼ teaspoon of caster sugar and a pinch of mashed garlic with a little salt. Drizzle this over the leaves, toss together very gently and serve.

Fine Leaf and Herb Salad with Lemon Oil Dressing

method

For 4 people, use 225 g (8 oz) of baby salad leaves mixed with herb sprigs such as flat-leaf parsley, tarragon, chervil, chives, fennel herb and dill. Simply drizzle over a little lemon olive oil or extra virgin olive oil and some salt and toss together until all the leaves are lightly coated. This doesn't need any vinegar or pepper.

Bitter Leaf Salad with Mustard Dressing

method   Bitter salad leaves and a dressing heavily flavoured with mustard go together pleasingly. To serve 4, use about 225 g (8 oz) of curly endive, chicory, dandelion, baby spinach leaves or radicchio, either individually or mixed. Wash them and then spin dry. Whisk together 1 tablespoon each of Dijon mustard and white wine vinegar, then gradually whisk in 5 tablespoons of extra virgin olive oil, some salt and freshly ground black pepper. Toss just enough of this through the leaves to coat them lightly and serve straight away. This goes extremely well with oily fish such as mackerel and herrings.

Patricia Wells' Cheesemaker's Salad

When I originally looked at the dressing ingredients for this salad – shallots steeped in red wine vinegar with double cream – I thought it wouldn't look very good and would taste harsh, but I was quite wrong. I should have known that Patricia Wells would be on to something special. She is American and has lived in France for ages, yet still has an infectious enthusiasm for the recipes she finds, in the same tradition as M. F. K. Fisher. She's got an unerring nose for great recipes and her own recipes are excellent, too. This is from her book At Home in Provence.

serves 4   **2 shallots, thinly sliced and separated into rings**
1 tablespoon good red wine vinegar
1 head of mild, delicately flavoured lettuce,
     such as butterhead
2–3 tablespoons double cream

method   In a large, shallow salad bowl, toss the shallots and vinegar together. Set aside for at least 15 minutes and up to 4 hours to soften the shallots. At serving time, add the lettuce, toss to coat with the vinegar and shallots and season with some fine sea salt. Add the cream, spoon by spoon, tossing gently to coat the leaves. Taste for seasoning and serve.

Little Gem Salad with a Garlic and Sherry Vinegar Dressing

method   For 4 people, cut 5 Little Gem lettuce hearts into quarters lengthways. Put them in a large, shallow dish, cut-side up. Gently heat 6 tablespoons of extra virgin olive oil in a pan, add 1 finely chopped clove of garlic and cook for a few seconds until the garlic starts to colour. Take off the heat and leave to cool, then whisk in 4 teaspoons of sherry vinegar and some salt to taste. Spoon over the lettuce hearts and sprinkle with freshly ground black pepper.

If you are like me, you will view a recipe with a cross-reference to another recipe at the back of the book with a sinking heart. It means finding even more ingredients, and doing some work in advance. However, it has to be said that fresh homemade stocks, sauces, pastes and other essentials are often so much better than shop-bought and these, in this chapter, are well worth the effort.

Take the masala paste. The secret to the best Indian and South-east Asian food is often just a matter of using fresh aromatic curry pastes, alive with ginger, garlic, tamarind, chilli and roasted cumin and coriander. My friend Rui in Goa, has a vast spice grinder, the size of a cement mixer, going every day and that's why his food is so good. In Singapore there's a restaurant called the Banana Leaf Apollo and I have very fond memories of eating fish-head curry there. The occasion was made so vivid by the presence of an ancient, belt-driven, stone-wheeled grinder, which was busy crushing cloves, cinnamon and cardamoms for the curries. The aromas and flavours from the open kitchen floated into the restaurant all through our long humid lunch. Our bowls of grouper's head curry and banana leaves laiden with pickles, and the poppadoms handed to me out of a deep, rusty biscuit tin, tasted so fresh … so vibrant, and alive.

Stocks, sauces and essentials

Your recipes will taste so much better if your stocks and sauces are freshly made. Most of the pastes will keep for a few weeks in the fridge and still taste better than anything shop-bought. Other recipes, oddities like preserved lemon, roasted tomatoes and salt cod, are here because you won't buy anything as good. This is the chapter on which everything else hangs.

Stocks

Fish Stock

makes

1.2 litres

(2 pints)

1 kg (2¼ lb) fish bones, such as lemon sole,
    brill and plaice
2.25 litres (4 pints) water
1 onion, chopped
1 fennel bulb, chopped
100 g (4 oz) celery, sliced
100 g (4 oz) carrot, chopped
25 g (1 oz) button mushrooms, sliced
1 sprig of thyme

method

Put the fish bones and water into a large pan, bring just to the boil and simmer very gently for 20 minutes. Strain through a muslin-lined sieve into a clean pan, add the vegetables and thyme and bring back to the boil. Simmer for 35 minutes or until reduced to about 1.2 litres (2 pints). Strain once more and use or store as required.

Chicken Stock

makes

1.75 litres

(3 pints)

Bones from a 1.5 kg (3 lb) uncooked chicken,
    or 450 g (1 lb) chicken wings
1 large carrot, chopped
2 celery sticks, sliced
2 leeks, sliced
2 fresh or dried bay leaves
2 sprigs of thyme
2.25 litres (4 pints) water

method

Put all the ingredients into a large pan and bring just to the boil, skimming off any scum from the surface as it appears. Leave to simmer very gently for 2 hours – it is important not to let it boil as this will force the fat from even the leanest chicken and make the stock cloudy. Strain the stock through a muslin-lined sieve and use as required. If not using immediately, leave to cool, then chill and refrigerate or freeze for later use.

Vegetable Nage (Stock)

makes
approx
2.5 litres
(4 ½ pints)

1 fennel bulb
1 large onion, peeled
4 celery sticks
A handful of button mushrooms
½ teaspoon salt
1 teaspoon black peppercorns
2 bay leaves
3 sprigs of thyme
½ teaspoon fennel seeds
300 ml (10 fl oz) white wine

method   Roughly chop all the vegetables and put them into a pan with the salt, peppercorns, herbs, fennel seeds and enough water just to cover everything. Bring to the boil and simmer for 20 minutes. Take the pan off the heat and add the wine, cover and leave somewhere cool overnight.

The next day strain the stock into another pan and use or store as required.

Sauces

Hollandaise Sauce

serves 4

2 tablespoons water

2 egg yolks

225 g (8 oz) *Clarified Butter*
   (see p. 239), warmed

Juice of ¹/₂ lemon

A good pinch of cayenne pepper

³/₄ teaspoon salt

method

Put the water and egg yolks into a stainless steel or glass bowl set over a pan of simmering water, making sure that the base of the bowl is not touching the water. Whisk until voluminous and creamy. Remove the bowl from the pan and gradually whisk in the clarified butter until thick. Whisk in the lemon juice, cayenne pepper and salt. This sauce is best used as soon as it is made but will hold for up to 2 hours if kept covered in a warm place, such as over a pan of warm water.

Quick Hollandaise Sauce

method

Using the same quantities as above, put the egg yolks, lemon juice and water into a liquidizer. Turn on the machine and then slowly pour in the butter through the hole in the lid. Season with cayenne pepper and the salt.

Mayonnaise

This recipe includes instructions for making mayonnaise in a liquidizer or by hand. It is lighter when made mechanically because the process uses a whole egg, and it's very quick, but I still prefer making it by hand since I like to do as much as possible in the kitchen by hand. You can use either sunflower oil or olive oil – or a mixture of the two, if you prefer.

makes
300 ml
(10 fl oz)

1 egg or 2 egg yolks

2 teaspoons white wine vinegar

¹/₂ teaspoon salt

300 ml (10 fl oz) oil

method

To make the mayonnaise in a machine, put the whole egg, vinegar and salt into a liquidizer or food processor. Turn on the machine and then slowly add the oil through the hole in the lid until you have a thick emulsion.

To make the mayonnaise by hand, make sure all the ingredients are at room temperature. Put the egg yolks, vinegar and salt into a mixing bowl and then rest the bowl on a cloth to stop it slipping. Using a wire whisk, beat the oil into the egg mixture a few drops at a time until you have incorporated it all. Once you have added the same volume of oil as the original mixture of egg yolks and vinegar, you can add it more quickly. This mayonnaise will keep in the fridge for about a week.

Mustard Mayonnaise

See the recipe for Mayonnaise *above if you prefer to make it by hand.*

makes
300 ml
(10 fl oz)

1 tablespoon English mustard

1 egg

1 tablespoon white wine vinegar

³/₄ teaspoon salt

A few turns of the white pepper mill

300 ml (10 fl oz) sunflower oil

method

Put the mustard, egg, vinegar, salt and pepper into a liquidizer. Turn on the machine and then gradually add the oil through the hole in the lid until you have a thick emulsion.

Aïoli

makes
175 ml
(6 fl oz)

4 garlic cloves, peeled
½ teaspoon salt
1 medium egg yolk
2 teaspoons lemon juice
175 ml (6 fl oz) extra virgin olive oil

method

Put the garlic cloves on a chopping board and crush them under the blade of a large knife. Sprinkle them with the salt and then use the flat of the knife blade to work them into a smooth paste. Scrape the paste into a bowl and add the egg yolk and lemon juice. Using an electric hand mixer, whisk everything together and then very gradually whisk in the olive oil to make a thick mayonnaise-like mixture.

Tapenade

makes 1
small jar

75 g (3 oz) pitted black olives (drained and
** rinsed if preserved in brine)**
4 anchovy fillets
25 g (1 oz) capers, drained and rinsed
3 garlic cloves, peeled
75 ml (3 fl oz) olive oil
Freshly ground black pepper

method

Put the olives, anchovies, capers and garlic into a food processor and pulse 3 or 4 times. Then turn the processor on and add the oil in a thin, steady stream through the lid. Stir in black pepper to taste, spoon the mixture into a sterilized glass jar, seal and store in the fridge for up to 3 months. Use as required.

Essentials

Preserved Lemons

The lemons must be small ones or they just won't fit or fill the jar.

makes
1 jar

3–4 small lemons per 500 ml (17 fl oz)
  Kilner jar
75 g (3 oz) salt per jar
Fresh lemon juice

method

Cut the lemons almost into quarters, leaving them attached at the stalk end. Sprinkle as much salt as you can into the cuts, push them back into shape and push into the jar, stalk-end down, packing them in tightly – they will fit with a little persuasion. Sprinkle over the rest of the salt, seal and leave for 4–5 days, giving the jar a shake every now and then, until they have produced quite a lot of juice. Then top up the jar with the lemon juice so that the lemons are completely covered, seal and leave for a couple of weeks before using.

Oven-roasted Tomatoes

serves 4

750 g (1½ lb) ripe plum tomatoes
1½ teaspoons sea salt flakes
Freshly ground black pepper

method

Pre-heat the oven to 240°C/475°F/Gas Mark 9. Cut the tomatoes in half and place them cut-side up in a lightly oiled shallow roasting tin. Sprinkle over the salt and some pepper and roast for 15 minutes.

Lower the oven temperature to 150°C/300°F/Gas Mark 2 and roast them for a further 1½ hours until shrivelled to about half their original size and concentrated in flavour. Remove and serve warm, drizzled with a little olive oil if you wish, or leave to cool.

Roasted Red Peppers

method   You can do this one of two ways: either spear the stalk end on a fork and turn the pepper in the flame of a gas burner or blowtorch until the skin has blistered and blackened; or pre-heat the oven to 220°C/425°F/Gas Mark 7 and roast the peppers for 20–25 minutes, turning once, until the skin is black.

Leave the peppers to cool and then break them in half (saving any juices from the centre if appropriate to the dish) and remove the stalks, seeds and skin.

Skinned, Seeded and Diced Tomatoes

method   Plunge the tomatoes into boiling water for about 30 seconds. Transfer them to a bowl of cold water and then peel off the skins. (You can also remove the skins by spearing the tomatoes with a fork and turning them over a gas flame until the skin splits.) Cut them into quarters and remove the seeds. Cut the flesh into small, neat dice.

Salting Fresh Cod

method   Sprinkle a 1 cm (½ inch) layer of salt in a plastic container, put the cod on top and then completely cover it in another thick layer of salt. Cover and refrigerate overnight. The salt will have turned to brine by the following morning. The next day, remove the cod from the brine and rinse it under cold water.

Tamarind Water

method   Take a piece of tamarind pulp about the size of a tangerine and place it in a bowl with 150 ml (5 fl oz) warm water. With your fingers, work the paste into the water until it has broken down and all the seeds have been released. Now strain the slightly syrupy mixture through a fine sieve into a bowl and discard the fibrous material left in the sieve. It is now ready to use.

Clarified Butter

method Place the butter in a small pan and leave it over a very low heat until it has melted. Then skim off any scum from the surface and pour off the clear (clarified) butter into a bowl, leaving behind the milky white solids that will have settled on the bottom of the pan.

Beurre Manié

method Blend equal quantities of softened butter and plain flour together into a smooth paste. Cover and keep in the fridge until needed. It will keep for the same period of time as butter.

Pastes

Laksa Spice Paste

makes
1 jar

25 g (1 oz) dried shrimps

3 red finger chillies, roughly chopped

2 lemongrass stalks, outer leaves removed,
the rest roughly chopped

25 g (1 oz) candle nuts or unroasted
cashew nuts

2 garlic cloves, peeled

2.5 cm (1 inch) fresh root ginger,
roughly chopped

1 teaspoon turmeric powder

1 small onion, roughly chopped

1 teaspoon ground coriander

Juice of 1 lime

2 tablespoons cold water (or enough to
make a smooth paste)

method
Cover the dried shrimps with warm water and leave them to soak for 15 minutes.
Drain and put into a food processor with the rest of the ingredients. Blend to a
smooth paste.

Thai Red Curry Paste

makes
1 jar

5 large red finger chillies, roughly chopped

2.5 cm (1 inch) fresh root ginger,
roughly chopped

2 lemongrass stalks, outer leaves removed, the
rest roughly chopped

6–8 garlic cloves, roughly chopped

3 shallots, roughly chopped

1 teaspoon ground coriander

1 teaspoon ground cumin

1 teaspoon *blachan* (shrimp paste)

2 teaspoons paprika

$\frac{1}{2}$ teaspoon turmeric powder

1 teaspoon salt

1 tablespoon sunflower oil

method
Put everything into a food processor and blend to a smooth paste.

Vindaloo Curry Paste

makes
1 jar

40 g (1½ oz) medium hot dried red chillies

1 small onion

1 teaspoon black peppercorns

1½ teaspoons whole cloves

7.5 cm (3 inch) piece of cinnamon stick

1 teaspoon cumin seeds

2.5 cm (1 inch) fresh root ginger

4 tablespoons roughly chopped garlic

A walnut-sized piece of tamarind pulp,
   without seeds

1 teaspoon light soft brown sugar

2 tablespoons coconut vinegar or white
   wine vinegar

method   Cover the chillies with plenty of hot water and leave them to soak overnight.
     The next day, pre-heat the oven to 230°C/450°F/Gas Mark 8.
     Place the unpeeled onion on the middle rack of the oven and roast for 1 hour, until
the centre is soft and nicely caramelized. Remove and leave to cool, then peel off the skin.
     Drain the chillies, squeeze out the excess water and then roughly chop them. Put
the peppercorns, cloves, cinnamon and cumin seeds into a mortar or spice grinder and
grind to a fine powder. Tip the powder into a food processor and add the roasted
onion, chillies, ginger, garlic, tamarind pulp, sugar and vinegar. Blend to a smooth paste.

Goan Masala Paste

makes
1 jar

1 teaspoon cumin seeds

2 teaspoons coriander seeds

2 teaspoons black peppercorns

1 teaspoon cloves

1 teaspoon turmeric powder

100 g (4 oz) red finger chillies,
   roughly chopped

1 teaspoon salt

6 garlic cloves, roughly chopped

1 teaspoon light muscovado sugar

1 tablespoon *Tamarind Water* (see p. 238)

5 cm (2 inches) fresh root ginger,
   roughly chopped

2 tablespoons red wine vinegar

method   Grind the cumin seeds, coriander seeds, peppercorns and cloves to a fine powder.
     Transfer to a food processor with the rest of the ingredients and blend to a
smooth paste.

Some thoughts on the ingredients

Anchovies

These come either salted or preserved in oil and in all the recipes in this book, I mean anchovies in olive oil. Not every tin of anchovies in oil is the same. The best are in olive oil but most are tinned in vegetable oil so check out the tin and generally the more you pay, the better the quality will be. You can also buy marinated anchovies similar to the recipe on page 115 in some good Italian delicatessens.

Asafoetida

This is a very pungent resin from a plant, *Ferula assa-foetida*, grown in Afghanistan and Iran. It smells awful in its raw state but once incorporated in a dish it adds a pleasant, unusual background taste and also acts as an important anti-flatulent in lentil dishes. The rather taboo subject of flatulence caused by pulses is well understood in Indian and Thai cookery and counteractive and effective ingredients abound. Asafoetida can be bought as a pure resin, or powdered and is often mixed with rice flour. The resin is very strong so use it sparingly and just scratch a little straight from the lump with a knife. The powder is much milder so can be used by the pinchful. It can only be found in Asian grocers but if you do get hold of some, make sure you keep it wrapped in lots of clingfilm or the smell will permeate everything else in your cupboard. It will last indefinitely.

Blachan (dried shrimp paste)

This is a pungent paste made from fermented prawns. It smells awful but is one of the essential ingredients in Far Eastern cuisine. It is either sold in hard slabs or cakes from which you chip off small pieces, or in a soft paste-like form in cans and jars (or from plastic washing-up bowls as in Thailand) and keeps indefinitely without refrigeration. It is always cooked before eating and is either fried in oil during the first stages of the dish, on its own or as part of a curry paste, or it is grilled or roasted if being added to other uncooked ingredients as in some sambals.

Black olives

There are some very good black olives, and some very bad ones. No wonder so many people dislike olives, because it's not until you've tasted a good one that you can see what all the fuss is about. Some of the best olives in Italy come from Liguria and Tuscany but the Greek Kalamata olive also has a distinctive, strong, salty flavour. Quite a few of the recipes in this book call for pitted olives. Removing the stones yourself from some good-quality olives will give you a much better flavour than the already pitted ones.

Black pepper

It is remarkable how pepper can differ in flavour. In Goa I came across black peppercorns which also had a hint of allspice and cloves, and in my kitchen back here in Padstow we use Wynard black pepper from the Kerala region of India which has large grains and a wonderfully aromatic, spicy flavour. It is important to always freshly grind pepper as it loses its flavour very quickly. I have found that pepper grinders with a Peugeot grinding mechanism are the best and you must only ever grind in one direction. Twisting the grinder back and forth wears it out very quickly.

Capers

These are the matured but unopened flower buds of a Mediterranean bush, *Capparis spinosa*, which are preserved in vinegar or salt. This process allows their piquant flavour to develop and it complements all types of fish. One type of caper in vinegar are the small *nonpareilles* ones from Provence. Tapenade, the black olive paste made with capers (amongst other things), takes its name from the Provençal word for capers, *tapéno*. Sicily produces very good salted capers. Once a jar of the capers in vinegar is opened, keep it in the fridge and make sure the remaining capers are kept covered by the liquid. You will need to rinse a little of the salt off salted capers so that the finished dish does not become over salty.

Chillies

Chilli sauce (see Sauces p. 246)

Dried chilli flakes This is a convenient, commercially prepared form of crushed dried red chilli. It doesn't add a specific flavour but is a useful way of adding a little background heat. It is also more appropriate in sauces than cayenne pepper because it doesn't colour the sauce, gives more of a chilli flavour than just some heat, and can easily be strained out at the end if you wish. It's in most supermarkets alongside all the other jarred spices.

Dried choricero and ñora peppers These are two types of mild, sweet dried red chillies from Spain which are a main ingredient in romesco sauce, the creamy-textured, bread-based sauce served there with fried fish. There is no real substitute for these chillies but you can buy them mail order from the Cool Chile Company (see p. 249 for the address).

Fresh chillies The range of fresh chillies available in supermarkets is getting better and I hope they will soon be sold by their name rather than just green or red. This will allow recipe writers to accurately specify the flavour and heat required. There are over 100 different types of chilli in the world but we see very few of them in the UK at the moment. Not all chillies are searingly hot and any chilli can be rendered milder if the ribs and the seeds are removed first. These are the parts that contain the hot oil called capsaicin. In 1912, a man called Scoville measured this capsaicin heat, or 'pungency', in units ranging from 0 to over 15 million to indicate the heat of each chilli. Modified versions of his rankings have been adopted over the years, and I've taken a standard range from 1 (very mild) to 10 (very hot), used by Mark Miller in his chilli book. The hottest chilli in the world is the *habanero* chilli which registers 10, and next the scotch bonnet (9), both favoured in Caribbean cooking. Curiously these are often available in the supermarket, possibly because they also look quite pretty, a bit like mini multi-coloured peppers, rather than because of their flavour. Another very hot chilli is the tiny red and green Thai birdseye chilli (7–8) which you tend to use whole as they are a bit small for deseeding, so a little will go a long way. You will also probably come across the long, slender red and green chillies called Dutch chillies, sometimes called Lombok (6) which come from Holland which offer a pretty average kick acceptable to most people's tastes and which I refer to as finger chillies in the recipes. The best general-purpose chilli is the *jalapeño* (5.5) which is beginning to appear in the UK.

Nam prik (see Sauces p. 246)

Pasilla chillies In Mexico, chillies usually have a different name when fresh to the name given it when it is dried, which is a bit confusing. *Pasilla* is the dried name of the *chilaca* chilli. The *chilaca* is about 15 cm (6 inches) long, black, shiny and smooth. The dried *pasilla* chilli tastes of smoke and liquorice and is very popular with seafood in that beautiful country. It's not too hot either. Incidentally, the dried version of the *poblano* chilli is called *ancho* and is the main ingredient in *mole* sauce after chocolate. I saw a chicken dish described as 'Chicken and Mole' on a Mexican menu which appealed to my puerile sense of humour.

Sambal oelek (ulek) This literally means crushed chillies and is a coarsely crushed mixture of chillies and salt. If you can't find jars of it under this name, you will easily find small jars of minced red chilli paste alongside the other spices and herbs in the supermarket, and it's essentially the same thing.

Sweet chilli sauce (see Sauces p. 247)

Chinese rice wine
This is used extensively in China and is made from glutinous rice, yeast and water. It is usually only available from Chinese supermarkets but a dry sherry such as a fino or manzanilla makes a very good substitute.

Chorizo sausage
This is a coarse pork sausage flavoured with paprika and garlic which is used widely all over Spain. The best ones are the small, deep red sausages about 10 cm (4 inches) in length, which are sold in strings, and although not cheap, a little goes quite a long way. The flavour is well worth the extra expense.

Coconut
Creamed coconut This is the thicker cream from coconut milk, chilled and sold in a small, hard block. Small amounts, chipped from the block, are useful for thickening sauces and curries towards the end of cooking but it does not have the same fresh taste of canned or fresh coconut milk.

Coconut milk Coconut milk is not, as some people believe, the liquid from the inside of the coconut (which is in fact called coconut water) but the liquid extracted from coconut flesh. This can be bought in cans from almost every supermarket these days and is used in most soupy Thai curries and a lot of southern Indian, Sri Lankan and South-east Asian dishes. By not shaking the can before opening, you can lift off the thicker cream that forms on top of the milk and use it separately as required. But in most cases, as in this book, just shake the can before using. I have tried many different brands of coconut milk over the years and my favourite to date is made by Amoy. It has a good colour and nice consistency, appropriate to all of my dishes.

Coconut vinegar (see Vinegars p. 248)

Coriander root
This is still very hard to come by in the West but it is a very important part of cooking in Thailand and the Far East. Try in your Asian grocers, or simply buy large bunches of fresh coriander and use more of the lower, thicker stalks than you normally would.

Cornmeal
This is made by grinding dried kernels of hard varieties of corn and comes in two textures – fine or coarse. The finer one is usually used for breads, cakes, batters etc and the coarser one for coating fish and shellfish for frying, as in the recipe for *Deep-fried Soft-shell Crabs in a Cornmeal Crust* on page 219. It also comes in different colours – yellow, white and even blue from the south-west of America, but when mentioned in this book, I mean the yellow one.

Crème fraîche
Crème fraîche has a high butter fat content and slightly sharp taste which matures as the cream gets older. It goes well in both savoury and sweet dishes, the younger, fresher-tasting one being more appropriate for sweeter dishes. The taste comes from lactic acid.

Curry leaves

These are the leaves of a small tree from the hilly regions of India and they have an aromatic, spicy flavour. They are used in curries when fresh. When dried they're not worth bothering about – a bit like dried parsley. Fresh leaves can be found in Asian grocers and sometimes in larger supermarkets. They can be frozen in plastic bags for later use. There is no real substitute so simply omit them if you can't find any.

Curry pastes

You will not always have the time, or all of the ingredients to make your own curry paste, but there are some very good ready-made ones around these days. I have tried quite a few over the years, but my favourites to date are made by Pataks. They have a very wide selection, but as long as you always have a mild one (I like their garam masala and korma pastes), medium hot (the rogan josh paste is a good one) and a Madras one you should be able to make a passing resemblance to any curry, though you can never really match a freshly-ground paste.

Dried black beans

Beans are essential to the Mexican diet and there this bean is known as the *frijole negro*. Much loved by the Mayans it is always cooked with a herb called *epazote*. It is also known as the black kidney bean and should be treated in a similar way to the red variety, i.e. boiled vigorously for 15 minutes before being left to simmer until tender. If you don't find them in the supermarket you should have more luck in a health food shop.

Dried porcini mushrooms

Drying mushrooms concentrates their flavour and they are almost more valuable dried than they are fresh. They need to be reconstituted in water before using, and remember to save this liquor for stocks and sauces because it has such a great flavour. I like the idea of fish with 'gravy' and gravy in this case to me is the flavour and colour of stock cooked with dried porcini. See the recipe for *Seared Swordfish with Mushroom Gravy and Garlic and Olive Oil Mash* on page 172.

Dried shrimps

These are sun-dried peeled shrimps which are used in many dishes from China and the Far East, such as the *Green Papaya Salad* on page 54. They are sold in Chinese and other Asian grocery shops and come loose, sealed in plastic bags. They should have a deep salmon pink colour and give slightly when squeezed. If they are dark, rock-hard and smell of ammonia leave them well alone.

Galangal

This is a rhizome root related to ginger and is available in most oriental food shops and some good supermarkets. It has much longer, thinner stems than ginger however, with paler skin and pink spikes on the end of each one. It will keep well in the fridge for up to 2 weeks. Ginger is a perfect substitute.

Hominy grits

This is white corn that has been treated in an alkaline solution so that the skin of the kernels dissolves. It is then dried, enriched with some of the nutrients lost during the processing and then ground. Most supermarket grits are ground a little too fine so look for coarse-ground, whole-grain grits. When cooked they take on a texture not unlike that of polenta, or cornmeal as it is called in America, which would make a good substitute, although much more yellow in colour than true grits. They are traditionally cooked in water or milk but I like to use stock and add plenty of seasoning to give them much more flavour than you would normally find in the States.

Ibérico and Serrano ham

The Spanish adore ham, and no wonder as they produce some of the best in the world. Ibérico ham is considered to be one of the most superior cured hams of Spain, taken from the Ibérico negro pig which has been allowed to run free in the oak forests, getting plenty of exercise and feasting on acorns. This gives the fat a golden colour and marbles the meat to make it incredibly tender and full of flavour. Serrano ham is another cured ham but it's not quite as good as Ibérico and comes from farmed pigs rather than those allowed to run wild. It is also far leaner than the more expensive hams, but it's still very good and excellent for cooking with. It would be a bit of a waste to use the very best cured hams for cooking – these are better saved for eating on their own, perhaps with a glass of chilled manzanilla sherry so that you can savour their distinctive and fine flavour. Serrano ham is easily available in the supermarket now, but Ibérico ham is still only found in specialist shops and Spanish delicatessens, but as these are both quite similar to the Italian Parma ham or French Bayonne ham you could use either one of these instead if you wish.

Kaffir lime leaves

These are the leaves of a gnarled and thick-skinned lime which has almost juiceless fruit. They are not easy to come by but you should find them in a good Thai grocery shop. Buy them up when you see them and store them in a plastic bag in the freezer until needed. The fresh leaves are quite distinctive in shape, having a double leaf on each stem, and add a fantastic flavour of lime to all Thai foods. They can be used whole in curries but are removed before eating. You can also finely shred them so they can be eaten. They're an important ingredient in most Thai curry pastes. Dried leaves are sometimes available in jars but they give an inferior, less-authentic flavour. The only alternative is to add a strip of pared lime zest and a little freshly squeezed lime juice towards the end of cooking.

Lemongrass

This is the thick, moist stem of a tropical grass which has a lovely lemony taste and smell. When cooked it imparts a fresh citrus taste and there is no real substitute. A little freshly grated lemon zest is the only alternative. Supermarkets are getting better at stocking it and if it's not on its own on the fresh herb rack, it's often included in packets of mixed Thai herbs.

Noodles

Flat rice noodles You might be lucky to find these in some of the larger supermarkets but, as yet, they are not so easy to come by. They are readily available, however, in Asian grocers. Because they are very delicate and break up very easily, they should be soaked first for about 1 hour in cold water, not hot, to reconstitute them. They can then either be dipped into boiling water for 2–3 seconds if being served like pasta, or can be added to a dish like the *Pad Thai Noodles with Prawns* on page 64 and cooked with the other ingredients for a minute or two until tender and heated through.

Medium egg noodles These can now be found in every supermarket, usually alongside the rice and pasta. They are yellow in colour and are sold dried, in looped nests, which need to be loosened into separate strands once they have been soaked. Contrary to the instructions on the packet, I think they are best dropped into a pan of boiling water, brought back to the boil and then removed from the heat and left to soak for 4 minutes. This way they do not get too soft, but rather retain a little bit of bite like perfectly cooked pasta.

Vermicelli noodles Sometimes labelled stir-fry noodles, these are available from both supermarkets and oriental grocers. These, too, are sold dried, and need to be soaked before using but it is important not to let them get too soft or they tend to stick together in one lump. Just drop them into a pan of boiling water, take the pan off the heat and leave them to soak for just 1 minute. Use straight away or they will eventually stick back together again.

Okra or Ladies' fingers

This is a vegetable that people either love or hate due to the fact that it becomes very soft and slimy in the centre after long cooking. However, it is very popular in Creole, Caribbean, Indian and Greek cooking. In Creole cooking, it is an indispensable ingredient in gumbo (see page 208) where it is chopped up into small pieces so that the slimy interior can escape and thicken the stew. In Indian cuisine, where it is called *bhindi*, it is added to bhajis, curries or split open, stuffed with a mixture of spices and deep fried. I was in a supermarket and I saw a well-dressed oriental girl by a tray of okra, taking them one at a time into her hand and snapping the pointed tips off each one. Intrigued, I asked her what she was doing, and she said that if they gave a nice snap then they were fresh – if they bent over they were old and stale and not worth buying.

Olive oil

There are two main categories of olive oil – ordinary olive oil, and extra virgin olive oil, and both are essential ingredients in central and southern Italian cooking. You can buy a Greek brand of ordinary olive oil, and olive oil from numerous other European countries, but I prefer the Italian ones, especially those from Tuscany, and those from the Provençal region of southern France. Cold-pressed, extra virgin olive oil is the oil taken from the first pressing of the olives and must have no more than 1% acidity (and the best has 0.5%). It has a deeper green colour and a more assertive and fruity flavour. Some believe that you should not cook with extra virgin olive oil, but rather reserve its use for salads etc. However on a recent trip to Naples they used nothing else but, and in most of my dishes in the Italian chapter, I have used a well-flavoured, though not exceptionally expensive, extra virgin oil in all the recipes. After extra virgin oil is pressed, there are all sorts of 'virgin' oils produced, of varying qualities. In descending order of quality, you get *soprafino* virgin, fine virgin and virgin, the last of which can have up to 4% acidity. Ordinary olive oil, which comes from subsequent pressings and is processed and then flavoured with a little virgin olive oil, is fine for deep-frying and mayonnaise, where the flavour of extra virgin olive oil would be a little overpowering and would also work out quite expensive.

Palm sugar

This comes from the sap of the coconut palm and in Thailand we bought it in attractive little cakes shaped like flying saucers. They were, however, very hard and needed to be broken up and then softened with a little water before use. Palm sugar has a rich caramel-like flavour and a good substitute is light muscovado sugar, or soft brown sugar at a push.

Pasta

Surprising though this may seem, the Italians do not use fresh pasta as much as the dried variety. There are two brands that I would recommend, although most supermarket pasta is perfectly acceptable. Look out for De Cecco, which comes in a turquoise blue and yellow packet, or Voiello, which is made in Parma, Italy. I like to cook my pasta in lots of boiling, well-salted water, and cook it for the least time possible to keep it *al dente*. It should definitely still have quite a bit of bite left in it when you come to drain it.

Pickled ginger

This is made in both Japan and China and can be found in oriental grocers and some larger supermarkets. The Japanese one usually comes in small clear plastic boxes and is salmon pink in colour, and often slightly sweetened. Chinese pickled ginger is usually white and unsweetened. It is an essential accompaniment to sashimi, but is also nice added to stir-fries as in the recipe for *Jack's Mud Crab Omelette* on page 88.

Polenta

This is the name given to the yellow cornmeal of Italy which is made into the porridge-like mixture and used to accompany fish, game and meat dishes. It is available finely and coarsely ground but for the recipes in this book, I am referring to the coarser variety, which has a better texture when cooked. It is available in most supermarkets these days, usually stacked near to the pasta.

Rice

Basmati rice This comes from the state of Haryana, north of Delhi, in the northern regions of India and has a distinctive flavour and delicate texture. Pick it over for small stones etc first, then rinse in cold water to remove the excess starch if you wish. It swells up to three times its length and has a fantastic smell during cooking which always reminds me of India. Tilda rice is as good a brand as any.

Risotto rice This includes Arborio and Carnaroli rice, as well as Maratelli, Roma and Vialone. Most rice labelled as risotto rice is usually Arborio and as with many ingredients, you will get a better quality rice if you pay just that bit more for it. Risotto rice is a short grain rice, essential for making a risotto because the outside of the grains breaks down during cooking, thickening some of the liquid, but the centre still retains some bite and gives the finished dish its classic creamy texture. There is no real substitute for risotto rice, but happily it is now widely available. Carnaroli is the variety favoured by restaurant cooks because it keeps its bite for longer – a bit more forgiving if you neglect the pan for a minute or two.

Thai jasmine rice As the name suggests, this is a jasmine-scented rice from Thailand. It is similar in appearance to basmati rice and tends to cling together in small lumps during cooking. It is the perfect accompaniment to all the Thai and Far Eastern dishes in this book and for instructions on how to cook it, see page 226.

Saffron

Some of the best saffron in the world comes from the La Mancha region of Spain and is the most expensive and highly prized spice in the world. It is the deep red-orange stamen of the purple crocus, three of which are removed from the centre of each flower by hand and dried to prevent it rotting before being packaged and sold on. It is sold in stamen or powdered form, but I prefer the stamens which have a fresher flavour and it is also easier to judge the quality when intact. Saffron also comes from Iran, which is said to be comparable in flavour though the stamens are slightly shorter, as well as India and Morocco. Last time I was in Goa I bought a large quantity of saffron off a beach trader. I was very clever; I made him let me smell it and dissolve a little in some water, and yes it was saffron. I came away with 6 packets of the world's most expensive marigold petals.

Salt

It might seem a little odd to have salt in this section of the book, but as with all ingredients, salts differ. Most salt that we buy is rock salt which is removed from underground seams, processed and crystallized to varying degrees of fineness. This includes 'cooking' salt, and 'table' salt which is often mixed with iodine and magnesium carbonate to prevent it from absorbing moisture from the atmosphere and becoming lumpy. Coarse rock salt has simply been allowed to crystallize into larger crystals and can be used in a salt mill. Sea salt, as you would imagine, comes from the sea. The sea water is trapped in enclosed areas known as salt pans, where it is left to evaporate and crystallize. *Fleur de sel* is the first layer of salt scraped off the top, which is full of impurities and minerals which give it a more complex flavour, and a mauve colour when fresh. Maldon salt from Essex comes in small flakes and has a good flavour and looks good sprinkled on top of foods for presentation.

Salted black beans

These beans are still only available in oriental food shops and either come in cans, or loose, packed either into cardboard tubs or plastic bags. Because they are preserved in salt they need a brief rinse under cold water before using. They are much used in Chinese cookery, so much so that I would identify them as one of the definitive flavours.

Sauces

Chilli sauce This is very similar to sweet chilli sauce but without the sugar. As this is a popular ingredient in many cuisines, such as Indian, Mexican, Jamaican, American etc, you can get an endless variety of sauces and they vary greatly in heat and flavour. When we were in Charleston, South Carolina, we bought one so hot we had to sign a waiver against all claims for any damage incurred on eating it. So go slowly and start with the milder ones until your taste buds adjust. Some sauces have garlic and ginger added too, but in all recipes where it is called for in this book, I mean one made from just chillies, vinegar and salt.

Dark soy sauce This is not a new ingredient but I just wanted to give you some advice about which one to buy. It is made from fermented and salted soya beans and in my opinion the best one to go for is the Japanese variety called Kikkoman which is slightly richer with a deeper, slightly sweeter flavour than the average soy sauce. Chinese 'Superior' soy sauce is also worth seeking out in Chinese grocers.

Ketjap manis (Sweet soy sauce) This is very different to normal soy sauce and the two are not interchangeable. It is an Indonesian-style soy sauce to which sugar and a special blend of spices have been added to give it a sweet but piquant taste. It is also much thicker than normal soy sauce.

Light soy sauce This is lighter in colour, thinner and much saltier than dark soy sauce and is usually used when it is desirable not to change the colour of a dish.

Nam prik This name is given to a wide variety of cooked or uncooked chilli-hot sauces or dips. The most common is a cooked *nam prik*, a sweet, hot, oily sauce made of chillies and shrimps and sold in bottles or jars. Again, you'll find this in Asian grocery shops, and sometimes large supermarkets if you're lucky.

Sweet chilli sauce This is basically a chilli sauce made with chillies, sugar, vinegar and salt. There are a number of makes on the market but the best one by far is 'Lingham's Chilli Sauce', and as they say on the label, it is made from 100% fresh chillies with no preservatives, no tomato paste or purée, no added flavourings and no food conditioners. And it tastes great, especially with grilled sausages.

Thai fish sauce Also called *nam pla* in Thailand, this is a clear, amber-coloured liquid derived from the salting and fermenting of anchovies and other small fish. It adds that unmistakable taste found in much Thai food, as they use this sauce like we use salt. It is an essential ingredient and there is no adequate substitute. It is getting easier to find these days but if you don't find it in your supermarket, please ask them to get some in. My favourite one is called 'Squid brand' and comes in large bottles, but always make sure you buy one which has a light, clear colour. If the liquid is dark it will be old and over-assertively fishy.

Seeds

Fennel seeds I share a passion with the Italians for fennel seeds. They have a sweet aniseed flavour and they go exceptionally well with both fish and meat. They can be a bit difficult to get hold of but you should find them in a shop with a serious spice rack.

Fenugreek seeds These peculiar-looking flat, oblong, mustard-brown pulse-seeds should be used sparingly in Indian dishes because they are quite bitter. However they do add a characteristic flavour and are one of the many spices which are ground together to make curry powder.

Mustard seeds Black mustard seeds lose their heat and take on a nutty flavour when they are lightly fried in hot oil and are used in some Indian curries and salads. Yellow mustard seeds, apart from being the main ingredient of mustard, are one of a number of spices used to make the 'shrimp-boil seasoning' on page 199 and add a pleasing hotness to the dish.

White poppy seeds These small, creamy-white seeds are usually ground to a powder and used to thicken curry sauces. They add a nutty flavour, especially if they are lightly roasted first. A good alternative is ground almonds.

Sesame oil

I use both cold-pressed and roasted sesame oil. The cold-pressed oil is light, delicate and fragrant and ideal for dishes where you don't want the flavour to overtake the dish. The roasted (or toasted) sesame oil, pressed from toasted sesame seeds, is much stronger and should be used sparingly or in robust dishes full of spice. It is never used on its own as a cooking oil, but is usually mixed with some lighter oil such as sunflower for use in stir-fries etc. Otherwise it is added at the end of cooking to give the dish that characteristic delicious nutty flavour.

Shiitake mushrooms

These are also known as Chinese black mushrooms and are now available both fresh and dried. The fresh mushrooms, which you now quite often see in the supermarket, have brown, shallow caps which should be plump and smooth, not shrivelled or pitted, and creamy-coloured gills. The dried mushrooms are usually sold in large plastic bags in oriental grocers and need to be reconstituted in hot water before using. The stalks are often removed before cooking because they tend to be very tough but do save the soaking liquor for use in the sauce or stocks because it will have a good flavour.

Sichuan (Szechwan) pepper

This is a characteristic flavour of Chinese cookery which manages to be both peppery hot and yet slightly tart and has the effect of numbing the mouth a little. Also called anise pepper, it is not in fact a true pepper but comes from a type of ash tree and is one of the five ingredients which go together to make Chinese five-spice powder. Simply use regular ground black pepper if you don't have Sichuan pepper.

Snake beans or Yard-long beans

These are literally very long beans, about 3 feet in length, which are sold at oriental greengrocers, twisted into loops for selling. It is the fresh bean from which the dried black-eyed pea is derived, and they have a very tender texture, with a flavour often likened to asparagus, hence another of its names, the asparagus bean.

Star anise

This is a very useful spice for fish cookery. When whole, it is an attractive seed pod shaped like a star, hence its name, and also comes in powdered form. It is another of the spices which go together to make five-spice powder. It is quite easy to get hold of and is always on sale in oriental food stores. I often add some to a fish stock for a subtle hint of aniseed.

Tamarind pulp

This is used in many types of Indian and Thai dishes where its acidic, scented flavour acts like lime or lemon, both of which can be used as an alternative. It can be bought in two forms. I prefer to use the raw pulp which has been scraped from the inside of the pods and compressed into rectangular blocks, seeds and all. You need to knead this pulp with some warm water to dissolve it and release the black, rock-hard seeds. The liquid can then be strained off and used as required. See page 238 for instructions on how to make Tamarind Water. The alternative is to use ready-made tamarind paste but I find this does not have such a good, fresh flavour as the pulp.

Thai holy basil

Holy basil, or *bai krapow* as it is called in Thailand, is an indispensable ingredient in many Thai dishes. The leaves are smaller and darker in colour than Mediterranean basil, and tinged a reddish-purple. It has a more intense taste and must be cooked to release its full flavour. It is best used in strongly flavoured dishes such as curries and stir-fries containing chillies.

Thai pickled radish

Known as *chi po* in Thailand, this salty pickle is made from mooli, or white radish as it is also known. The vegetable is rubbed with large amounts of salt and left overnight to allow the salt to draw liquid out from the root. This liquid is kept. The vegetable flesh is kneaded, squeezed dry and left in the sun to dry out. At night the flesh is returned to the briny liquid produced from the soaking. This process is repeated three more times, then the vegetable is left to dry and sealed in plastic bags, by which time it has turned from a white crunchy root into a soft, slightly shrivelled, pale brown pickle. To use, a very small amount is cut into very thin slivers and tossed into the dish towards the end of cooking to heat through at the last moment, as in the recipe for *Pad Thai Noodles* on page 64. The pickle will keep, well sealed in a glass jar, once unpacked.

Tomatillos/Mexican green tomato/tomate verde

This essential ingredient to Mexican cookery is not in fact a tomato but is related to the cape gooseberry or physalis. They are prepared by removing the papery husk and rinsing. They are usually cooked and not skinned. When in season, they are available from Peppers by Post (see p. 249 for the address), but otherwise the nearest thing would be a green tomato mixed with a little freshly squeezed lime juice.

Tortillas

There are two types of tortillas – wheat and corn. We can now get flour tortillas quite easily in supermarkets, alongside other Mexican ingredients, or in the bread section with the naan and pitta breads. However the corn tortillas needed for the recipe for *A Feast of Mahi Mahi,* on page 214 are only just beginning to appear. I don't care for tinned tortillas.

Vinegars

Apple balsamic vinegar One of the reasons for the success of modern Australian cooking is the emphasis placed on really good ingredients and the length that chefs will go to to find something unique and exciting like this vinegar, i.e. long and slowly matured cider vinegar. You might be able to find it in some delis; otherwise substitute balsamic vinegar.

Balsamic vinegar This is a dark, smooth vinegar made only in and around Modena in northern Italy. It is aged in oak casks and the longer it is aged the better it gets, and the more expensive it becomes. Use a young, cheaper vinegar for cooking, and leave the good expensive stuff for dressing salads etc.

Coconut vinegar Also known as coconut toddy or palm vinegar, this is one of the most common vinegars used in South-east Asia. Produced from the sap of the coconut palm, it is milky-coloured with a mild, slightly fruity flavour which is an important element in dishes such as the *Shark Vindaloo* on p. 36. White wine vinegar is an adequate substitute.

Rice wine vinegar This is a clear white vinegar called for in many Chinese dishes and is one of the main ingredients in the classic sweet and sour sauce. It is not easily available outside an oriental grocers but a good substitute is to mix three parts white wine vinegar with one part water and a little caster sugar.

Sherry vinegar This is good in cooking but not so good in cold salad dressings as I find it a little too strong. (Sherry and balsamic vinegars are my favourites for hot dressings, which I love with fish.) As with so many vinegars, there is so much variation between the best and the worst. I like Vinagre de Jerez 'Gran Gusto'. Jerez is famous for its sherry and equally so for its vinegar.

White wine vinegar Good white wine vinegar is very important for salad dressings. Two vinegars which I particularly like are one by Martin-Pouret from Orléans and one from Bordeaux by Menier, both imported into the UK by Bouchard Aîné of London. Both are produced by the Orléans method which takes more time and uses good-quality wine, making them more expensive, but they are well worth the cost. Wine is poured into barrels, some vinegar is added together with a vinegar culture and the barrels are left open to the air, where the culture slowly turns the alcohol in the wine into vinegar. Cheap vinegar is made by mechanically oxygenating wine with a culture in a tank kept at blood temperature. This is a quicker process but produces a harsher-tasting vinegar without any subtle flavours.

Useful addresses for ingredients

Asian and Chinese ingredients available from:
Wing Yip (London) Ltd
395 Edgware Road
London
NW2 6LN
Tel: 0181 450 0422
or
550 Purley Way
Croydon
Surrey
CR0 4RF
Tel: 0181 688 4880
or
375 Nechells Park Road
Birmingham
B7 5NT
Tel: 0121 327 6618
or
Oldham Road
Manchester
M4 5HU
Tel: 0161 832 7215

Couscous and other Moroccan grocery items
are available, mail order, from:
Le Maroc
94 Golborne Road
London
W10 5BS
Tel: 0181 968 9783

Dried chillies and other Mexican ingredients
are available, mail order, from:
The Cool Chile Company
PO Box 5702
London
W11 2GS
Tel: 0870 902 1145 *or*
E-mail: dodie@coolchile.demon.co.uk

Indian ingredients available, mail order, from:
Patel Brothers
187 91 Upper Tooting Road
London
SW17 7TG
Tel: 0181 672 2792

Italian ingredients available from:
I. Camisa and Son
61 Old Compton Street
London
W1V 5PN
Tel: 0171 437 7610

Olive oils and vinegars available, mail
order, from:
The Oil Merchant Ltd
47 Ashchurch Grove
London
W12 9BU
Tel: 0181 740 1335 *or* Fax: 0181 740 1319

Spanish ingredients available from:
R. Garcia and Sons
248 Portobello Road
London
W11 1LL
Tel: 0171 221 6119

Spices available, mail order, from:
The Spice Shop
1 Blenheim Crescent
London
W11 2EE
Tel: 0171 221 4448

Tomatillos and fresh chillies are available,
mail order, from:
Peppers by Post (Michael and Joy Michaud)
Sea Spring Farm
West Bexington
Dorchester
Dorset
DT2 9DD
Tel: 01308 897892 *or* Fax: 01308 897735

Most of the other ingredients are available,
mail order, from:
Stein's Delicatessen
8 Middle Street
Padstow
Cornwall
PL28 8AP
Tel: 01841 532221 *or* Fax: 01841 533566

Index